ROUGH
JUSTICE

ROUGH JUSTICE

Do we have the law we deserve?

HER HONOUR
WENDY JOSEPH KC

PENGUIN BOOKS

TRANSWORLD PUBLISHERS
Penguin Random House, One Embassy Gardens,
8 Viaduct Gardens, London SW11 7BW
www.penguin.co.uk

Transworld is part of the Penguin Random House group of companies
whose addresses can be found at global.penguinrandomhouse.com

First published in Great Britain in 2024 by Doubleday
an imprint of Transworld Publishers
Penguin paperback edition published 2025

Copyright © Wendy Joseph KC 2024

Wendy Joseph has asserted her right under the Copyright,
Designs and Patents Act 1988 to be identified as the author of this work.

The appendices contain public sector information licensed under the
Open Government Licence v3.0 © Crown copyright

Every effort has been made to obtain the necessary permissions with
reference to copyright material, both illustrative and quoted. We apologize
for any omissions in this respect and will be pleased to make the
appropriate acknowledgements in any future edition.

A CIP catalogue record for this book
is available from the British Library.

ISBN
9781804992661

Text design by Couper Street Type Co.

Typeset in 10.01/13.69pt Adobe Minion Pro by Jouve (UK), Milton Keynes.
Printed and bound in Great Britain by Clays Ltd, Elcograf S.p.A.

The authorized representative in the EEA is Penguin Random House Ireland,
Morrison Chambers, 32 Nassau Street, Dublin D02 YH68.

No part of this book may be used or reproduced in any manner for the purpose
of training artificial intelligence technologies or systems. In accordance
with Article 4(3) of the DSM Directive 2019/790, Penguin Random House expressly
reserves this work from the text and data mining exception.

Penguin Random House is committed to a sustainable
future for our business, our readers and our planet. This book
is made from Forest Stewardship Council® certified paper.

This book is dedicated with love and respect to my darling husband Iain, without whom it would never have been written, but who died before it was published.

CONTENTS

Preface		xi
Introduction		1
PART 1:	The Evil That Men Do	7
PART 2:	The Way to Dusty Death	85
PART 3:	The Quality of Mercy	163
PART 4:	No Evil Angel...	243
Conclusions		309
Appendices		315
Acknowledgements		349

PREFACE

THE OLD BAILEY IS a place where you learn about more than the law. You learn a lot there about suffering. About life, too. And death. By day its courtrooms resonate with these things, but at night it echoes to a different heartbeat. They say ghosts walk here. And certainly if ghosts walk anywhere, it might be here, for in this corner of the City of London, more people have died than in most places. Men, of course, in their tens of thousands, but women and children too. Hearts have burst, throats been cut, plague and typhus have raged. Starvation. Misery. And hangings. Many, many hangings. Because in this place – where now we spend the days patiently sifting facts in order to achieve some form of justice – for seven hundred years stood Newgate Prison.*

For much of that time the courthouse in the little street called Old Bailey was adjacent to the prison and joined to it by an underground tunnel. Many thousands of cases were tried there. You can read about them in the Old Bailey archives, because between 1674 and 1913 their details were carefully documented and recorded. Brutal acts of killing and rape, mean or desperate acts of dishonesty, acts of madness. They filled the courts down the years and are still filling them today.

Some things over those years have changed. As a society, we have softened our approach to punishment – no more castration, disembowelling, beheading and quartering. No more flogging, whipping,

---

* Appendix A.

PREFACE

branding or pillorying. No more hanging.* As our moral perspective has shifted, we have removed from the criminal calendar some offences we think should never have been there at all – you can no longer be prosecuted for consensual homosexual acts, nor for trying to kill yourself.† We are a more thoughtful society now. But – and here's the important question – are we a more just one? Are we, after centuries of trying, any closer to achieving justice?

That question is what this book is about. I have taken areas where the courts have notoriously fallen short over the years, including rape, domestic violence and child cruelty. These are tough subjects to address because their victims are so often women, the very young, the mentally ill or the physically frail. But isn't a measure of our justice system, and of our society, how we protect those among us least able to protect themselves? How have we set about giving them the justice they need? Have we got it right?

I have worked in the criminal courts for not far short of half a century. I have both prosecuted and defended, and perhaps more significantly I have sat as a judge for almost fifteen years, ten of them at the Old Bailey. I have seen the law played out a thousand times but – let me make a confession – despite all the years I have spent in the system, I do not really know what the word 'justice' means.

It's a strange word. A glance at a dictionary suggests that 'just'

---

* In 1965, the Murder (Abolition of Death Penalty) Act abolished capital punishment for all offences except treason, piracy with violence, and arson in royal dockyards. By 2004 even these had gone.
† The Sexual Offences Act 1967 decriminalized homosexual acts between consenting adult males. An Act of 2000 reduced from eighteen to sixteen the age at which a person may lawfully consent to certain homosexual acts. The Suicide Act 1961 decriminalized the act of suicide so that people who tried and failed to kill themselves could no longer be prosecuted for the attempt, though it remains a crime to enter a suicide pact or to help bring about another's suicide.

behaviour involves the fair and reasonable treatment of people, and that 'justice' means having those qualities. But the same dictionary* describes the 'justice system' as no more than 'the legal system used by a country to deal with people who break the law', and that 'bringing someone to justice' is to arrest, try and punish them in that system's law courts. Somewhere along the line, the addition of the word 'system' has drained away the words 'fair and reasonable'. So if a country had thoroughly unjust laws, the courts applying those laws would still be working in a justice system . . . of sorts.

Of course, that's not us – is it? The criminal justice system in the UK tries so hard to be fair – doesn't it? In Commissions and in legislative departments, in universities and in Parliament, brains whirr and computers click and ink runs dry as work is done to make the justice system 'better'. In more recent times, enough statutes and rules have been drafted to sink a battleship and enough guidelines, textbooks and Practice Directions to mop up the resulting mess. How, after all that effort, could our courts *not* be delivering better justice for all?

I've put a question mark at the end of that last sentence because I am genuinely asking the question and genuinely interested in the answer. It's an important issue, and it's one that – because of all the years I have spent in the courts and particularly at the Old Bailey – I may be in a better position than many to examine. But anyone can wander through the public galleries of the Old Bailey as it does its daily work; and anyone can access its online archives, which cover nearly 200,000 trials held in its courtrooms. Anyone can look at the sorts of cases I have identified – and ask themselves 'was justice done?'

As in my first book, *Unlawful Killings*, out of respect to witnesses, defendants and the bereaved who have already been through enough,

---

* *Collins English Dictionary.*

I haven't written about their actual cases. Rather I have created the stories in this book by drawing details from many different trials over which I did preside. Where, however, I refer to similar cases in the archives of the Old Bailey, these are directly taken from real trials recorded there. You can, if you want to, go and read about them, just as I did.

INTRODUCTION

MAYBE A GOOD PLACE to start is to ask what a criminal court is actually designed to do. Essentially, there are two things. The first is to produce a verdict. The second, where that verdict is guilty, is to produce a sentence. The courts play no part in the investigation of the crime beforehand . . . that is the responsibility of the police and prosecuting authorities. They play no part in what happens afterwards . . . that is the responsibility of the prison, probation and other services. The courts' business is to produce verdict and sentence . . . and we all know what that means. At least, we think we do. But if you read on, you might be surprised.

First, the verdict. In the Crown Court a defendant is 'arraigned' – asked if he/she is guilty or not guilty – and if he/she pleads 'not guilty' a jury is sworn to try his/her case. The jurors listen to the evidence, retire to their room to consider it and come to a conclusion. Generally* there are only two verdicts which a jury can return – guilty or not guilty. At the Old Bailey, where we deal with very serious cases, that conclusion usually means the defendant will either go down to the cells to start a long sentence of imprisonment, or walk out of the courtroom into the world where the rest of us live. So the jury's verdict is critical – not only to the defendant but also to the victim or (if the victim has been killed) to the bereaved family and friends. It is also critical to our society as a whole. After all, if

---

* But not always – see Appendix B.

juries repeatedly got verdicts wrong, our streets would be full of dangerous criminals and our prisons full of the righteously indignant. The verdict is the culmination of the trial – the point towards which everyone has been working; it's what the whole performance is about. But what do those words 'guilty' and 'not guilty' actually mean?

The self-declared aim of our criminal justice system is that juries should convict the guilty and acquit the innocent. It sounds good. It sounds obvious. Except that is *not* what we ask our juries to do. Not exactly. We ask them to do something subtly but essentially different. Jurors are instructed only to convict those whom the prosecution has made them *sure* are guilty – and to acquit everyone else. The 'everyone else' includes not only those the jurors are sure were not guilty, but those whom they think were possibly, probably or even very probably *guilty*. If, at this point, you think you need to reread that last sentence, do; but it won't change. If a juror concludes a defendant almost certainly committed a murder, abused a child, defrauded a pensioner . . . it is the duty of the juror to acquit that defendant, because 'almost sure' isn't the same thing as 'sure'. I have heard defence counsel say this to bemused jurors a thousand times. And counsel are right, because that's the law.

It is the law – no doubt about that – but is the law just? Is it justice if a defendant who is very probably guilty walks free because the prosecution has failed to make a jury *sure* of guilt? You could argue that it is not. But would it be better if a defendant who just might be innocent were sent to prison? You could argue that isn't just either – particularly if you were the defendant in question. You can't have it both ways. The system has to decide which way to bend, and in this country we bend in favour of the defence. Before anyone can be convicted of anything, the prosecution must make the jury sure of guilt.*

---

* Appendix C.

INTRODUCTION

This isn't a mere whim – a kindness to defendants; there are at least two positive reasons why we have adopted this standard. One is that, in bringing the prosecution, the Crown has all the resources of the State behind it. Even though (in more serious cases) legal aid is given to a defendant to prepare his response to the Crown's case, still the Crown is the Big Beast. The second reason is that we believe (it seems) that it is better for nine guilty men to go free than for one innocent man to be convicted. You could argue against that too. And I suppose you would if you were the parent of a child sexually abused by a paedophile whom a jury had previously acquitted of abuse of another child. But to change the standard of proof would mean having in our prisons quite a lot of people who were in fact innocent. The State would be sanctioning the removal of their liberty because they might be guilty and . . . well, what sort of country would that be?

So when jurors say 'guilty', it means they were sure of guilt, and when they say 'not guilty', it means they were not sure of guilt. And that's it. They may get it right, they may get it wrong. Either way, the system of justice has been carried out.

Next, the sentence. If a defendant is acquitted, the judge's job is finished. Functus, we call it. Don't ask. Sometimes Latin is just best forgotten. But if a defendant is convicted, the sentence must follow. And this whole question of 'sentencing' also deserves a lot of thought. The process requires the judge to look at the Guidelines and Directions, which in turn requires weighing up the harm done and assessing the offender's culpability. The more serious the harm and the more culpable the defendant, the heavier the punishment. The Sentencing Council* dutifully lists the purposes of sentencing as

---

* The SC declares itself to be an independent non-departmental public body whose main function is to issue guidelines on sentencing, which the courts must follow unless it is in the interests of justice not to do so.

(i) punishment, (ii) preventing the offender from committing further crimes, (iii) deterring others from similar offending, (iv) to reform and rehabilitate, and (v) to make the offender give something back to society. But – let's get real – for the worst crimes, the weight is on punishment; on the appropriate length of sentence. Whether the prison system manages to fit in rehabilitation, education, help with mental illness or anything else during the currency of the sentence is not thought to be a problem for the court. The shutter comes down. Bye bye, birdie.

In fact in almost all general and legal dictionaries, the definition of 'sentence' involves the word 'punishment', and its association with words like 'retribution', 'revenge' and 'vengeance'. But is that what we really want? A lot of people certainly do. When victims plead for justice they are often saying 'make him hurt like I am hurting'. When the deceased's family and friends say 'give us justice' they may mean 'make him suffer like my dead boy suffered, make his family suffer as we, the bereaved, are suffering'. And it's what most of us would feel, isn't it? Individually, we can entirely empathize with that position. But is it what we want as a society?

Over all the centuries and all the cases that have been tried at the Old Bailey, each verdict and sentence has been reached by the playing-out of our system of justice; but I'm betting an awful lot of those involved would say justice wasn't done. Defendants will have said there were wrongful convictions, complainants that there were wrongful acquittals. Prisoners will have said their sentences were too harsh, while victims that they weren't nearly harsh enough. And I'm also betting that this is especially so where the wrongs alleged happened with no independent witnesses, behind closed doors, where most allegations arise of physical and sexual violence towards a partner, a child, the elderly. It is the intimate drama of these lives I want to look at – these lives which have been publicly dissected at such cost to all those concerned. And I want to ask the question: are we achieving justice for those involved? Are we even coming closer to it than we were in the past? And if not, why not?

In order to examine the issue, I began by concentrating on just those sorts of cases where the most vulnerable are involved . . . but as I have worked through them I have found, again and again, that those at the forefront of the stories were women or girls. And so – with no disrespect to others – there is a focus in this book on the fate of the female in the face of the system we call 'criminal justice'.

1: The Evil That Men Do

BETTY JAMES IS SITTING *in her kitchen. There are four plates warming in the oven. She has set out a bottle of vinegar and another of tomato sauce. In her childhood she might have thought there was something biblical about this – the bitterness, the blood – but Betty doesn't allow herself such foolish thoughts any more. She has been sitting there for some time, and in the warmth of the centrally heated December evening, the bread is beginning to curl, the butter to glaze. In the living room her husband is watching noisy football, but in the kitchen everything is quiet. There is only the tick of the clock on the wall. She glances at it again, surreptitiously, as if she doesn't want it to know she is becoming rather . . . well, anxious. Yes, she acknowledges anxious, but not yet worried, because of course Jason will take good care of Susan. He is a careful driver. And it's only a couple of miles from the church hall where, every Friday night, her daughter goes to Guides. Susan is in the Red Rose Patrol, which Betty James thinks sounds nice. And every week Jason picks her up and stops to buy fish and chips on the way home. He buys it for all of them, because Jason is nice too. So nice. They really don't know what they would do without him; really can't think how they managed before he came into their lives. So if he is late there must be a good reason. Perhaps there's a queue at the fish shop. Yes, that will be it. Jason is waiting for a fresh batch of chips. Better to wait and get them fat and golden. He will be here any moment now. Is that his car she can hear? She thinks it is, and relief bubbles inside her. She is about to get the plates out of the warming oven when there is a ring on the doorbell. Susan never rings the bell because she has her own key, on a little key ring that her father has adapted so it clips on to her belt.*

Betty goes to the front door because when the doorbell rings, what else can you do? From the television in the living room there is the throaty roar of a crowd of football fans who have nothing to do with her but who have somehow come into her home. Her fingers fumble on the latch. She opens it. She did not know how frightened she had been until she sees Susan standing there. The child is alone. A plastic carrier bag hangs from her hand, heavy with fish and chips.

'Susan!' Relief brings irritation. 'Did you forget your key?' And then, 'Where's Uncle Jason?' And finally, because Betty can no longer ignore the fact that tears are pouring down her daughter's face, 'What's wrong?'

CHAPTER ONE

Long and bitter experience has taught me that in life there are two things you cannot argue with. One is Fate, the other is bollards.

Even without these things, today would not be a good one because I have to deal with The Queen v. Jason Godmer, and I don't want to. It's the not-wanting-to that has made me put off the final preparations for it. And now the morning has come and I still have things to sort out before I can go into court. So I am impatient to get to my room, which makes me impatient with the man driving into the Old Bailey ahead of me, which tempts me to tailgate. Which brings me to the bollards.

They lie in the roadway that leads to the judges' entrance. If you wait your turn like an orderly and proper judge, they lie peaceably enough. But if you are a person of evil intent they are meant to leap up and smash through the underside of your car. Tailgating is, to their minds, evidence of evil intent. And so . . .

. . . and so I arrive in my room late, sad, and considerably poorer than I was when I left home. The security man comes with me. I tell him I wasn't tailgating, I was only saving him the trouble of putting the bollards up then down again. He tells me that whatever I call it, if I follow another car through, the bollards – which answer only to a higher and automated authority – are beyond his control. He fetches me a cup of tea and a sweet biscuit. I have had a nasty shock, he says – but not nearly as nasty as the one my car has suffered. Poor faithful beast, its day is done. Functus. But mine has barely begun. And there is still the case to cope with.

The security man goes and I turn to my computer. I am wretched even before I begin on Jason Godmer, and he's not likely to improve things. I first met him some weeks ago at a preliminary hearing when his counsel raised three spurious arguments of law. He did so apologetically and I knew it was at the instigation of his client. But it is counsel's business to deal with his client. If he can't, today's hearing will be difficult. So I put bollards behind me. And it is at this point that my other nemesis, Fate, comes knocking at the door.

It is a quiet knock. My fellow judges favour the perfunctory rap before walking right in. Ushers tend to tap with feet or elbows, their hands being full of missing papers or mugs of coffee. The list officers*, the clerks, security and catering staff are all identifiable from within by the way they announce themselves from without. But this particular quiet knock is in a language I cannot read.

'Come in,' I say, and the court manager appears. Everyone loves the court manager. He comes by to chat. Generally he arrives with a smile and good gossip. But not now. Now he comes with a problem. In fact, he comes with thirty-two problems. And an interpreter. A large delegation of Chinese judges have come a very long way in order to understand how our criminal justice system works – and the judge who was going to host them has the flu.

I listen to this tale of woe with an expression of sympathy but I know what he's up to, this wily old court manager, and I have no intention of giving it to him.

'I am sorry for your difficulties,' I say. 'I am sorry for your thirty-two delegates and their interpreter. I am sorry for anyone with flu. But I have a lot to do.'

The court manager draws up a chair and sits on it. 'Your case isn't listed until 11 a.m. You have plenty of time.'

'I have plenty of work to fill it.'

---

* The people in charge of listing cases.

'Please,' he says. 'I'm having a difficult morning.'

'So am I.'

'Ah, yes,' he says. 'You have broken the bollards. There is a queue of traffic stretching back to Ludgate Hill. Fortunately, the Chinese have arrived by tube.'

By the time he leaves my room, I have inherited the entire delegation (plus interpreter) and must consider myself fortunate I haven't had to take on the flu too.

As it happens the Chinese are charming; touchingly eager to understand our rules of law and the way evidence is presented in our courts.

'In our country,' I say, 'it isn't the judge who decides if a defendant is guilty or not guilty. It's the jury. When the trial starts, each juror swears to "reach a true verdict according to the evidence". It is part of the judge's job to ensure that the evidence the jury receives will lead them to that "true verdict" and not away from it. Jurors must hear all that is necessary in order to focus on the issues in the case. They must not hear what may divert or prejudice rather than inform.'

No pressure on the judge there, then.

My counterparts from across the world nod and the interpreter, encouraged, asks what else must judges in this country do?

'Well,' I say, 'a judge is rather like a referee, overseeing the contest, making sure that both sides behave according to the rules.'

The interpreter struggles with this. 'Like football?'

'Um . . .'

He takes this for a 'yes' and interprets rapidly while my visitors nod and make notes. I wonder how much damage I have done to international understanding. Or how much good. I wonder if I should tell them the truth – that judges here, like everywhere, must sometimes deal with cases they would rather not; must hear what they don't want to hear; see what they don't want to see.

'You put bad people in prison,' says the interpreter.

I nod. I don't say, 'And sometimes I must put people who are not so bad in prison too.' Nor do I say, 'Sending even very bad people to prison doesn't improve them, nor does it put right the wrongs they have done. It just marks society's disapprobation, and keeps them away from the rest of us for the period of the sentence. Which, I suppose, is something.' I do not say these things but I think them, and I think about Jason Godmer and about Susan James and the part I am to play in the lives of these people who at present I barely know, and who do not know me.

CHAPTER TWO

ALL I KNOW ABOUT Jason and Susan is what I gleaned from the earlier hearings – that Susan came home one Friday evening in distress. Later that weekend she told her mother that Uncle Jason had raped her. Police were called and Uncle Jason was arrested and interviewed. Unlike many defendants who say 'no comment' to every question asked, Uncle Jason had a lot to say. He was indignant. He was hurt. Susan was a fantasist. When told that she had genital injuries consistent with assault within the previous seventy-two hours and inconsistent with fantasy, he said that she must have had 'to do' with someone else. When asked why she would wrongly accuse him, he said that on the drive home from Girl Guides, she was rude to him and he threatened to stop visiting the house. She knew how much he did for her mum and dad – how much he gave them, and helped them. She was frightened they would be cross with her. She must have blamed him to deflect their anger. Nothing happened, he said. Absolutely nothing of the sort that Susan claimed. Not, at least, with him.

Beyond this I know nothing, so back in my room and with just a little time before I have to go into court, I open the Digital Case System where all the information about cases is stored. I begin by looking for a photograph of Susan. Many years ago I prosecuted murders in front of a wise judge who always asked to see a photograph of the deceased as they had been in life. It was right, he said, to have in one's mind's eye those who weren't there any more. It's a habit I have fallen into. It can tell you a lot to see how someone looked before – back in that place to which neither the victim nor the defendant can ever return.

The police have obtained from Mrs James a school photograph of her daughter taken in September, just before Uncle Jason came into their lives. In it she looks like any eleven-year-old – striking only in her normality. Perhaps she is rather small for her age. And is there something fragile about her, or is that my imagination? Judges shouldn't have imagination. It does no good. The back of the photo has been reproduced too. On it the distraught mother has written 'Susan Before Things Happened to Her'. Is that how her parents think of it? If so, I hope they will forgive me for saying they have got it wrong. Things didn't happen to Susan. Because 'Things' don't just happen. Not 'Things' like that. They are perpetrated. And if (but only if) Susan is telling the truth, the perpetrator was Uncle Jason.

So now I have images in my mind of Jason Godmer and of Susan James, both still strangers to me, but how much better will I know them by the end of the day?

As it happens, the answer is not much. I have barely set to work when from the corridor I hear a scuffle and low, indignant voices. I open the door. My ushers stand there. Leonie is young, new to the building. Martin has her in tow because, having been with us for many years, he knows all there is to know about the job. Leonie is clearly keen to learn.

'He's at it again,' says Martin.

I know well that when Martin complains with a shake of the head, he is cross with the prosecution; when he complains with a frown, he is cross with the defence. Now he frowns. And shakes his head.

'Bloody man,' he says.

Whatever 'bloody man' he is talking about, I don't want him teaching young Leonie this sort of thing. I invite him to put it a different way. He gives me a long look.

'Right you are, My Lady. I'll put it this way. The gentleman in the dock wishes to sack the gentleman who is representing him. The gentleman prosecuting says if there is to be sacking, he'd be grateful if it could be done quickly because any delay will be upsetting for the child. The defendant says it's upsetting for him too and would the prosecutor mind his own business, while the gentleman who is to be sacked doesn't seem to know what to say.'

I shake my head. 'Bloody man.' We aren't due to sit until eleven o'clock, but it is clear I had better see counsel straight away.

In court the dock seems smaller than usual, perhaps because Jason Godmer and his indignation occupy a lot of space. Physically he is a large man. His clothes stretch disturbingly over his bulk. But neither fury nor flesh are indicators of guilt, and eight months on remand in one of HM's prisons doesn't leave anyone looking their best. When I enter court his barrister is at the side of the dock, apparently trying to post reason through a slit in the security glass. Now he scurries back to his place in counsel's row.

I bow. I sit. I wait.

'My Lady . . .' It is Mr Purvis, the prosecutor, who has got to his feet. He is a man with a comfortable paunch who looks old enough to be father to the young defence counsel. 'We apologize for asking you to come into court early, but the defendant has indicated a course which, if he pursues it, I fear will make today's hearing impossible. And if there isn't to be a hearing, I would like to send the child witness away.'

The defence barrister is nodding in agreement. It is not the same one who represented Mr Godmer on the previous occasion. Perhaps the first one is exhausted by his three failed submissions of law. Or perhaps Mr Godmer is. Anyway, today the solicitors have sent someone else to represent their client. If they are hoping this will make him happier, they are wrong. Mr Godmer has apparently taken against today's offering. He is shaking his head in a motion directly contradictory to that of his counsel.

'I know my rights,' he yells across the courtroom.

Privately, I doubt he does. Or at least, I doubt he knows the limits of them. But let's see. I look for the young counsel's name on the list before me and find it. Mr Webley. Oh Lord. I bet they called him 'Wobbly' at school. Somehow I just know this is not going to end well.

'Mr Webley, your client seems a little . . . upset. Would you like to tell me what is going on?'

'I'll tell you.' The voice, belligerent, challenging, is, of course, coming from the dock. 'I want to change my whole legal team,' yells Jason Godmer. 'I don't want to be represented by that tosser.'

Mr Webley, fresh-faced as a schoolboy, looks pained. I really can't allow counsel to be abused in this way. On the other hand I need to get Mr Godmer to listen to me, and that won't happen if I start weighing into him. I settle for moderation.

'Mr Godmer,' I say, 'I seriously doubt that Mr Webley is a . . .' I cannot bring myself to say it. I cannot bring myself to look at the poor man. 'And even if he were, do you have a more cogent reason for wishing to sack him and your whole legal team?'

'I don't trust him. I don't trust any of them. I'm an innocent man. I'm—'

'Of course,' I say. 'All defendants are innocent unless and until a jury decides they are guilty. Your lawyers are there to help you avoid that outcome.'

'Well, I want a different lot.'

'I see.' I glance through the paperwork. 'You are in receipt of a legal aid order assigned to a particular firm of solicitors. Do you want to sack your present lawyers and have the legal aid order amended so that others can represent you?'

'That's it,' he says, poking the inoffensive air. 'That's it exactly.'

I pause because I know that what I am about to tell him will make his eyes goggle. But it is something he needs to hear. 'I wonder,' I say reflectively, 'if you have considered Part 3 of the Criminal Legal Aid (Determinations by a Court and Choice of Representative) Regulations 2013?'

Mr Godmer, obligingly, goggles.

'And in particular, have you considered section 14, which deals with "change of provider"? No? Then perhaps I can help you. Section 14 subsection (1) says that once a defendant has selected a provider of legal services in criminal proceedings, there is no right to select a different one in their place.' Mr Godmer opens his mouth to share with me his thoughts on subsection (1) but I get in first. 'Subsection (2) has better news for you. It says the court can allow you to make the change if – but only if – it determines the original lawyers can no longer provide effective representation . . .'

Mr Godmer points at Rupert Webley, as if resting his case on this subject.

'. . . either because there has been a breakdown in the relationship between you and them, or for some other compelling reason.'

I give him a moment to absorb this, then I turn to the barristers and ask if they agree I have properly summarized the law. Both confirm I have.

'So, Mr Webley, do you know of any reason why you cannot continue to work with this defendant?'

Mr Webley looks as if he would very much like to have such a reason but honesty compels him to admit he does not.

'Mr Godmer, do you have anything to say?'

It turns out that Mr Godmer has a deal to say. His thrust is this: 'They have sent a kid to do a man's job and I want shot of the lot of them. I want a whole different set of lawyers and if you won't give them to me, I'll have to go it alone.'

Now, his going it alone – acting without lawyers – is the very last thing I want. It's a difficult and delicate case. Jason Godmer doesn't know the half of how hard this is going to get, both for him and Susan James. To have him conducting his own defence will be a nightmare. What to do then? First I must give him and Rupert Webley time – probably the rest of the day – to try to resolve their differences. Tomorrow I will have them back to see what progress they have made. If there is no resolution, I will need to consider how to protect both child and defendant. Susan has already been brought to court once to no purpose. I can't let the same thing happen again. So I will send her away till the following Monday, by which time I will surely have sorted out Jason Godmer.

'Mr Godmer,' I say, 'you need time to reflect. You certainly need to talk to your counsel. I'm adjourning your case till tomorrow. We'll see how things look then.'

Mr Purvis gets to his feet. 'But what should I tell Susan?'

I cannot have a child brought to court then treated as if her time, her stress, her feelings do not matter. She is owed an apology, and who to give it but me? I must go and speak to her. I could take counsel with me but the position of one of them is – to say the least – tenuous. I debate the matter with myself and make a decision.

'Mr Purvis, Mr Webley, I intend to go to meet the witness. I will not speak of what has happened. I will simply explain that there has been an unavoidable delay and apologize for it. Does either of you have any objection?'

Mr Purvis does not.

Mr Webley does not.

There is a low rumble from the dock. Thunder is in the offing. I rise and leave court before the storm can break. I take Leonie with me, leaving Martin to clear the courtroom of the shambles that Mr Godmer has made of my morning.

Susan is in witness support – a section of the Old Bailey dedicated to the use of witnesses, their families, and the bereaved in homicide cases. I find her in the room for young witnesses. It is full of things to absorb a child's attention, but when I look through the open door, Susan is sitting on a small sofa, staring into space. The books beside her are unopened. The ubiquitous teddy bear lies on its side. A volunteer support worker is talking quietly to her but she gives no sign of hearing. I look for a long moment, shocked into silence, because I barely recognize this child as the one I saw in the photograph. The gentle eyes are hardened with shadow. The elfin frame has grown heavy. The pale skin is lardy. Even if she has suddenly reached puberty, surely it could not account for this ... this ... what? The child she was has disappeared and another is here in her place.

'Hello, Susan.' I take off my wig and set it down on the low table. I do not sit on the same sofa where she is – keep your distance, is the rule. Don't crowd the child. So I take a chair, tell her my name, and that I'm the judge. She nods. Her eyes are blank.

'Thank you for coming today,' I say. 'I'm glad you have because now you know what it's like here.' I smile at her, and at the lady from witness support. 'It's OK, isn't it? Not too bad?'

I expect her to smile back. To say it's nice in this room. But Susan only stares.

'I'm afraid I have some rather bad news,' I say. 'We've got a bit of a problem – just one of those things and nothing for you to worry about. But we aren't going to be able to hear your evidence today.'

There is no reaction from her. Has she heard?

'Do you understand?'

She nods briefly.

'So I'm going to ask you to go home now and come back again next Monday.'

She doesn't move, but slowly her eyes fill with tears. And slowly the tears spill over the lashes and run down her cheeks. Leonie stifles a sob and runs from the room. The lady from witness support provides a tissue for the child. I would like to put my arms around her so that she feels some human comfort, but that is strictly forbidden. And wholly inappropriate. Because this is a child who – if she is telling the truth – has had other inappropriate arms put around her. A judge isn't a counsellor or a social worker or a parent or a friend. A judge – at the end of the day – is just a judge.

CHAPTER THREE

WITH THE TRIAL DELAYED, I now have plenty of time to prepare the wretched case.* I also have time to look for a new car but somehow that seems to have lost its importance. How to understand what I have seen? This is a child who is suffering. I can't say what from – I can't say if she has been traumatized by abuse, or is frightened because she is lying. I can't say if she is depressed or if she is in the throes of some other mental illness. But I can see this is not normal. She has been waiting eight months for this moment and it has taken its toll. Now she must wait longer.

I am saddened by the state of this girl and upset that I must prolong her torment. I am cross with Jason Godmer because . . . well, because he is making my life difficult. But I am paid to deal with difficulties and he is a man to whom I owe a huge responsibility. He deserves justice. He must not only get it, but be seen to get it. Besides, I am cross with myself for feeling it would be easier just to let him have new solicitors, and maybe I could slip this one through . . . but the rules are strict for a good reason, and the same rules must apply to everyone. If you allow one defendant to have an unwarranted change of lawyers just because he is difficult, it will only encourage other defendants to be difficult.

Still, it is my job not only to make myself think what it is like to be Susan James, but what it is like to be Jason Godmer too. I remind myself that he is innocent and will remain innocent unless he is

---

* Judges are salaried and get the same pay whether they are sitting in their rooms or in court.

found guilty. And for that, the prosecution must prove its case against him by making a jury sure that Susan is honest and reliable.

'Honest' and 'reliable' are big words. They are meant to test the character of all sorts of witnesses and this one is very young to bear the weight of them. But young as she is, everything, for Jason Godmer, hinges upon her. Everything for him hinges on the jury not believing her. If they do, he will go to prison for a very long time. If they don't, he will walk free – back to whatever life he came from. For her there is, of course, no walking free. Whatever has or hasn't happened – she will bear the burden of this trial for ever.

How many children in the position of Susan James have there been over the centuries? How many men like Jason Godmer in the dock? And how many juries have, at the end of the day, achieved a 'true verdict'? Perhaps it is this thought that makes me do what I do next. Or perhaps it is the unexpected expanse of time at my disposal. Whatever it is, back in my room and at my computer, my finger hovers over the icon which admits me to the Digital Case System; but my mind is not with my finger. It is wondering about all the children who have been through what Susan James is going through, and worse. After all, we are only asking Susan to do what countless others have done. And we do it better now than we did in the past, don't we? Suddenly, I want reassurance that we do. My finger moves from the DCS button across the screen. It wants to show me I am not presiding over needless anguish. It wants to show me that things aren't as bad as they used to be. It leads me to a website that deals not with current Old Bailey cases, but with ones from the archives. And who am I to argue?

So I enter the website and in the 'search' section I select 'sexual offences – rape'. In 'key words' I type 'eleven years old'. Then, on a whim, I add the word 'Susan'. There is a pause, a blank screen, a long second while I think there is nothing to be found – then up she comes from the depths of the past where she has been a long time hidden. Up to the surface comes another little girl and with her, linked for ever by their histories, another defendant who stood in the dock at the Old Bailey.

The entry is dated 15 October 1735. The defendant is a man called Julian Brown. He was indicted for 'Ravishing and Carnally Knowing Susan Marshall, an Infant of Eleven Years old'. The incident was alleged to have happened on 11 April that same year, so Susan Marshall waited only a little over six months for the trial . . . much less than 'my' Susan. In this respect we seem to have made no progress at all. A point to The Past. But surely, in every other way, the system has improved since the eighteenth century. We have learned so much. We try so hard. Just look. And I access the detail of Julian Brown's case to do just that.

Almost three hundred years ago Susan Marshall walked into a courtroom at the Old Bailey, just yards down the street from where I am now. She climbed into the witness-box. Perhaps she was so short they had to bring a chair for her to stand on so she could be seen. Along one side was the judge's Bench, higher than any other structure in the courtroom except the dock, so that she had to look up at the jowly man sitting there in his robes and wig. Beside him a line of dignitaries had come to see the fun. In the well of the court were rows of barristers waiting for the many cases that would be dealt with that day – for justice in that court was swift, with dozens of trials to be got through in any session. Opposite her in the jury-box, twelve strangers, all men,* scrutinized her with judgemental eyes because, after all, that is what they were there for. The public

---

* It wasn't until 1920, following the Sex Disqualification (Removal) Act 1919, that women were regularly sitting on juries, though even then they, like men, had to meet 'property qualifications' to do so.

galleries on every side were crowded. She had to speak up in front of all of them – probably more people than she had ever before seen at one time. And just across the courtroom, in the dock, Julian Brown. Mr Brown who had done these things to her . . . or hadn't. Mr Brown whose eyes met hers and whose expression she could not read. I allow my own eye to move to the end of the account. The verdict. Acquitted. Either that little girl lied to the court, or the system let her down badly.

What must it be like to stand up in front of so many people and draw out of your head the memories and organize them in a logical form, and find the words to convey them to strangers? In such circumstances, the pressure on any witness to say all that must be said is enormous. There is a risk that the giving of evidence becomes a test of nerve. When the witness is a child or mentally frail or confused, it is even more difficult. I told the Chinese delegation that it is the judge's job to ensure the jury gets the best possible evidence – but how is that to be achieved? It must have been obvious to those sitting in the courtrooms of the past that something needed to be done. No doubt there was a lot of heart-searching. But heart-searching doesn't help. Not unless practical steps are taken. It took a long, long time for us to work out the answer, but in the end we did find a better way than that which young Susan Marshall had to endure. And when we finally got there, the solutions were so simple.

It was the Youth Justice and Criminal Evidence Act 1999 (yes, I do mean 1999) which finally introduced a range of 'special measures' for vulnerable witnesses.* Among the first, easiest and most obvious of the measures is the use of a curtain drawn around the witness-box so that the witness is screened from everyone in the courtroom except the judge, jury and the barrister asking questions. She cannot be seen by or see anyone else – particularly not the

---

* See Appendix D.

defendant. Any 'Susan' giving evidence after this and utilizing this 'special measure', wouldn't have to see the eyes of a defendant upon her, the subtle shake of his head, his threatening frown or pleading smile. Even in 1999 there were those who argued against this development, claiming the defendant was disadvantaged by it, but we have been using the curtain-screen for nearly a quarter of a century now, and no one says that any more. This must surely make the task of getting into the witness-box easier for Susan James than it was for Susan Marshall? A score point for The Present – an equalizer.

But the 1999 legislation went further than that. In certain circumstances,[*] including where a child gives evidence of being raped, it provides for some witnesses to be outside the courtroom altogether, in a room (usually, but not always, elsewhere in the building), linked by a video/TV connection to the courtroom itself. So a witness like Susan can, these days, be seen on video screens by everyone in court, while she sees only the face and hears the voice of the person – judge or barrister – speaking directly to her.

These measures are meant to assist a vulnerable witness without taking away any of the defendant's rights to a fair trial. Of course, the judge has to ensure the jurors aren't prejudiced against the defendant by any of this. I have done it hundreds of times. 'It's a purely administrative matter,' I say. 'That's just the way we do things, day in, day out, in courtrooms up and down the country. It must never be held against a defendant, because it is nothing to do with him.'

So here is another way in which we have achieved something that helps a witness give better evidence to the jury. Another score point to The Present.

---

[*] See Appendix D.

CHAPTER FOUR

THE CURTAIN AND THE remote witness room can both ease the stress of giving evidence in front of the defendant and a roomful of strangers, but neither of them helps with the central problem – that of remembering and recounting the events themselves.

How did witnesses – especially the young – manage in the past? How did Susan Marshall cope? Perhaps the answer is spelled out at the end of the account of the trial in that word 'acquitted'. But as it happens, I can tell you more than that about how it went. At least, I can tell you pretty much what she said on that day 288 years ago. I can do it because, as now, a record was kept of the evidence. In 1735 there was a scribe to do it. Later there were stenographers, and in due course a digital recording system. But one way or another, over the years, the words of numberless witnesses have been caught and preserved. Here is what Susan Marshall said as Julian Brown stared at her from the dock.

On Friday Night my Mother sent me to the Prisoner's Shop. – He keeps a Chandler's Shop* the Corner of Plum-tree Court in Dyot-street, – for two Red Herrings. When I had them, the Prisoner bid me carry them home, and come back again, and he would give me one for myself. So I came the second Time, and he bid me go into his Back Room, and he would bring me a Red Herring, but

---

* A chandler's shop in the eighteenth century dealt primarily in candles, but also sold oil, soap and probably paint, etc. and, apparently, red herrings.

he brought me a Dram of Anniseed* and made me drink some of it. Then he set me on his Lap, and put his Hand up my Coats, and threw me on the Floor, and – and – I screamed out, and called him nasty Rogue. But he said, Hush! hush! I do so to my Wife. And then he made me promise to tell no body, and so I did not speak of it till Monday; but then I told Mrs Bathaway, for I was so sore that I could not go about; and she told my Mother.

The scribe has made a real attempt to capture her as she speaks . . . her hesitations . . . the 'and – and – I screamed out'. This is Susan Marshall's voice as she gives her account of the incident, her evidence-in-chief. How long did it take her to say this? A few minutes? Barely that. So short a time to collect herself and make sure she says all she needs to. So short a time to remember all that happened six months before. And if she is telling the truth, so difficult for her to disentangle the hard fact from the trauma and the emotions that followed. The difficulties the system posed for any witness – and particularly for the vulnerable – are obvious.

Susan Marshall was facing a problem intrinsic to our way of criminal justice. For centuries we have depended on witnesses standing in a courtroom to recall and describe what happened months, sometimes years, before. Despite the many advantages of our system, speed isn't one of them. Long periods can pass between the allegation of an offence and the trial. Time must be allowed for each party to prepare their case – to find witnesses, instruct lawyers, research the law and draft applications and submissions. More months may go by if courts are overburdened with work and cannot provide an early trial slot. We know now that as time passes, memory fragments. It can be lost, or suppressed, or distorted by constant reliving

---

* A dram is a small quantity, usually of alcohol. Aniseed here refers to a sweet alcoholic liqueur probably tasting of liquorice.

in flashbacks or in nightmares. Again and again I have seen thoroughly honest witnesses who have no reason to lie, swear to facts which – when tested against the CCTV or other incontrovertible evidence – prove to be fiction. Memory, upon which so much of our trial procedure depends, is a porous and fallible thing. But, here's a strangeness – although we have known for many decades that memory is a fragile thing, we seemed unable to adapt and are stuck with the old procedures.

It wasn't until that same statute of 1999 that we found a way to help witnesses with this problem of loss of accurate memory, and even then – even now – we only make it available to some witnesses. The new procedure was designed to help those who are particularly vulnerable – the young, those with mental health issues or those who must talk about traumatic events or things of a very personal nature – in short where age, incapacity, fear or distress threaten to undermine the witness's evidence. Like the 'screen' and the 'remote witness room' it is so simple, so obvious a solution. And like them, its initial detractors have melted away with the passage of time. It's a procedure we have come to know as Achieving Best Evidence or ABE – because that is precisely what it is designed to do. The magic is contained in section 27, which says that a judge who, having regard to all the circumstances of the case, thinks it right, can direct that a video recording of an interview of the witness be played to the jury as that witness's evidence-in-chief.* The important words are 'a video recording of an interview'. It refers to a recording made when the witness – the Susan – made her first detailed complaint to police.

Of course, the interview must be carried out in a way that prevents unfairness. Inevitably there has grown up a whole protocol as to how it must be done. But with section 27, the ABE interview was born and it is designed to do exactly what it says. Here's how it

---

* See Appendix E.

generally works: as soon as possible after a complaint is made – typically within a day or two – the 'vulnerable witness' is taken to a special suite of rooms equipped with audio and recording devices. There, in as relaxed an atmosphere as can be contrived, he or she is interviewed by a trained officer. The witness is allowed to recount an event, then the officer questions them to draw out the detail. Everything that takes place in the room is recorded so that witnesses cannot be prompted, coached or led into their evidence. It must come from them. But they can be helped to focus on what is relevant. And in due course, when the trial takes place, this recording can be played to the jury as the witness's 'evidence-in-chief'.

This is what happened with Susan James, and the procedure has given her the chance to give her best evidence before her memory was lost or corrupted. How much luckier she is than complainants like Susan Marshall. 'My' Susan was interviewed on the Monday afternoon following the events of the Friday evening. The recording is available to the lawyers, and to me. And now, at last, I settle down to watch it.

On my computer screen the scene is frozen in the past. A push of another button will unspool time, but I don't do that yet. I study the opening image. There is the interview room, big enough to avoid claustrophobia, not so big as to lose the child in it. One camera is trained on the sofa where she sits. Another will follow her if she stands or moves around or even if she makes a dash for the door. Everything in the room is designed to be comfortable, but Susan is not comforted. She sits on the edge of the sofa, very small, very stiff, very still. She stares through a mane of straight fair hair. She is the child in the school photograph. My finger hovers over the play button. It does not descend. Not yet. I want to understand this little girl. I want to understand Jason Godmer too. And defunct cars, visiting Chinese judges, everything else, must wait their turn because here is what is important. Here, where a child is saying 'he raped me' and a man is protesting 'she's lying, fantasizing'. And however the system dresses it up with barristers and wigs, with submissions of law and subclauses of statutes, in the end it is between these two accounts – the child's and the man's – that a jury must decide. I reach out to click play.

She is sitting where she has been put, under the full scrutiny of the camera. She is holding a teddy bear. These rooms are equipped with a good selection of soft toys and presumably the kindly interviewing officer has given her this bear for comfort. Susan holds it in her lap. She stares at it as if she can't think what it is doing there.

The female officer begins with the introductions and formalities, and then she sets about the required checking that her witness understands the difference between truth and lies.

'If Mummy left a jam tart on the kitchen table and you ate it,' she says, 'and when Mummy asked, you said it wasn't you who took it, is that the truth or a lie?'

This would test the Chinese interpreter. It seems to challenge Susan too. She looks at the officer as if the woman is mad.

'My mum doesn't make jam tarts,' she says. 'They're bad for your teeth.'
'Yes, but—'
'And I don't like jam.' Suddenly Susan has had enough of this. 'And I don't steal,' she says. 'And if I did, I wouldn't lie about it.'

I hear her words, and with them, echoing somewhere in the future, the thud of defence counsel's heart dropping. Either Susan is a consummate actress, or she is about to tell the truth as far as it is in her power to do so. And so she describes that Friday night.

'Uncle Jason,' she says, then stops. The officer waits patiently. Susan tries again. 'He said the car was making a funny noise.' Susan said she couldn't hear it but Uncle Jason stopped the car and looked under the bonnet. He said the car needed to cool down, though Susan didn't see why because they had only been driving for five minutes. He said they should play a game. He got into the passenger seat and sat her on his lap, facing him, her legs apart over his thighs. And then . . . and . . . and . . .

Susan may have known a lot, but she didn't know about this. This was beyond her. But she knew she was hurt and she knew it was wrong and she knew – she thought she knew – she should have screamed and pushed him away.

. . . but it was Uncle Jason who was so kind and he had cuddled her before in the car, though not like this. And she hadn't told Mum then. And she hadn't told Mum when he said she was beautiful and special. In fact, she had been rather pleased. So perhaps it was all her fault and Mum would be so cross . . . and then they had got the fish and chips and he told her to stop crying and when she couldn't he got very angry and pushed her out of the car and drove away.

The officer nods. She hasn't interrupted at all but now Susan has got herself to the end of her first account, the officer must ask questions – not leading the child but allowing her to explain. She begins with what Susan had been wearing.

'My Guide uniform, of course.'
  'Of course – but is that a skirt or trousers . . . ah, a skirt. And underneath?'

> 'Knickers,' says Susan. 'Just knickers. Until . . .'
>
> 'Until?' asks the officer. And out comes the story of how Uncle Jason had removed them. 'And Uncle Jason's clothes?' asks the officer, 'did they come off or stay on?'
>
> Susan thinks about this. 'He was wearing red tracksuit bottoms,' she says. 'He . . .' She demonstrates lifting her bottom as she sat. 'He pulled them down so they were round his ankles.'
>
> 'And where exactly was the car when this happened?' asks the officer.

I had been wondering the same thing myself. Defence counsel will wonder, too. Surely Godmer couldn't have done this at the side of a road where any passer-by could see? Is this an indication the child is lying? But Susan does not hesitate. She says,

> 'Behind the park. He said that if the car broke down on the main road it would hold up all the traffic so he had to go to a place where it could cool down without obstructing the highway.'

'Obstructing the highway' . . . not the words of an eleven-year-old, surely. A sign that she was indeed repeating what he had said to her? Again the officer has had the same thought.

> 'Did he use those words, Susan? Did he say "obstructing the highway"?'
>
> The child nods.

And so it goes on, each step of the account examined and every inch of information extracted. Where she stops in her account, unable to describe exactly what he had done, with fingers, with penis, now the officer draws it all from her and makes a good job of it. Finally she says,

'Is there anything else you can tell me, Susan? Anything else you remember?'

Susan looks down, sees the teddy still in her lap, places it carefully to one side. 'He was hot,' she says. 'He was sweating. And the drops of sweat fell on me.'

The camera is on her. It captures what surely she could not have invented. A perceptible shudder at the memory.

The recording lasts about forty minutes and during it the trained and skilled police officer aims to ensure it contains all that Susan James can say about what happened to her. And once she has done that, the words are caught. They can't get distorted. Things can't get confused. Details can't be forgotten. It's there for all time – or at least for as long as it is needed. Forty minutes of careful exploration. Another point to The Present.

CHAPTER FIVE

I SPEND THE REST of the morning watching the ABE recording; listening to the eleven-year-old Susan talking to that police officer and thinking about the twelve-year-old Susan whom I had met in witness support earlier. What will the jury make of the difference between the two? The child in the ABE is a picture sad enough. Properly understood, I suspect the child I have seen today is even sadder. But how will it look to the jury who try Jason Godmer? We are so used to seeing actors on television where the good are beautiful, where the honest gaze straight into the eye of the camera. The Christian ethic associates suffering with goodness. We are conditioned by art from the Renaissance onwards to associate truth with beauty. But in my experience suffering distorts, both inside and out. A liar can be as good-looking as a truthful person. Tears and sleeplessness and poor eating produce an image that needs to be understood. Eyes that won't meet the jurors', or an inability to answer questions, must not automatically be taken as signs of dishonesty, for they may be quite the opposite.

I try to look at the ABE interview with the eyes, the mind, the heart of the juror who will have to weigh up Susan's account against that of the defendant who made an immediate and indignant denial of wrongdoing. What else will the juror have to throw into the balance?

Surely there was evidence from Susan's mother. If the complaint was a true one, Mrs James had seen her child within half an hour of the incident, and had then spent the weekend with her. A jury might feel they could rely on Mrs James. In the DCS I find her. She had spoken to police that same Monday, her witness statement signed with a shaking hand. Poor woman. She told police this:

> 'Uncle Jason isn't Susan's real uncle, not even a blood relation. Susan's dad met him in a pub a couple of months ago and they got talking. He called round and soon became a regular visitor to the house. He has more money than we do and he was very generous. He brought little presents. He has a car and was generous with that too. He drove me to the shops. He helped in all sorts of ways. He made our lives easier. We came to depend on him.'

In no time at all Uncle Jason had become indispensable to the Jameses. I've heard this so often – of abusers working their way into the family of a child who has caught their eye. But I have fallen into a trap here. Just because others have done this, I mustn't assume Uncle Jason has. The law says he is an innocent man and he will remain so unless and until a jury says otherwise. So, back to Mrs James's account.

> 'Soon, it became a regular thing for him to collect Susan from Guides on a Friday evening. He was so reliable. And on the way home he would buy fish and chips for us all. He seemed such a nice man. It was such a good arrangement. However, by December Susan was saying she didn't like Guides any more. I told her it was good for her and that Uncle Jason was kind to drive her and even kinder to buy fish and chips for us. Susan said she didn't like fish and chips. I told her that was silly because everyone likes fish and chips. After that she didn't say any more.'

Poor Mrs James has had to think of all this, and of the missed opportunities to protect her child; and she has had to recite it to the police and see it recorded in writing for consumption by strangers.

The weight of her failures lies heavy upon her. But you don't see what you can't conceive of, and it is clear that Mrs James has now been forced to see what was previously beyond her imagination.

Her statement explains how the arrangements went on and if Susan was quiet on Fridays, quieter on Saturdays, she always seemed fine by Sunday and the family put it down to the stress of the school week. Christmas came and Uncle Jason was his usual jolly, generous self. He was helping Susan's dad find a better job. He gave Susan's mum a hand with digging the tiny garden so she could plant vegetables in the spring. The household settled into the new year, and Susan said nothing more to trouble her parents until that Friday evening. So at last Mrs James gets there.

> *'She and Uncle Jason were late home from Guides. I had begun to worry, but then I heard his car, and when the bell rang I went to the door. Susan was standing alone on the step. She was holding the bag of fish and chips. Tears were running down her face.'*

Of kindly Uncle Jason there was no sign.

> *'I asked where he was but she didn't answer. Her dad asked if she had upset him – been rude to him, or been naughty – and she only cried more. She said she had a headache and went to bed. She didn't want any supper. Susan's dad tried to phone Uncle Jason but there was no answer so he left an apologetic message though he didn't know what he was apologizing for. In the morning Susan didn't want to get up. She was very pale and said she had a stomach ache.*
>
> *'I thought she was sickening for something,' said her mother. 'I thought I'd see how she was next day. But next day she only wanted to stay in bed.'*

It wasn't until that afternoon that the Jameses' world began to unravel. Mrs James described it like this:

'After lunch – Susan ate almost nothing – I collected the laundry from the basket in the bathroom and began to load the washing machine. Susan's knickers were with the week's washing. She wore clean underwear every day, seven pairs to be washed every week. I pushed them one by one into the washing machine, until something caught my eye. I looked more carefully. One of the pairs was bloodstained. Not heavily, but enough to be noticeable. I put them into the machine with the others and altered the setting to a higher temperature because of the stains. It was stupid but I wasn't thinking – at least I was thinking, but not about rape. I was thinking about Susan's age and . . . well, she was young but . . .'

Even as Mrs James had pressed the button to start the cycle, she had paused. Susan was a sensible girl and knew what was what. Surely her behaviour couldn't be . . . and anyway, there was only one pair of stained knickers. And as she watched the water sloshing into the machine and the clothes slowly turning and turning, something inside her turned too, into liquid fear.

All this is either set out in Mrs James's statement to police, or there to be drawn from between the words. She had left the washing machine to do its worst and gone up to her daughter's bedroom. When she came out twenty minutes later, her world had turned upside-down. There is no suggestion anywhere that she disbelieves or even doubts her daughter's word. After all, there was the girl's condition when she got home, and there is the underwear. The idea that there might be another perpetrator than Jason Godmer seems never to have crossed Mrs James's mind. And why would it, when Susan says it was Uncle Jason?

But how do juries look at such evidence from a mother? Do they think, 'well, who knows their child better?' or do they think, 'what mother would publicly doubt her daughter?' And of course mothers do believe their children, don't they? Wouldn't you? At least on a matter of this gravity. Mrs Marshall, when she gave evidence back in 1735, had believed her Susan. And in her case, too, there was stained underwear. Ah, how little changes in nearly three hundred years. Of course, sometimes children do lie, but surely, you might think, they do not lie about something like this. And yet . . . and yet . . . If a jury cannot be sure a victim of rape is telling the truth, it is a terrible thing. But if a man is wrongly convicted, isn't that worse? And unless and until a jury says otherwise, Jason Godmer is an innocent man.

I worry about it till lunchtime, then I go down to the judges' dining room. What do you call a gathering of judges? A pride? A murder? Today there are no guests to be entertained so we have set aside wigs and gowns and look neither proud nor murderous, only hungry. Bread rolls are passed round. There is a crisis when it is discovered the butter is missing. Butter is sent for. The crisis passes. Enquiries are made about weekend plans . . . plenty of work, some relaxation. S says he intends to finish reading a most interesting exposition of modern slavery. H says, 'Each to his own.' I say that I have a child sex case and the possibility of a defendant representing himself – no barrister, no solicitors. I am hoping for advice or comfort but H only says, 'Pass the pickle.'

I shake my head. 'Mr Godmer wants to conduct his own defence.'

'Well, he can't,' says H.

S expresses surprise that H's constitution can cope with pickle in this quantity, then adds, 'I rather think Mr Godmer can conduct his own case except, and here,' he lifts a forefinger, 'here is the critical point. He can't cross-examine the complainant.'

'That,' says H through a deal of onion, 'would seem to be the whole point of defending oneself.'

S is right, of course. I know, because I have checked. If Jason Godmer insists on dispensing with his lawyers, I will have a difficult situation to deal with because yet another change designed to protect vulnerable witnesses is a prohibition on a defendant himself (or herself) cross-examining a complainant or any child witness in proceedings for sexual offences.*† Another point for The Present.

It's old news to most of us around the lunch table but a Young Recorder‡ who has joined us for the week is aghast. Battered cod hangs forgotten on his fork. 'But surely,' he splutters, 'a man charged with rape can't be expected to let the allegation go unchallenged because he has fallen out with his lawyers.'

'Obviously not,' says S. 'But you have to bear in mind Part 23 of the Criminal Procedure Rules 2015.'

The YR tries to look as if he and his friends talk of little else, while S, a kindly man who will not mortify unless mortification is absolutely called for, explains. Following sections 34 and 35 of the 1999 Act, rules were made for its practical implementation. Part 23, to which S refers, says that if the defendant is representing himself, as is his right, the court must explain the limitation on this right in terms he can understand. Easier said than done. Especially when the defendant is Mr Godmer. The judge must then tell him he can arrange for a lawyer to carry out the cross-examination on his behalf, or the court will – if it is necessary in the interests of justice – appoint such a lawyer for him. There are pages and pages of these rules and S's exposition sees us through to the cheese. The expression

---

* YJCEA 1999 s34, see Appendix F.
† YJCEA 1999 s35, see Appendix F.
‡ A recorder (not to be confused with the Recorder of London or others who, as the senior judges in an area are called, the recorder of that area) is a barrister who has been appointed as a part-time judge sitting perhaps three or four weeks a year on less complicated cases. Such a recorder will in this way learn judgecraft, and mop up any routine cases that have crept onto the Old Bailey list.

on the Young Recorder's face suggests he will not be applying to sit at the Bailey again. Some people think that life is too short for Part 23. Others agree.

Back in my room, and having nothing else to do, I think I'll just see how they dealt with this in 1735. I had left Susan Marshall, her short account of what happened in the room behind the chandler's shop, completed. I join her again as Julian Brown gets to his feet. It seems he has no barrister to represent him, and no Part 23 to prevent him, because he turns to face his accuser and begins. And with his very first question – here's the surprise – we can actually hear his voice. Just as the scribe had tried to capture Susan Marshall speaking, so he set about recording the defendant's heavy accent.

'*Vat 'our it vas ven you come to mine Shop?*' said Julian Brown.

And Susan answered: '*What Hour? It was between Nine and Ten at Night.*'

He then asked her about the number of visits, said she never came a second time that Friday and never went into his back room that evening. She insisted she did. After asking some other questions, Mr Brown established that in the days following, she returned to his shop. He demanded to know why she would do that if he had raped her. She said, '*I went with two or three of my Play-fellows to drink a Dram.*'

The point he was making would not have been lost on the jury then any more than it would be today. Why would she willingly have returned to the scene of such a terrible thing . . . except that when you have seen enough of these cases, you begin to understand how hard it is for a young victim to accept what has happened and how great the temptation is to simply pretend it hasn't. And to go on pretending until the reality – the soreness, the injuries, the pregnancy, the trauma – can't be ignored.

So it isn't the revisiting of the chandler's shop that surprises me.

It's the reference to children drinking drams. I read and reread it. Surely she can't be saying what she seems to be saying. Can 'dram' have meant something different in 1735? But she herself had mentioned a dram of aniseed – and how else could that be drunk but as a spirit or liqueur? It's one thing for an eleven-year-old to be wandering London at midnight in search of red herrings – it's another for her to be out drinking strong liquor.

Whatever his point, Mr Brown was satisfied and sat down. Susan Marshall left the witness-box. And I must redraw the parameters of the world. We have made progress in other respects than the giving of evidence. Whether Susan Marshall was deterred by questions asked of her by the very man she was accusing is a moot point, but at least Susan James will not have to deal with this.

CHAPTER SIX

THE NEXT MORNING, I am back in court with Jason Godmer. His solicitor is there too. But not Mr Webley, who has stepped aside. Or been thrust. I don't need to check the name of his replacement, because I know her. Mary Benyon has been in my court before, and I like her sensible, no-nonsense approach. She is so tall that I imagine in the cell she will be able to look him in the eye. She is as thin as he is broad. She scorns make-up and her hair is cut rigidly short. She is straight as a die and she is vastly experienced in this sort of work. Jason Godmer has done well to get her. I suppose I and the public have done well too, because the legal aid order remains with his original solicitors and after all, it's up to them which counsel they instruct. And Susan James has done well because the cross-examination will be carried out neatly and efficiently. In fact everyone is fine except poor Mr Webley, whose self-confidence and bank balance may have taken knocks they can ill afford.* Still, life is a learning curve. As someone ... I can't bring to mind who ... observed, 'them's the breaks'. And surely, now, we can get on with the case.

Miss Benyon rises to her feet. 'My Lady, I understand there were some difficulties yesterday, but they are now resolved. We needn't trouble Your Ladyship with any further application and are ready to proceed.'

---

* Not only will he have lost the future fee, but may well have to share what he has already earned by way of preparation with whoever must now prepare the same work again.

Very good. She must have worked hard overnight to get up to speed for today's hearing. 'Thank you, Miss Benyon.'

'And I thought Your Ladyship might wish to use this morning for a Ground Rules Hearing?'

'An excellent idea, Miss Benyon.' And it is.

Have I told you about Ground Rules Hearings? This is another development since the days when Susan Marshall struggled to put her story together. Another point for The Present. Another measure designed to level the playing field for vulnerable witnesses and defendants – to enable them to participate fully in the hearing. It is part of 'fairness', of 'dealing justly' with every person involved in the trial. It allows the judge to make directions for the way in which a vulnerable witness is questioned.* Before the GRH, the judge will receive a report – often from an intermediary,† perhaps with input from a school or doctor – about a witness's ability to use and follow language, how long they can concentrate for without a break, and how they will cope. It is then up to the judge to make orders for the conduct of the hearing. Possible directions a judge can give include:

- when and how witnesses should refresh their memory by seeing their ABE
- when and how judge and counsel should meet the witness ahead of the hearing
- whether the witness needs the help of an intermediary while giving evidence
- the number and length of breaks
- the manner and duration of questioning to avoid over-rigour or repetition

---

* See Appendix G.
† See Appendix G.

- what questions are 'off-limits'
- the use of age-appropriate language
- the avoidance of complicated sentences or tags at the end of them.

In this case the report says Susan James is an equable child. What does that mean? Does it mean she doesn't feel strong emotion, or only that she doesn't express it? And if the latter, what will happen when she is pressed – as pressed she will be – in cross-examination? I read on. The intermediary has concluded Susan's abilities are consistent with her age and although she is apprehensive, she will be able to cope with the court process if appropriate adjustments are made. She will be able to understand and answer questions provided we avoid complex language and sentence structure. The report continues 'changes of subject should be flagged up for her so she does not get confused' and 'she should be given ten-minute breaks every thirty-five to forty minutes so she can concentrate properly'. All of this is easily dealt with. It does not cause the sort of problems that present with a witness aged five, or one older but with the mental age of a young child, or one with mental health issues. Still I am worried. The picture painted by the report does not, somehow, match the distressed child I saw the day before. But I am not the expert. And anyway, how can I explain what I saw? I close my eyes briefly, hoping for an answer, but none comes.

'Good. Let's deal with the Ground Rules Hearing.'

So we do. There are no disagreements from counsel about how Susan James should be questioned. No one wants the intermediary to attend the trial. No one raises difficulties. I make the appropriate orders.

'Good,' I say. 'Is there anything else I need to consider before I adjourn this hearing to Monday, when the witness will attend for cross-examination?'

'Yes,' says a strident voice.

I'm getting used to this from Mr Godmer but Miss Benyon is still learning about the problem that is her client. She suppresses a sigh. 'Would Your Ladyship give me a moment?'

I nod. As far as I'm concerned she can have as many moments as she needs to sort him out. There follow one, two, three minutes of whispering through the glass partition of the dock – furious from him, mollifying from her – before she returns to her place in counsel's row. The expression on her face is the one I have seen on Mr Webley's, and on his predecessor's before him.

'Well?' I say.

'Not entirely,' says Miss Benyon. 'It seems Mr Godmer has been checking the Rules. And the Advocate's Gateway toolkits.'*

I allow my eyebrows to rise.

'My Lady, he has been checking the authorities in anticipation of the possibility of representing himself.'

I don't ask how he has got access to a law library. Perhaps there is a black market in such things in prison. Perhaps you can exchange the Rules for a reefer, the entire Advocate's Gateway for an illicit phone call. Or perhaps they have a stock of the things free at the point of need.

'He believes the Ground Rules Hearing should take place a week before the witness gives evidence. He makes the point that since it is Friday today, the witness cannot be cross-examined until next Friday.'

I give Mr Godmer a look which he modestly deflects. I give serious thought to climbing down from the Bench and going over to the dock and . . . but no. Instead, I open my copy of the Rules. I send for copies of the Gateway and the relevant toolkit. It turns out that

---

* The Advocate's Gateway toolkits provide guidance on good practice for advocates dealing with those who have communication needs.

Mr Godmer is right about the toolkit but ... always look further, always dig deeper, and when I do I discover the source for the toolkit is the Criminal Procedure Directions. And Direction 3E.3 says only that discussion in advance of the trial is preferable so that advocates have time to adapt their questions to the witness's needs. Any references to 'one week' would seem to be advisory rather than mandatory.

Mr Purvis nods briskly. Miss Benyon says that is one interpretation. I take this as agreement. I say (is this pusillanimous?) that although a week's notice would be best if Mr Godmer were represented by someone inexperienced, he is in fact represented by Miss Benyon. 'Miss Benyon, who has ...' I stop myself from saying 'who has been dealing with Godmers for years' and replace it with 'who has graced these courtrooms for so long. Surely you, Miss Benyon, do not need time to adjust your thoughts to accord with my directions? They are, after all, very common ones.'

They are.

'Surely you can manage?'

She can.

'Very well. Susan will return to this court at ten o'clock on Monday morning to be cross-examined.'

And on this note, I remove myself from the courtroom before Mr Godmer can think of any other rule of law with which to derail my trial.

CHAPTER SEVEN

I'VE SPOKEN OF THE cross-examination of Susan James a good deal because, of course, even after the pre-recorded evidence-in-chief came into existence, the witness still has to come to court to be cross-examined. But now we seem confident of getting this done on Monday, you may be wondering why I haven't yet mentioned the jury. The answer is simple. There isn't one. Not yet. And there won't be on Monday either. And this, too, is new.

Let's go back to the 1999 statute – the one called the Youth Justice and Criminal Evidence Act. Section 27 introduced the concept of the ABE interview, which records evidence-in-chief at the time of the initial complaint. In the decades that followed, thousands of witnesses in rape cases, many hundreds of children like the Susans, having benefited from the ABE procedure, still had to face cross-examination in the course of the trial. True it is that after 1999 they might be helped by a curtain around the witness-box, or even better, be allowed to appear in the remote witness room. But still, they had to wait for months, sometimes years, for the trial in which they were cross-examined. Often they were unable to begin counselling until that ordeal was over. And all this additional grief was, in truth, unnecessary because the very next section of that very same piece of legislation enabled pre-recorded pre-trial *cross-examination*. The law was there from as far back as 1999, but was not brought into force until recently.*

---

* After 'pilot' cases in a very limited number of Crown Courts, a statutory instrument of 2020 (no. 888) led to a substantial number of courts across the country (including the Old Bailey) beginning to use the provision more or less regularly.

Of course, cross-examination cannot take place at the same time as the ABE interview because after the ABE must come the arrest of the defendant, the police interview, the charge. The defendant must then have an opportunity to instruct lawyers, to prepare his case and to seek witnesses of his own. All this takes time. But once both defence and prosecution are ready, where there is a section 27 ABE interview, section 28 permits a visual record of cross-examination or re-examination* to be made under the eyes of a judge and then to be admitted before the jury when the trial ultimately takes place.

The legislation was all there, ready to be used, yet we didn't use it for decades. Why not? Concerns were expressed about the undermining of the trial process. Problems were envisaged with early preparation of the defence case. And with finding counsel available for both earlier and trial hearings. Lawyers worried that evidence presented in this way would carry less weight. All these anxieties led to delay. But finally we have taken a deep breath and put it into effect and ... you guessed it, the difficulties have proved far less than were feared.

It is this very section 28 procedure which will take place on Monday morning. In Susan James's case it won't achieve all it should have done, because Jason Godmer has caused so many delays that the trial is due to start in a few weeks' time anyway. But at least she will be spared coming to court when the atmosphere is made fraught by the trial itself – and at least some weeks are saved.

And so Monday morning arrives. The defendant is in the dock, arms folded across his chest, staring around the courtroom. There aren't many people present beyond those involved in the case, but the public gallery is open, and other court users from time to time wander in and out. The barristers are in their places. It is

---

* See Appendix H.

time for them to meet the child. The ushers lead the way to the witness suite.

Susan is sitting on the sofa where I saw her before. Her face is still pale and blank. Leonie pushes a tissue into her hand though I can see no immediate need. I introduce counsel to her. If they are surprised by her appearance, they show no sign of it. They remove their wigs, say hello, smile. I explain to her what they will do once the hearing starts. She stares at them with that same absent look, and I worry again about that intermediary's report – whether there is something we are missing or whether she has deteriorated in the time since the report was compiled. But there is nothing to be done. I ask Leonie to take the child to the remote witness room.

'Me?' says Leonie. 'You think I can do it?' She is pink with pleasure.

'I don't see why not. And I think Susan will be better with a young woman rather than an . . . rather than Martin.'

Martin nods. 'I'll sort out the video equipment in court,' he says.

So Leonie stays to deal with Susan and the rest of us leave. On the way back downstairs Martin says, 'It can't be easy for Miss Benyon or any barrister, cross-examining a kid like that.'

'No,' I agree. 'Not easy at all.'

Martin goes to wrestle with the technology while I wait to be told all is ready. And soon it is and we are back in our places in the courtroom. There are more people in it now. A couple – they look like tourists – come into the public gallery. Police officers who have worked on the case gather near the door. Martin and my clerk bend over the equipment, turning dials and pushing knobs. The camera that links us to the remote witness room is trained on me. A journalist wanders in and sits in the press-box. He takes out a notebook and prepares himself for the morning's hearing, though he will not be able to use this material until the trial itself begins.

Martin flicks a switch and the video link flickers into life. Susan's face appears on the screen. I open my mouth to say hello to her and to explain what is about to happen when suddenly there is chaos. Mr Godmer is on his feet. He is shouting. A prison officer is trying to contain him but he will not be contained. Martin reaches out to the link equipment, looks up at me and at my nod, terminates the connection. Susan's bewildered face disappears. How quickly these things can erupt. They can be serious, violent. Defendants and dock officers can be hurt. But Jason Godmer seems more intent on gaining attention than on causing harm. Second and third dock officers appear from behind the green baize door. In moments he is held between them, purple in the face but firmly restrained. He is, however, still yelling at me, at Miss Benyon, at anyone who will listen.

'There's no need to shout, Mr Godmer. We have an excellent amplification system. You are coming across loud and clear. If you will be calm, I will permit Miss Benyon to come to the dock to speak to you. Yes?'

A pause, then he nods.

'You may speak to him through the glass, Miss Benyon. No further, mind.' I cannot risk counsel being injured. But there is no danger of that, it seems. She listens while he pours into her ears his woes. She stands back, looks around the courtroom, speaks to him again, then returns to her place.

'My Lady,' she says, 'I wonder if my client could be taken to the cells so that I can speak to him privately. There is a matter he wishes me to raise, and I need to understand his reasons.'

Susan is waiting. Any further delay is likely to disorient her. But clearly something is upsetting the defendant and I don't want another outburst while she is being questioned.

'Miss Benyon, if this is more time-wasting . . .'

'I really think,' she says, 'there is something that Mr Godmer feels he needs to speak about to me.'

'Very well. I will rise.'

Now Mr Purvis heaves himself to his feet. 'My Lady. This is grossly unfair. I . . .'

'Mr Purvis, I'm going to give Miss Benyon fifteen minutes. She will then explain what this is all about. If it proves to be a groundless interruption she knows . . . Mr Godmer knows . . . I will take a dim view of it.'

Mr Purvis shakes his head but he has made his objection and he can do no more.

Fifteen minutes later I come back in the courtroom. 'Now, Miss Benyon, perhaps you can tell me why Mr Godmer behaved as he did?'

A pause. A shake of the head. 'I can tell Your Ladyship *what* caused it, but I'm not sure I can explain *why*.'

'Try,' I say.

This time she gives an apologetic glance at the press-box where the reporter still sits. He is one of our regulars, known to us all. He has a round and innocent face above which his thinning hair is neatly combed. Everything about him bespeaks common sense and a decent respect for the job he does.

'I'm afraid,' says Miss Benyon, 'Mr Godmer takes exception to having a journalist in court.'

The journalist stops tapping. He clearly cannot believe what he thinks he just heard. He inserts a finger in one ear and wiggles it. He turns to the dock. We all do. Jason Godmer glowers.

'My client,' says Miss Benyon, 'wishes me to express his deep concern. He believes these proceedings should not be reported by the press.'

The clue is in the language she has chosen. She does not say that she is raising the objection, but that she is instructed to do so by her client. She gives a pointed and anxious look at the dock as if to remind me that she is the third barrister to try dealing with Mr Godmer, and that if I want this child to be cross-examined anytime today I had better cut her some slack and let her say what he wants her to. And after all, he may have a point. He does seem to have been making a close study of the law. I think of Susan, waiting. But . . .

'Shall we look at the law in Archbold,* Miss Benyon?' I watch the defendant reach down to produce the textbook from somewhere around his feet. He begins furiously turning pages. I get in first.

'I don't know what Mr Godmer has in mind, but the open justice at the heart of our system means generally the public have a right to attend court, and the media to report hearings fully and contemporaneously. Some restrictions apply.' I am aware I am making the law sound like a special offer at the supermarket. I hasten to add, 'I remind the reporter that publication of any matter likely to identify a complainant of sexual offence – in this case Susan – is automatically prohibited during her lifetime[†] and nothing said by her today can be published until her evidence is put before the jury in the course of the trial.'

The reporter nods. 'Of course, My Lady.'

'Well, there you are, Miss Benyon. That seems to dispose of the basics.'

Miss Benyon shakes her head. 'I'm afraid it isn't Susan about whom my client is concerned.'

'No surprise there,' says Mr Purvis, and tries to look as if he hadn't.

Miss Benyon ignores him. 'It's the identification of himself as defendant to which Mr Godmer objects.'

---

* Archbold (and another source, Blackstone) are the leading textbooks for criminal practitioners in our jurisdiction, and some others too.
† Section 1 of the Sexual Offences (Amendment) Act 1992.

Mr Purvis sighs. 'My Lady, there is no section of any statute which would protect Mr Godmer from identification.'

'Where's the justice in that?' yells Mr Godmer. 'Why should the kid be protected when I'm not? I'm an innocent man – the judge said so. Why should my name be published or my picture when I'm not guilty?'

I don't like having my own words quoted back at me. But . . . 'Mr Godmer, it would help if you would let Miss Benyon do the talking for you. She really is rather good at it and has more experience than you. She also knows the law.'

'But it's not fair,' he shouts again.

A lot of people agree with Mr Godmer on this point – including, in the not-so-distant past, a lot of MPs. In fact, the Sexual Offences (Amendment) Act 1976 introduced anonymity for both complainants and defendants in cases involving certain sexual allegations. However, anonymity for defendants was repealed by the Criminal Justice Act 1988. There has been a deal of to-ing and fro-ing on the subject ever since.

'I don't make the law, Mr Godmer. I only apply it. Let's just see what it says on this point.'

'I can tell you,' he announces. 'It says the court has an inherent power to regulate its . . . its . . .'

'Its own proceedings?' I say faintly.

'That's it. And I want you to do some regulating.'

'Mr Godmer, we are all impressed at your diligent research.' Well, I am. 'I do have such a power. But it must be exercised in accordance with the general principle, which is in favour of open justice. There is no specific rule to set against that principle. Quite the reverse. As the law presently stands, defendants have no general right to anonymity once they reach the age of eighteen.'[*]

---

[*] Appendix I.

He shakes his head vehemently. But wishing won't change the law.

'Now if you can show me that your trial will not be fair unless I abrogate the general rule, I am happy to consider the matter.'

He turns the pages of Archbold at great speed. I only hope he isn't looking up 'abrogation'.

'Miss Benyon, is there anything further you wish to submit?'

'No,' says Miss Benyon sadly.

'Mr Purvis?'

'No, My Lady.'

'Very well, if the media wish to report Mr Godmer's name or print his picture, they may do so. And if we ever get to the end of this trial, and Mr Godmer is in the unhappy position of being convicted, he can take my ruling to the Court of Appeal Criminal Division and complain about it. Now – can we please get on.'

Miss Benyon treads her weary way, yet again, to speak to her client at the back of the court. Why is it that all Mr Godmer's barristers seem to shrink under the burden of representing him? But she returns to tell me there will be no more interruptions. I am about to express gratitude when I see her fingers are crossed.

CHAPTER EIGHT

AND SO WE TRY again.

The video link is re-established. Susan reappears on the screen. Her face is as blank as a mask. The strain of delay is telling.

'Susan, we are ready to begin now. First I'd like you to read out some words – they are a promise that you will tell us all the truth and only the truth. And then Miss Benyon will ask you some questions. Do you understand that?'

She doesn't reply. She is very pale. There is a sheen of sweat on her forehead. 'Are you feeling all right, Susan?' Stupid question. Of course she isn't. Perhaps things will be better once we start.

'Leonie, would you give Susan the card with the words on it for her to read?'

The child takes the card and stares at it. After a moment she reads out the words. Her voice is painfully flat.

'Susan, do you understand the words you have read?'

She nods. 'I must tell you everything and no lies.'

'Yes.' That's it. 'Now you will see Miss Benyon on the screen. You won't see anyone else. But I will be listening to what she asks you, and to your answers. If you need anything or want a break, just tell me or Leonie. Is that OK?'

Susan makes the smallest inclination of her head. It will have to do. I tell Miss Benyon she may begin.

'Hello, Susan,' says the barrister. Seconds pass during which the recording device captures silence. No doubt the jury will pore over this in due course. It is one of the things about the use of a screen in the courtroom. Jurors are used to watching them in their own homes and analysing every flicker on the face of the hero or villain. They watch in court in the same way. If a witness pauses, hesitates, it will be dwelt upon – has she forgotten a detail or is she inventing an answer? Is she genuinely puzzled at what she is being asked or stumped because she has no answer? Has she forgotten or had there never been a memory in the beginning because the complaint is untrue? For all the advantages of this new system, it has its disadvantages too – and one of them is that it may lead a jury to overinterpret in a way appropriate for soap dramas but not for real life.

'Susan?' Miss Benyon seeks to get her attention.

Susan tears herself away from some inner thought and looks into the camera.

'When you first met Uncle Jason did you think he was very kind?'

'No,' says Susan, looking down.

'Wasn't he kind to Mummy and Daddy?' asks Miss Benyon.

Susan chooses not to answer.

'Didn't he help them?'

No answer.

'He did, didn't he?'

Susan gives a heavy sigh. 'Yes,' she says.

'He took Mummy shopping?'

'We managed OK before he came. Mum and I went shopping on the bus.'

'But he made things easier for Mummy . . . for Mum?'

Grudgingly, Susan nods.

'And that was kind, wasn't it?'

I would remind Miss Benyon to avoid tags at the end of questions but Susan doesn't need help on this.

'Maybe,' she says, 'he just wanted Mum to trust him. So that he could . . . could get me alone.'

'It's what you say now, but it's not what you thought then, is it?'

Susan frowns. 'I don't know what you mean.'

I intervene. 'Miss Benyon, find another way to ask your question, please.'

Miss Benyon shakes her head. 'I'll move on if I may, My Lady.'

And she does. She sets about a systematic examination of the contents of the ABE, during which Susan becomes more and more silent. Unable or unwilling to answer. It could be the genuine distress of a traumatized child. But it could be a sulky pre-teenager. And Miss Benyon only needs to be able to say to the jury that it *might* be the latter. Susan is playing into the hands of the barrister who, no doubt buoyed up by this, suggests that nothing improper happened in the car at all. Susan stares.

'Do you agree with me?'

Susan puts her head down, elbows on the table, hands over her eyes. She isn't coping with this. I don't know how long she can keep going and I am anxious to get this finished in one sitting if I can. So, 'Move on, please, Miss Benyon.'

Miss Benyon does. Next, she turns to the car's front seat, which she says was too small to accommodate Uncle Jason and Susan in the way the girl had described. Susan mutters something inaudible. Miss Benyon asks her to speak up. Her voice comes, faint but distinct.

'I was smaller then,' she says.

Miss Benyon suggests that nothing bad happened in the car, that they were playing games and she had been happy to do so.

Susan says nothing. If this is to stand as her evidence for the jury she needs to answer, but she has retreated somewhere inside herself.

'Susan,' I keep my voice neutral, 'is Miss Benyon right? Were you happy in the car?'

'I was crying,' she whispers.

'Ah, yes,' says Miss Benyon. 'The tears. You were certainly crying when you got home.'

Susan nods.

'But by then you had been rude to Uncle Jason and he was upset...'

No answer.

'...and you knew he would tell your parents...'

Nothing.

'...and you were afraid they would be cross with you.'

The smallest movement of Susan's head. Miss Benyon pauses, gives her every opportunity to agree or disagree but Susan does not speak.

'If something really happened in the car – something you didn't like and which made you cry – why didn't you tell Mummy when you got home?'

Again nothing. I won't let this go on much longer. But if I stop it before Miss Benyon has had a chance to ask her questions, what then?

The barrister tries again. 'Why not, Susan? Answer my question, please.'

'I don't know.'

'You don't know!' Miss Benyon adopts an expression of mock surprise, though she could hardly have hoped for a better response. Uncle Jason is smiling and nodding.

Suddenly Miss Benyon seems to lose patience. 'You didn't tell your mum that night, nor the next day, nor the next. You didn't tell her or anyone. You didn't mention it until your mum asked you about the state of your knickers.'

'Miss Benyon,' I am giving her a warning. 'Remember the Ground Rules.'

'I apologize, My Lady.' But Uncle Jason is grinning, and perhaps she can feel his encouragement because she persists. 'Still,' she says, 'I would like an answer to the question why Susan didn't make a complaint. It is of course a central point in my client's case that she had nothing to complain about.' Her voice has risen. She leans forward, her long body angled against her lectern, more intense with every word. Good advocates have a beast inside them that can scent blood, and the stench of it is strong in the nostrils of this one.

'Really, Miss Benyon!' She is going way beyond what is appropriate with a witness like this. 'You know the Rules. I expect . . .'

But it doesn't matter what I expect. Miss Benyon and I, in the exchange between us, have lost sight of the child. Never do that. Never stop watching. But I did. And at the critical moment. At least, it is critical for Susan, because she can take no more. With one quick movement she stands up and pushes away the table.

'Susan,' I say. But it is too late.

Leonie has leapt to her feet but that is too late as well.

'Go away,' screams the child. 'Go away all of you.' And she picks up her chair and smashes it into the television screen.

I have no idea what she does after that because the link is disconnected. I don't even know if she can still see or hear us, though that seems unlikely.

'Take the defendant down to the cells,' I say sharply. 'Someone from witness support should take care of Susan. She is not to leave the witness suite. I shall rise. Leonie is to come to my room and report on what is happening and anything that Susan may have said after the link was broken.'

I am furious with Miss Benyon. I wouldn't have expected it of her. She is so steady. I thought I could trust her. But am I being unfair? After all, her job is to represent her client. Until that final point, she had conducted herself and her cross-examination with care and respect. I remember Martin saying 'what must it be like to question a kid like that?'. I did it often enough when I was at the Bar. Being an advocate isn't an easy job. Counsel can be under huge pressure too. And perhaps it wouldn't have mattered how she had spoken. Perhaps Susan had just had more than she could take.

CHAPTER NINE

IN MY CHAMBERS I sip cold coffee and wonder what are the chances of getting Susan back into the witness room today – or ever. And whether I should even try. The child had been so upset. After all, Miss Benyon has had a good opportunity to test her. What has she lost by Susan withdrawing from the proceedings? The damage – if damage there be – is to Mr Purvis's case. He hasn't had the chance to re-examine – to ask those questions arising out of cross-examination – his chance to put Susan's evidence back on the prosecution track. Without this his case may be severely weakened. He can be sure that Miss Benyon will stress to the jury that the point at which Susan finally 'lost it' wasn't in dealing with events in the car. It was in response to questions about why she hadn't told her parents straight away. Because – Miss Benyon will say – if the complaint is true, why didn't she tell her mum when she got home? And what will the jury make of that?

I see this again and again. Complainants who don't make their complaint at the first opportunity and defendants who say it has been made up later. We – the lawyers, the jurors, even the public – place such reliance on a victim making their allegation at an early stage. We even have a special category of evidence for it – it's called 'recent complaint'.* But Susan is one of an endless stream of women

---

* At common law, the fact that a complainant of sexual attack had made her complaint at the first reasonable opportunity could be admitted at trial to show consistency with her evidence. This was called 'recent complaint'. Section 120 of the Criminal Justice Act 2003 provides such evidence can now be admitted to show not just consistency but also the truth of what she says.

and girls who fail to say they have been raped until days, weeks, sometimes years, have gone by. It's nothing new. Back in 1735 Julian Brown asked the same question Miss Benyon has asked today.

'*Why,*' he said, '*did you not complain before Monday?*'

And Susan Marshall's reply? '*Because I was afraid my mother would beat me.*'

And why should she think her mother would beat her? Because, I suppose, she thought she would be blamed. How often do women and girls feel that somehow these terrible things are their fault? Perhaps because – before the event itself – they enjoyed the attention a man paid to them? Or perhaps because he has seduced all those around her into thinking he is a nice, a kind person? Then there is the prospect that once the words are spoken, everything will change – that if she speaks out, she will be in new and uncharted territory. She may be anxious that her home will be torn apart, all certainty and security gone. Sometimes there is the fear of being disbelieved. Often there is terror of retribution from the wrongdoer. And sometimes a victim just doesn't know how to say what has happened – there is shock and trauma and a plain inability to put it into words. In the light of all this, perhaps we should not be surprised at a delay in making an accusation. Perhaps we should rather be surprised that any complainant ever comes forward straight away.

That Susan has had enough becomes increasingly clear. The messages from the witness suite are of her distress. She refuses to come back to face Miss Benyon and any more of her questions. She hates Miss Benyon. She hates Uncle Jason. She hates everyone. She wants to go home. I could insist on speaking to her myself, but would that do any good? Or would it do more harm? I accept the reality. There is no way I am getting this child back into the witness room today.

I return to court and tell counsel.

'But . . .' Miss Benyon is on her feet.

I want to say 'but me no buts'. I want to say 'this is all your fault for going beyond the Ground Rules I set down, for asking multiple questions that she couldn't cope with'. I want to say a great deal more, but I don't. I give her the opportunity to say what she wants to – that she hasn't finished her cross-examination.

'Oh yes, you have,' I say. 'At least for today.'

I order that Susan should be taken home and that she and all those concerned should be told they must not speak about her evidence until I make a decision as to how things will proceed. I do this because I must protect the integrity of the trial process if I can. But the decision must be taken quickly, because whatever happens in the trial – and whether Jason Godmer is ultimately convicted or acquitted – Susan needs help and must get it soon.

'I intend to give the child time to calm down and to see if, over the two weeks that remain before the trial date arrives, she is prepared and able to return to finish her evidence. If so, well and good. But if not, we will have to decide what to do. Miss Benyon, you are welcome to try to persuade me your client is disadvantaged, but you will have an uphill task. You have put your case. You have tested her extensively.'

'I could have put more,' she says. 'There are other important matters. My client is disadvantaged if I don't complete my cross-examination . . .'

At this Uncle Jason nods vigorously. 'Go on,' he mouths to her.

And she does. 'I may have to ask that the proceedings are stopped as an abuse of the court's process* and that a verdict of not guilty is recorded because the trial is not fair.'

---

* The court has an overriding duty to prevent injustice. To this end it can stop (or stay) a prosecution if to allow it to continue would be an abuse of the process of the court. This arises if either it is impossible for the defendant to have a fair trial or if it is necessary to protect the integrity of the criminal justice system.

'Yessss,' says Uncle Jason.

I feel my eyes widen as I say, 'Is that so?'

Miss Benyon has the grace to blush.

'What other matters were you thinking of asking her?'

'Well . . .' She hesitates.

What's she up to now? Or rather, what's he up to?

'My Lady, I was thinking of making an application to cross-examine the witness about how else she might have sustained her genital injuries. Other sexual encounters.'

This comes as news to me – and if any such application had been in the offing, it should have been flagged up by her well before this. The law – the dear old Youth Justice and Criminal Evidence Act 1999, this time section 41* – does not permit cross-examination about previous sexual experience without leave of the court. But Miss Benyon knows this as well as I do. So I content myself with raising an eyebrow and wait to hear more.

'The information upon which I would wish to cross-examine,' she says, 'has only recently come to my attention, and I have an application to make under section 41. If it is successful, and if Susan does not return to be cross-examined on it, and if—'

'That's a lot of "ifs". Supposing we take them one at a time. Let us see first if there is anything in the new material that would warrant this cross-examination.'

'The child has physical injuries,' says Miss Benyon. 'If there is some other explanation – some other potential perpetrator . . .'

'I've already said we will take this stage by stage. Let's start with what it is you have discovered. What do you want to ask Susan about?'

In the dock, Mr Godmer has his arms in the air. He is waving Archbold – no mean feat given the size and weight of it. 'What

---

* Appendix J.

about section 41?' he shouts. His tone is that of the heckler at a political meeting who calls out, 'What about Potiphar's wife?' If he spent last night reading section 41 of the Youth Justice and Criminal Evidence Act 1999, I can't criticize his thoroughness. 'Mr Godmer, you have my word that if section 41 becomes relevant, it will be given the fullest consideration. But the question of section 41 does not arise until I am satisfied that the material passes the first and basic test of admissibility – namely: is it capable of proving anything about the issues in this case?'

I have no idea whether the material does or doesn't pass this test, but Mr Purvis is looking smug and so . . . let's see. 'Now, Miss Benyon, what is this material?'

Miss Benyon closes her eyes. Composing herself, or praying?

'My Lady, the week before the alleged incident, the witness was kept in detention after school for her behaviour with another child, a boy in her year. She and the boy were asked after the morning lesson to remain in the biology laboratory to clean and put away equipment that had been used by the class. When the children did not appear at lunch, a teacher went to find them. They were discovered in a cupboard at the rear of the laboratory.' She pauses.

'And?' Whatever is she going to tell me? That two eleven-year-olds were found in flagrante delicto? In a cupboard?

'Well . . .' says Miss Benyon.

'Would it help,' Mr Purvis is all sweetness, 'if I were to read aloud the report upon which Miss Benyon relies? Just so we can all see the force of her application.' He doesn't wait for a reply. 'My Lady, police obtained in the course of standard enquiries at the school, a brief report of a detention that was given to Susan. Naturally I disclosed it to the defence. It is the content of this upon which Miss Benyon relies. And she is right that two pupils were asked to remain behind to clear up after a lesson. The teacher who went to the laboratory found them in a store cupboard at the rear of the block. The teacher's report reads thus: "Tom was on his knees..."'

Surely not. Surely not Tom and Susan. In the biology lab. But no. I should have had more faith in Tom. And Susan. Mr Purvis continues reading from the teacher's note.

'"Tom was picking up pieces of glass. Susan said she had dropped a beaker and they wanted to hide the evidence. Susan was reprimanded for carelessness and both were put in detention for seeking to conceal a matter that should have been brought to my attention. This is the seventh beaker to be broken in my lab this term and the matter is becoming serious."'

'A beaker?' I say. 'Miss Benyon, you want to tell the jury that Susan broke a beaker?'

From the back of the court Mr Godmer shouts, 'She says it was a beaker. But how do you know what they were up to?'

Miss Benyon and I both ignore him.

'Miss Benyon, are you suggesting this could possibly explain Susan's genital injuries?' I keep my tone even. I do not say, 'Dear woman, you are allowing your client to override your judgement.' It certainly won't help if I provoke Mr Godmer into thinking he can do better representing himself. But I don't need to hear any more.

'This material,' I say, 'is not admissible because it has no relevance to any issue in the case.' In the dock the defendant is on his feet, but really I have had enough of this. 'Mr Godmer, Miss Benyon has said all she or anyone else could on this point. I rule against her. You may add this to your list of appeal points should you ever need points to appeal.' I draw a deep breath. 'Moreover, I am satisfied that Susan's failure to complete her evidence cannot disadvantage the defendant or the defence case. But ...' and here's the rub, 'Mr Purvis, what about the position of the prosecution? You have not had the opportunity to re-examine the witness. It is your right to do so and you are entitled to ask me to get her back so that you can; but since she is your witness, you may take the view it is better to bear the disadvantage than to put her through any more.'

Mr Purvis gets to his feet and nods gravely. 'We ... that is the CPS, the police and myself ... have been considering the position,' he says. 'We have spoken briefly to Susan's parents. We would like to see if Susan will return voluntarily to finish her evidence.'

'Of course. But if she will not?'

'Then, unfortunate as the situation is, I do not think I can justify forcing her back to court or putting her through the stress of answering further questions against her will. If Your Ladyship is satisfied that there is sufficient in the recording already made to enable a fair trial, we for the Crown would be content with that.'

'In that case,' I say, 'the trial will remain fixed for Monday week. In the meantime, if Susan is willing to return to answer more questions I will consider recalling her. If she isn't, the trial will proceed with what we have, which will include the recordings made of the ABE interview and the section 28 procedure.'

Mr Godmer is making frantic signs to Miss Benyon, but she refuses to see them. No doubt she will go straight from court down to the cells. I wish her luck in what will follow.

CHAPTER TEN

THE TWO WEEKS PASS, and Susan still refuses to come back to court. She has told the kindly police liaison officer that she won't answer any more questions and that she doesn't want to think about any of this ever again. I have the power to make her. It is possible to use contempt proceedings against some witnesses who won't give their evidence ... to have them brought to court under arrest if necessary. But I have no intention of doing that to a twelve-year-old who may be a victim of rape. When she says she never wants to think about 'these things' again I'm sure that is what she genuinely feels now. I fear, however, that she must think of them again, because somehow she must be helped from the place at which she has arrived to a better place – or at least to one where she can learn to move forward. Whatever Uncle Jason has – or hasn't – done, Susan still has a life to lead and this ... all this ... must not be allowed to subsume the other things she can do and be. If healing is possible, she must be helped to heal. But the courtroom isn't the place for that. Mr Purvis must manage without her; and Miss Benyon is free to make what she can out of the incomplete evidence.

The day of the trial arrives and the court assembles. Although Miss Benyon is still representing the defence, Mr Godmer seems determined to have his input from the dock. He achieves this with a variety of gestures and comments. When I ask Miss Benyon whether we can go through a whole trial like this, she assures me that once we have a jury in court, her client will contain himself. She points out that he is under great stress because he is on trial for his liberty and ...

'And I'm an innocent man,' he reminds me.

Quite so. And Miss Benyon turns out to be right. I can only suppose she has spoken long and hard with him about his conduct in front of the jury, because from the moment the panel appears and twelve are called and are sworn in – from that moment he is a model of rectitude. Apart from the dark looks he keeps giving to the press-box.

So, off we go. Mr Purvis opens his case. It's simple enough and it takes him less than half an hour, then he moves on to the evidence. He begins with that from Susan which is, after all, the heart of his case. He plays the ABE interview and then the recording of the section 28 cross-examination – with the exchanges between counsel and me edited out. The jurors are totally focused on their screens, absorbed in the face, the words, every movement and gesture of the child who fills their vision. Of course, the cross-examination finishes abruptly, in a way no one would have wished – and they see this too. I had thought we might simply tell them that Susan had declined to answer further questions but Miss Benyon, on instructions from her client, wants the whole thing put before the jury, including the violent ending. It seems Mr Godmer wants them to see the sort of things Susan is capable of. There is no reason in law why I should withhold this part of the recording from the jury, and since the defence want it in evidence, it is played with the rest.

The twelve jurors – seven men and five women – are visibly surprised by the change in the child in the ABE and the one in the section 28 recording. They are clearly frustrated by her refusal to answer questions in cross-examination, and plain shocked by her violent outburst. Mr Purvis has some ground to make up, but he does have good material to work with and towards the end of this first day, he deploys it to considerable effect. He calls the doctor who examined Susan soon after her mother called the police. The doctor is as sensible and experienced as Miss Benyon herself, but, as a scientist, is cautious. She will not be tempted into going beyond the pure science. All she will say is something has penetrated the vagina of this eleven-year-old with force. Something has caused bruising around the labia and a tear in the hymen. The injuries were likely inflicted between twenty-four and seventy-two hours before the examination. In answer to Miss Benyon's enquiry, she agrees that 'likely' isn't 'certain'. She also agrees that she cannot say whether it was fingers or a penis or even an inanimate object that did the penetrating. Beyond this she cannot go. She certainly cannot say it was Jason Godmer who inflicted the injuries.

Where does Mr Purvis take us next? To another expert witness, this one a forensic scientist specializing in body fluids and DNA. If only there had been any. The witness shakes his head at the stupidity of people. If only, he says, the mother hadn't washed the clothing. If only she hadn't put it in a hot wash with bleach. Then he might have been able to recover DNA, even semen, from a perpetrator. But as it is, nothing can be safely interpreted from the limited laboratory results. To Miss Benyon's question whether he has come across cases where inquisitive eleven-year-old girls experiment with objects, he says it is outside his area of expertise.

'Well,' says Miss Benyon, 'let's see if you can answer this. Could a child – approaching puberty and curious about her body – have inflicted the injuries on herself?'

'Definitely outside my area of expertise,' says the witness.

Miss Benyon does not pursue the matter. She doesn't need to. The seed is planted in the jury's mind.

The diligent journalist is still in the press-box. He has not let the defendant's earlier attack deflect him from sitting through the day's hearing. He has kept writing despite the hard looks sent in his direction from the dock. But nothing can alter the evidence. And at the end of the first day Mr Godmer, for all his weight, goes down to the cells with a sprightly step. Mr Purvis's head, on the other hand, is down. The slump of his shoulders says it all.

Next morning brings a marginal reversal of things. Mr Purvis has brightened up. He still has the mother to come, and she is a patently honest woman. He must be thinking that the jury will like her. Mr Godmer, on the other hand, is looking less chipper. Perhaps he has seen the press reports. I certainly have. The case hasn't made the nationals, but has wide coverage online, especially in those titles local to the general area where all this happened. And although, in accordance with my orders, nothing is reported capable of identifying Susan, the defendant's full name, date of birth and photograph are there to be seen by anyone who looks. The photograph was one taken at the police station after his arrest. No doubt it is not the one Mr Godmer would have chosen for this embarrassing exposure. But there it is. Still, there is nothing in the national press, and nothing Miss Benyon can complain about.

Mr Purvis begins the second day by calling Mrs James. In the flesh she is smaller than I had imagined – a neat woman, tidily dressed, nervous but determined. She gets into the witness-box, takes the oath, speaks more loudly when asked to. She looks about the large room, catches sight of Godmer in the dock and flushes very red. She turns away from him and does not look back.

Mr Purvis takes her through her evidence-in-chief. She tells the jury all that she had put in her witness statement – tells them about Susan's coming home distressed, her strange behaviour over the weekend. She tells them how on Sunday afternoon she went to do the weekly wash, as she always did. She described how she saw the marks on the knickers. Susan was only eleven and had not yet had her first period. And she thought – didn't think – only after she had put the washing in the machine and turned it on, had it occurred to her – but she didn't really know what had occurred to her, only a horrible feeling that something was wrong. And by the time she had spoken to Susan it was too late because the spin cycle had started.

Mr Purvis is satisfied. Miss Benyon gets to her feet.

'This must be very hard for you,' she says gently.

Mrs James agrees.

'So I'll make it as short as possible.'

'Thank you.'

'In fact, I'll ask only one question. You found seven pairs of knickers in the weekly wash, and one of them was stained in a way that caused you concern. But which of the seven pairs had Susan been wearing on that Friday?'

'I'm not sure I know what you mean,' says Mrs James. If that is so, she is the only person in the room who doesn't. Can Mrs James link the bloodstained underwear to the Friday – the only day of the week when Jason Godmer had been alone with Susan?

Miss Benyon asks the question again and this time Mrs James sees the point. 'Well,' she says, 'I assumed . . .'

'Please,' says Miss Benyon, still gentle, 'please don't make assumptions. Just answer the question. Can you say which of the seven pairs of knickers Susan wore on that Friday?'

'Well . . . well . . . no. I can't. But . . .'

But Miss Benyon sits down, and after a moment's thought Mr Purvis declines to get up – for what question could he ask to put this right?

CHAPTER ELEVEN

The rest of the day is occupied with the last of Mr Purvis's case. None of it is likely to help him. There is evidence of the arrest – three officers called, each of whom describes Jason Godmer's look of astonishment, his protestations of shock, his denials. Then there was his arrival at the police station and his demands that he speak to someone, to lawyers, because this was all ridiculous. Then the police interview in which he expounded at length his theory of why Susan was lying about him.

As the afternoon progresses, Mr Godmer nods more, scowls less. Throughout it all the journalist scribbles furiously. But Mr Purvis has given up keeping notes, and Miss Benyon contents herself with marginal flourishes.

After we rise, I go down to tea. I am trying not to feel depressed. Because after all, why should I? I have no stake in the verdict. I have no way of knowing what is the right verdict. None of that is my business. My business is to make sure there is a fair trial.

From the biscuit barrel, S has taken a pack of Little Gems and is setting them out in an equilateral triangle across the tea table. From time to time H, in a fit of abstraction, picks up and eats the end of S's median bisector. There is little talk, and what there is stutters and fades. Interest is infused into the proceedings when H suggests we see who has had the worst day. There is competition on this front. One judge has spent the whole time in his room, waiting for a defendant to be produced from prison. Another has a jury in retirement, apparently unable to reach a verdict in 'the most obvious of cases'. Someone else has had a row with counsel, which he describes with a thump of fist on table so forceful that H's tea splashes out of its cup. We stare at the spreading stain.

'How is your difficult defendant?' asks H at last.

'Increasingly easy,' I say. 'He believes he is on the verge of a triumphant acquittal. Tomorrow he will get into the witness-box and tell the jury how innocent he is.'

'And is he?'

I shrug. How do I know? 'It's the system,' I say. 'But is it justice?'

S looks at me and shakes his head. 'The process,' he says, 'is all.' And with a sweep of his arm he pulls the little shining biscuits into a pile which he deposits in front of H.

And S is right. We have a process and it must be gone through. And so I arrive the following morning, ready for what is to follow. It begins with Martin. But instead of the knock on my door, he pushes it open and sticks his head in.

'Something's going up,' he says.

'Up?'

'Or down. Either way, something is happening.'

'Explain,' I demand.

It seems that Martin had found the reporter outside the courtroom door. He was looking for the officers in the case. They were sent for and he spoke to them.

'Didn't you hear what they were saying?'

Martin shakes his head. 'Not for want of trying,' he says. 'But it was all whispering. Then they asked me to get a message to Purvis to come double-quick. Which I did. Then there was more whispering. And Mr Purvis asked me to put out a tannoy for Miss Benyon. And then she came. And then they all disappeared.'

'What do you mean, disappeared?'

'Vanished,' he said. 'Gone. That was half an hour ago and now it's three minutes to ten o'clock. The jurors are in their room. The defendant is in the cells. But there's no sign of any of them.'

'Not even the journalist?'

'Not even him.'

A pause while we both reflect. I try to think what might have caused this – has Susan decided she wants to finish her evidence after all, or has something come to light about her credibility or . . . or . . . but speculation is pointless.

'Leave the jurors in their room. Apologize to them for the delay and say . . .' What message can I send them? I must not lie or mislead them but I have no idea what is going on. '. . . say we are sorting out an administrative matter.' That should cover it, I hope.

It is twenty minutes later when I receive a request from counsel to come into court.

'Miss Benyon, is all well with your client?'

I ask because the Jason Godmer I have come to know is absent. Instead there is a husk hunched into his seat, head down in a gesture that reminds me, strangely, of Susan.

'That remains to be seen,' she says.

The two barristers exchange looks.

'Would someone like to tell me what is going on?'

'May I ask,' says Mr Purvis, 'that the journalist who has been reporting on these proceedings comes to sit behind me? I may need to check things with him as I explain to Your Ladyship what has happened overnight.'

I struggle with my eyebrows and have them under control before the journalist arrives behind counsel.

'There has been a development,' says Mr Purvis. 'Late last evening a young woman contacted the journalist who sits behind me. Early this morning another contacted the police. Both had read the report of yesterday's court proceedings. Both had seen the photograph of the defendant. One girl is fifteen, the other sixteen years old. Both gave similar accounts of being sexually assaulted by the man in the photograph.'

'Mr Godmer?'

'That was not the name by which they knew the man. Both knew him as Jason Pritchard.' Mr Purvis pauses. I can tell from his face that he has another card to play. He produces it with a flourish. 'Pritchard,' he says, 'is the defendant's mother's maiden name.'

Oh, Mr Godmer. Chickens are fluttering home. Roosts are readying themselves.

'My Lady, if there is any strength in these allegations, it is of the utmost relevance to the current trial.'

'*If*,' says Miss Benyon.

This is the moment at which the Mr Godmer I know should have leapt to his feet and shaken his fist in support of that 'if', but this Mr Godmer doesn't move.

'So what do you want me to do, Mr Purvis?' As if I didn't know.

'May I suggest that we send the jury away for the rest of the day, while urgent enquiries are made? Both young women are willing to make statements and ABE interviews can be carried out later today. Given the length of time that has elapsed since they assert the assaults took place, it is unlikely there will be medical or scientific evidence, but consideration must be given to the credibility of their late complaints.' He tries to keep his voice even – contemplating the possibility that two other girls have each, independently, invented complaints against Jason Godmer. Tries and fails.

'Mr Purvis, if the girls prove not to be reliable, I assume we will continue with this trial?'

'That would be the Crown's wish, My Lady.'

'But if they seem to be credible witnesses?'

'Then the Crown may ask for the jury in the present case to be discharged, and that there is a future trial on the allegations made by all three complainants.'

'Miss Benyon?'

She shakes her head. 'I can't object to an adjournment until tomorrow,' she says, 'but the defence may object to any discharge of this jury.'

And from the dock? The old Uncle Jason briefly makes an appearance. 'It's not fair.' His cry of anguish echoes through the courtroom and follows me out of the door.

But what is 'fair'? What is 'just'?

If there are two more girls, unrelated to each other or to Susan, what are the chances of all three having invented a similar story against the same man? How much more likely does it make it that each is essentially telling the truth? Put another way – if the current trial proceeds and the jury acquits, not because they are sure Susan is lying, but because they cannot be sure she is telling the truth – how would they feel if it then came to light that two other unrelated girls had made the same accusation against the same man? How would you feel? Would it be you, then, who was howling 'it's not fair'?

Next day, Mr Purvis arrives with preliminary interviews from the two girls who have come forward. Everyone must have worked exceptionally quickly to produce this material in twenty-four hours. It is far from ideal, but it sets out the basis of what they are saying. Of course, the investigations are nowhere near complete – that will take some time – but there is sufficient to show both these girls are making cogent complaints, with remarkable similarities to those made by Susan James. In each case Jason Godmer had befriended families with daughters in their very early teens. He had found opportunities to be alone with the girls. In one case the incident had happened, as with Susan, in his car. In the other, in a park where he had driven her. One girl says she didn't come forward because she didn't think anyone would believe her, but that when she saw in the local paper he had done it again and to an even younger child, she had found courage. The other says she couldn't face talking about it, but the idea of him going on and on, doing it to other girls, was more than she could bear and so . . . Thank the Lord for sisterhood!

'Miss Benyon?'

This morning Miss Benyon is free to say what she thinks because her client has refused to come up to court. What Miss Benyon thinks is this.

'I doubt there is anything I can say to dissuade Your Ladyship from discharging this jury and ordering a retrial.'

'You're welcome to try, Miss Benyon.'

So she does. 'It would seem unfair,' she says, 'that Susan should have another chance to give her evidence.'

'She won't,' I say. 'Her evidence must stand as it is. The ABE and section 28 recordings would be her evidence at a retrial, just as they are at this trial. Anything else?'

'Um. It would be an additional strain on the witnesses in this matter if they had to give their evidence all over again.'

I give this some thought. 'The officers and experts can repeat their evidence without stress. It's their job. I do agree that it is unfortunate Mrs James would have to come to court again but if she is willing to . . .' I look at Mr Purvis, who nods emphatically, '. . . I see no injustice to the defence in it.'

Miss Benyon nods reluctantly.

'And of course,' I add, 'I will order a transcript of the evidence Mrs James has already given, to assist you in cross-examination should she say anything different on a future occasion. There will be a fresh trial. It will be expedited to ensure the earliest possible hearing date. And one more thing. Since Susan's active part in any trial is as complete as it is going to get, immediate thought should be given to counselling for her. I make no order about that. I can't because it is not my business, but it is common sense.'

And so, there will be two further prosecutions, and Mr Purvis will prepare an indictment alleging sexual assaults and rapes on three young girls. The evidence of each will undoubtedly support the others. And oh, Jason Godmer, justice – whatever that is – is on its way to meet you.

CHAPTER TWELVE

LATER, IN THE PRIVACY of my room, I revisit Susan Marshall. I feel I owe it to her. There are many reasons why in her case the jury may have acquitted. There are things we will come to later. But the simple fact is that an eleven-year-old girl was called on to stand in front of a large number of strangers and to speak of most intimate events, to do so and be tested upon detail six months after the incident, and to face publicly being called a liar. Wherever the truth lay in her case, she was unlikely to be able to give her best evidence.

Since those days we have made many changes, all designed to 'level the playing field' for vulnerable witnesses. We have brought in the curtain and the remote witness room, the ABE and the section 28 recordings, the Ground Rules Hearing, the rule against exploring a complainant's sexual history without permission of the court, the prohibition on public identification of a complainant in the media... but for all these changes, were it not for the other two girls who came forward at the last minute, might we still have been writing under the archived record of Susan James's case, the word 'acquitted'?

If Jason Godmer is indeed guilty of these offences, it isn't the changes outlined above that have brought us closer to a just result. In this area of law which deals with truly horrible offending, few of the guilty are brought to publicly face their wrongdoing and to pay for it. The material issued by those who support women in the crisis of rape shows that the number of offences hasn't dropped; but the number of convictions makes depressing reading. It behoves us to look very carefully at why this is. When we do, the reasons are not hard to see.

Before I consider them, may I be forgiven for saying this: in examining the trauma for victims of sexual offences, we mustn't underestimate the trauma for an innocent defendant. Although the number of false complaints may be comparatively few, there are undoubtedly some. And we shouldn't ignore the possibility that very occasionally a defendant has genuinely not understood that the woman did not want sexual contact. There can, of course, be no misunderstanding of the word 'no', only wilful deafness to it. But where the word is not said, circumstances can be surprisingly complex. In Spain they take the view that only 'yes' means 'yes'. There may be a lot of sense in this. But back to the question of why so few rapists are brought to justice. Here are some thoughts.

In the recent past various people have criticized juries for believing stereotypical myths against women leading to bias in favour of the defendant and wrongful acquittals. And so there has been a call by some for serious sexual offences to be removed from juries. Presumably those who raise this argument think a judge more capable of a 'right' decision; think that one legally trained mind is somehow better than twelve minds pooling their collective experience of life. Before we take so grave a step as depriving defendant, complainant and public of a jury, we need to be very sure that is the best thing to do. After all, the jury system has been widely regarded as the gold standard of fairness. That there can be a problem in sex cases was recognized as long ago as 2010* when the Court of Appeal endorsed the use of properly tailored directions by judges to counter this risk. There is now clear guidance for judges to give jurors.† This guidance warns against allowing false assumptions or misleading stereotypes about rape to affect their decision. There is a general warning – 'there is no typical rape, typical rapist or typical person that is raped. Rape

---

* R v. Miller [2010] EWCA Crim 1578.
† Appendix K.

can take place in almost any circumstance. It can happen between all different kinds of people. And people who are raped react in a variety of different ways'. Then there are specific warnings including that jurors *must not assume*:

- a delayed complaint must be untrue. Some people complain straight away but others may not out of shame, shock, confusion, fear of getting into trouble or of causing problems for others or of not being believed.
- if a complainant says something 'new' in the witness-box it must be untrue. Shocking, upsetting or traumatic experiences can affect the ability to take in and recall experiences. Equally, evidence consistent with a previous complaint isn't necessarily true.
- a victim should react in a particular way. There is no normal level of emotion or distress. Indeed, some people may be unable to show any reaction at all.
- because someone dresses in revealing clothes or is drunk, they are consenting to sex. Nor that either of these things can give rise in a defendant to reasonable belief in such consent.
- just because a person previously had consensual sex with the defendant, that she must have consented on this occasion. Nor that this gives grounds to a defendant to reasonably believe in such consent.
- just because a person let the defendant into her home and willingly engaged in kissing, that she must have consented to sex. A person is entitled to choose how far sexual activity goes, and to say no to anything further.
- just because a person did not struggle, that they consented. There is a difference between submission and consent (even reluctant consent).

So juries are given a lot of warnings against making assumptions. Is it true that, despite this, jurors remain biased against women complainants? The statistics suggest they are not – at least, that is the view of Professor Cheryl Thomas* after her careful research into all verdicts in England and Wales over a recent fifteen-year period. She found that on average jurors had convicted in 58 per cent of these cases; and that in the last few years, that average had risen to over 70 per cent. She suggests the increase may be because of changing social attitudes or improving prosecution techniques. She does not think it is because the CPS cherry-picked only the strongest of cases, though it is not clear what statistic allows her to say this. Whatever the cause, the recent conviction rate is higher than in attempted murder, manslaughter, GBH and threats to kill.

But if the problem does not lie with juries, where does it lie? It seems clear that (i) many who are victims of rape never complain to the police at all, and (ii) of those who do, many withdraw their complaint or do not see it through to the end of the trial process. The reasons for this are again easy enough to see. For example:

- while anyone – woman, girl, other – can be a victim, wrongdoers have always targeted those most likely to be afraid to complain, most likely to be disbelieved or to fear they will be disbelieved;
- for a woman or girl who has been physically hurt and/or mentally and emotionally traumatized, the telling of it – which the law requires if a complaint is even to be considered – can be an agony;
- the medical examination may feel like a further invasion;

---

* *Juries, Rape and Sexual Offences in the Crown Court 2007–21* by Cheryl Thomas, Professor of Judicial Studies, UCL: Director, UCL Jury Project

- there may be real fear of further invasion of privacy by the system's demands on investigating a complainant's private life, e.g. her mobile phone and diaries;
- the need to keep recounting detail brings back the pain without giving a chance to heal it;
- the long – sometimes very long – wait for trial, which drains the will;
- failures of practice, e.g. the CPS not making full disclosure, may lead to the case collapsing;
- if there is to be a trial, the witness will be challenged and treated as or even called a liar.

If these points are valid, the first problem to face is how we give victims confidence to go to the police at all. The second problem is how to ensure the CPS fulfils its duties to both prosecution and defence, so cases aren't lost through loopholes. The third is how to provide an efficient trial process, with the complainant's part concluded speedily. In short, we need to investigate properly, quickly, thoroughly and sensitively, respecting the rights of everyone involved.

If we could drive home these messages, would it make things better? Police, CPS and courts all acknowledge the need. They often claim to be working to that end and if they succeed, it certainly might help more women to come forward and support a prosecution. But is this any more than a sticking-plaster on a festering wound? Because if Jason Godmer had been acquitted despite all the things the court could do for Susan James, who *had* come forward and *had* seen it through to trial, how would more sensitive investigation, etc. have helped?

So maybe we should be asking ourselves if our present system just won't work for these sorts of cases. Do we need to start afresh with a clean whiteboard for them? Do we have the law itself right? Law is there to serve the public and the public needs to be able to trust it, but what member of the public can grasp the more than seventy sexual offences contained in the 2003 Sexual Offences Act? How do we make the atmosphere and procedure in the courtroom user-friendly while retaining the scrupulous standards appropriate for offences which can carry sentences of life imprisonment? Is it possible to balance the need for dispassionate judgement while giving victims a platform for closure?

The Spanish have come up with a neat idea . . . a specialist court for violence against women. No doubt there are plenty of criticisms which can be made of the current functioning of the Spanish model, but that doesn't mean we shouldn't give some thought to the concept. There might be real advantages in having a specialist court with specially designed facilities and specialist judges available to make swift decisions on preliminary matters and to make early section 28 recordings.

Of course, all this takes money and there could not be a worse time to be asking for it. Everything and everyone is hard pressed. I am no politician. I have no way of weighing the needs of justice against that of a sick child needing NHS care. Or anything else. But this much at least is clear: we have a problem and we do need to tackle it at its root, because while offenders are not brought before the courts and tried and convicted, they remain out here, with us, free to do it again. And by letting them get away with it, we – society – are tacitly encouraging others to think they can get away with it too.

2: The Way to Dusty Death

SHE IS TALL FOR *her fifteen years and broad too, her hair chopped brutally short. She wears dungarees and boots. There's a scowl on her face. Her mouth turns down as she scans the shelves. Something about her makes the man at the till watch her carefully, but he is reassured when he sees her select a bottle of bleach, a can of air freshener, a pack of cleaning cloths. At the till she adds a bottle of water to her purchases. He regrets having doubted her. Perhaps it is this that makes him try conversation as he puts the things into a bag.*

'Helping your mum?' he says.

She has been counting out her money, a lot of small change, but now she stops and stares at him. The frown deepens. She pushes the money towards him, picks up the bag and leaves. She does not wait for him to check the coins but when he does, it is right, to the penny.

CCTV cameras track her as she marches down the high street, but the cameras don't cover the whole stretch of road, and she disappears from their view. She might have gone into another shop or into one of the houses with their peeling paint. She might have turned around and slipped, in the shadows, back the way she came. Wherever she has gone, five hours later – give or take a few minutes – the CCTV cameras will find her out again.

When they do, it is already dark. You can only make out a moving shape until she is caught in the headlights of a car, suddenly, shockingly real. You can see then that she is dragging a suitcase. It is on wheels but still she is struggling with it. She disappears again. She isn't seen for another hour. And this time she turns up miles away, still dragging the suitcase, on the edge of Hackney Downs.

The Downs are quiet in the middle of the night. Even the drug dealers move noiselessly. But quiet is what she wants as she sets about her task. She doesn't just throw the pieces of body away. She looks for crannies and dips where she can nestle them. A lower leg here, a forearm there. She can't expect the body parts not to be found. She knows they will be. So what Lesley Brown is trying to achieve isn't clear.

Somewhere in the hours between midnight and the first glimmering of dawn, a fox trotting across the familiar grass finds unfamiliar meat. A bone with the thin flesh still attached. Fresh but unsatisfyingly bloodless. Somewhere after the sun rises, a man with a dog comes across the suitcase. The dog whines, backs away then comes back and paws the ground. The man, who trusts his dog, approaches the case cautiously. He unzips it and stares, unable to comprehend what he is seeing . . . but in the end he has to accept he is looking at a severed hand – which Lesley, frightened at last by what she is doing, has overlooked.

CHAPTER ONE

'How very unpleasant,' says S.

And it is. It's worse than unpleasant. The killing of an elderly woman is bad enough, but the dismemberment of her body and the discarding of it across Hackney Downs is obscene.

'And so stupid,' says S, 'because if she had left the body in the flat, they might never have caught her.'

This is true too. But if it weren't for defendants doing stupid things, a lot of them would never be caught. How many defendants have been arrested through their own carelessness? Burglars are forever dropping their Oyster cards at the scene of crime. Killers call their mums using cell sites within yards and moments of their offence. Drug dealers change their appearance by turning hoodies inside out – in full view of a CCTV camera. Lesley Brown had bought the cleaning materials in a small local store with an observant shopkeeper, then she had walked past three CCTV cameras in the short distance to Miss Sopher's home, and had done the same when she left. By then she was dragging a wheeled suitcase packed with the remains of the elderly woman she is now charged with murdering.

We know all this – S, H, I and every other judge at the tea table – because the list officer is telling us. The defendant is very young – only sixteen, and someone, somewhere has decided the trial must be expedited. The list officer needs a judge to hear it. He does his best to make it sound larky, a fun couple of weeks leading up to the Easter break, but we are too experienced to be taken in. A body chopped up and chucked about Hackney isn't fun. When the body is that of an elderly woman, it really is unappealing. The jury will hate it.

S sniffs disdainfully. 'Whatever did she think she was doing?'

I say, musingly and only because it crosses my mind, 'It's almost as if she wanted to be caught. How odd...'

The list officer interprets this as 'how interesting', claps me on the back, expresses gratitude that someone – here he eyes the others coldly – is willing to help him out and leaves before I can object. As he goes through the door he calls back, 'I'll put it in your court tomorrow morning for a preliminary hearing.'

When he has gone there is a silence. Then S, clearly thinking I am as stupid as Lesley Brown, says, 'Well done. You've got yourself a... what did you call it... a very odd case.'

But it is odd, I think. And interesting.

Next morning Esme, my usher, is in a chatty mood as she takes me down to my courtroom. 'You don't see too many girls charged with murder,' she says. 'Certainly not ones as young as this.'

I agree. You don't.

'It's the little ones that are always the most shocking,' she says.

I know what she means. There is nothing more disconcerting than seeing in the dock a child with something monstrous lurking inside him – or her.

As it happens, Esme and I are setting ourselves up for a fall because, whether or not Lesley Brown has a monster lurking inside, this is no frail child. This is someone who was able to lug a dead body about, and death weighs heavy. What's more, if the Crown is right, she killed the body and chopped it up. All this makes more sense on seeing the real Lesley than it did when we were only imagining her.

She sits in the dock like a stump of wood, closed to all approaches, especially those of Curtis Neil QC, her barrister. He is standing by the glass screen that separates defendants from the rest of us, talking to her through one of the narrow gaps in the glass. That is to say, he is talking at her. She just sits, letting his words wash over her, giving no sign of taking them in. All I can see of him is his long narrow back and the wig, grey and unravelling with age. He is so taken up with his client, he is unaware of my arrival on the Bench until a hiss from the dock officer alerts him. He hurries back to counsel's row, head moving from side to side, as if he is crossing a battlefield. The eyes of the girl in the dock follow him dully. It is obvious there is no rapport between them. This isn't surprising. Curtis Neil is an able advocate but he is old enough to be her grandfather. He comes from a world where they use different language. He will fight tooth and nail to win her case, not because he cares about her but because he cares about winning. He hates to lose. This makes him a very good man to have on your side. Very good, that is, for most defendants. But not, it seems, for this one.

His opponent in the case could not be more different. He is an equable man, not tall but with a comfortable paunch and the comfortable name of Tom Tidmarsh QC.* Mr Tidmarsh will set out the agenda for today's hearing and is politely waiting for Neil to take his seat, but Curtis Neil has an agenda of his own. He refuses to sit and at last, Mr Tidmarsh cedes the floor.

'Mr Neil,' I say, 'you have something you wish to raise?'

'I have an application, My Lady.'

Tradition and courtesy suggest Neil should tell his opponent this before he tells the judge but he clearly hasn't because Tom Tidmarsh looks surprised.

'In fact,' says Neil, 'I have several applications.'

Tidmarsh looks pained.

---

* QC is the abbreviation for Queen's Counsel. We are now all KCs – King's Counsel.

'Seven, in fact.'

Tidmarsh looks like a toddler presented with puréed sprout. I take up the cudgels on his behalf.

'Mr Neil, I have other things in my list today.'

'My client must take precedence over them all. She is barely sixteen years old.'

As a matter of fact she's not far off seventeen but little is to be gained by pointing this out.

'My client is deeply distressed.'

So are most people facing a charge of murder.

'And,' he throws down his trump, 'she has been formally deemed a victim of modern slavery.'

Modern slavery! I hear with my mind's ear S's voice. It is saying, 'Well, now, that *is* interesting.'

CHAPTER TWO

HERE ARE SOME FACTS about modern slavery. It's a problem, and it's growing. It began with people brought into this country, usually illegally, and then forced into servitude such as cheap 'housekeepers', prostitutes or on cannabis farms.

I eye Curtis Neil cautiously. 'In what context?' I ask.

The answer comes in two short words. 'County lines.'

Worse and worse. In the past few years modern slavery has taken a sinister turn, with young people – some very young – drawn into drug dealing. The victims are commonly teenage boys sent by drug gangs out of London into the counties. According to a government website, the term 'county lines' describes 'gangs and organized criminal networks involved in exporting illegal drugs into one or more ... areas within the UK, using dedicated mobile phone lines'.* Gang-masters exploit the vulnerable, especially children and young people, often with coercion, intimidation and violence. They use their victims to carry drugs, to store them, to sell them and then to bring back the proceeds.

The story of children taking drugs and dirty phones (the 'county lines') from conurbations into smaller towns, then carrying back to their 'masters' the cash profits, every penny to be accounted for, is horrifyingly common. There has been a huge increase in reported cases over recent years, though it isn't clear if that is because the slavery is increasing or because greater awareness has led to more reporting and more accurate recording.

---

* County Lines Programme overview – GOV.UK (www.gov.uk).

The first of the Modern Slavery Acts creating offences for this behaviour became law in 2015. But it has proved difficult to get the evidence to prosecute, and even if a case is brought, it can be difficult to secure a conviction – not least because victims often do not see themselves as such.

I allow my gaze to move from Curtis Neil to his client. She is slumped in her seat in the dock. She wears a prison-issue sweatshirt. Her cropped head is lowered, hands lifeless in her lap. She looks up but gives no sign of catching my eye. Her face is sullen. But now I wonder what lies beneath this. Most youngsters who are groomed and turned into dealers have been made vulnerable by their own life experiences, which have often exposed them to a world of grief . . . of physical and sexual abuse, of drugs and alcohol, and of mental illness. Is this what I am dealing with here, with this girl? She may not be the fey and wayward creature of Esme's imagination, but something has made her what she is. And she is, after all, only a child.

'Mr Neil, you said there was a formal finding that Lesley is a victim of modern slavery. Do you have anything in writing?'

He hands Esme a sheet of paper, which she passes to me. It begins, 'To whom it may concern'. This is a document meant to go with Lesley as she passes through various systems. It is written by someone who sees no easy way out for this girl. I read on. The document takes the form of a letter describing how, after Lesley – then aged fifteen – was reported missing to the police, the writer was appointed as her social worker. Lesley returned home after seventy-two hours and no one seems to have established where she had been. At this time Lesley was still attending school, where she was once regarded as an able pupil, likely to secure reasonable GCSE passes and to benefit from further education. However, her attendance had declined sharply and she had missed more than half the previous school term. The social worker noted that Lesley's mother was caring and attentive but was a single parent struggling financially and in other ways. When confronted, Lesley had been apologetic about running away and that seems to have been that. Despite her ongoing truancy, no one paid much attention to why she had disappeared until she was arrested in possession of a considerable quantity of crack cocaine. Crack is a class A drug, and the amount Lesley had was far too much for personal use. She was dealing. 'Possession of class A drugs with intent to supply' is a serious criminal offence. Only then was Lesley's behaviour over the preceding months more closely examined and her frequent trips out of London established. She had been going to seaside towns, often staying overnight. Her mother had never again reported her missing but now she confirmed that her daughter would return home dirty and hungry, silent and unhappy. To the social worker – who finally found time in her overwhelming workload to pay attention to Lesley – the pattern was a familiar one. Perhaps she had only missed it earlier because it is much rarer with teenage girls than boys. Lesley was couriering drugs across the country for dealers. When questioned, the girl would not say who had given them to her nor to whom she gave the proceeds of sale, but there was no doubt what was going on. She was involved in a drug gang. The social worker got together with the police. The criminal investigation was put on hold and the matter was sent to the National Referral Mechanism.

If you have never heard of this Mechanism, you will. It was introduced in 2009 to meet the UK's obligations under the Council of Europe's Convention on Action against Trafficking in Human Beings. After the Modern Slavery Act 2015 came into force, the NRM was extended to help identify and protect all victims of modern slavery in England and Wales. The Mechanism provides a Single Competent Authority (SCA), which is part of the Home Office. Potential cases can be referred to the SCA by a 'first responder'. Then a 'decision maker' will decide – theoretically within five days – whether there are reasonable grounds to suspect the person referred is a victim of human trafficking, slavery, servitude, or forced or compulsory labour. If so, the suspected victim is entitled to further help and assistance, including safe accommodation, financial support, use of the NHS and legal representation. A second stage may lead to a conclusive decision that the person is indeed a victim. For adults there is a requirement that they have been forced or deceived into their position but that is not so for children, who by definition are particularly vulnerable. Any child who is recruited, transported, transferred, harboured or received for the purposes of exploitation is deemed to be a victim of trafficking.*† The document before me says that the Home Office has decided there are Conclusive Grounds to accept Lesley is a victim of modern slavery. The social worker writes:

We had expected to support and encourage her in returning to school and in due course in higher education or in finding training and/or employment. Thereafter, if she chose to access services, we would have assisted her with developing independent living skills and monitoring her own emotional wellbeing. However while we were making these plans for her future, Lesley was arrested for the current serious matters which she now faces. If she is acquitted of these charges, we would still hope to assist in the ways described above. If, however, she were to be convicted, we envisage she would be in custody until she has passed the age when we would expect to offer this sort of support.

---

* National Referral Mechanism guidance: adult (England and Wales) – GOV.UK (www.gov.uk).

† It is intended that all children deemed potential victims will have an independent advocate to support and act in the best interests of the child on the issue of being trafficked, and in anticipation of this, various pilots are in place, but none of them will help Lesley. She must make do with Mr Neil, who, though a highly skilled criminal lawyer, is not a specialist in this field.

CHAPTER THREE

A VICTIM OF SLAVERY! It sounds incongruous in the modern world. Would that it were. I turn to the prosecutor.

'Mr Tidmarsh, do you dispute that this child is the subject of the finding described in the document?'

'No, My Lady. I don't. But the fact that she may herself be a victim of a different crime doesn't mean she isn't guilty of the crimes with which she is charged. It doesn't provide her with any sort of defence to murder or to disposing of the murdered body.'

'I didn't suggest it did,' says Mr Neil stiffly, 'but it is relevant to my submissions of law.' He draws himself up to his full height and turns from Tom Tidmarsh to me. 'My Lady, the court has the power, indeed the duty, to take all appropriate measures to facilitate the defendant's effective participation in the trial. Criminal Procedure Rules 2020, rule 3.2(2)(b).'

You don't say.

'Also the European Convention on Human Rights, Article 6.'

Well, well.

He hands Esme printed copies of the law. Silently she passes one to Mr Tidmarsh and one to me. We study them. Mr Tidmarsh pulls his wig down over his eyes. I have to restrain myself from doing the same. Mr Neil is nothing if not complete. I read:

Submission on behalf of the child defendant Lesley Brown

1. Defendant to leave the dock and sit in the well of the court with parent.

2. Defendant to have use of intermediary throughout trial.
3. Defendant to be given breaks every twenty minutes to facilitate concentration.
4. Barristers and judge to remove wigs and gowns so as not to frighten defendant.
5. If defendant gives evidence, to do so from a remote witness room.
6. Counsel to modify language and sentence structure to facilitate understanding of defendant.
7. To be confirmed.

I look at the list. 'I see you have been studying the Judicial College's "Youth Defendants in the Crown Court", Mr Neil.'

'A useful publication, My Lady.'

'And number seven?'

'I'm working on that one. As for numbers one to six, in relation to these, My Lady, the court is required to make an assessment of the defendant's needs and to adapt the processes so as to facilitate her participation.' In case I have missed the point or the law, he adds, 'Facilitating participation includes enabling the defendant to give his or her best evidence, to comprehend the proceedings, and to engage fully with his or her defence: Criminal Practice Directions I, 3D.2. Is Your Ladyship following me?'

'Every word, Mr Neil.'

After a little discussion, he is persuaded to park some of his submissions for later consideration but we must make a start somewhere, so we begin with the seating arrangements. Page 94 of the Judicial College's guidance is where it's at. We find the heading 'Who Should Sit with the Defendant'. We read,

> . . . a youth defendant should be accompanied by a parent or guardian at all court appearances. Where the defendant is

seated outside the dock, he/she should be permitted to sit with their parent or guardian or other suitable supporting adult, such as a social worker, who should be available throughout the trial: Criminal Practice Direction I, 3G.8. Where, for security or other reasons, it is necessary for the young defendant to be seated in the dock, the supporting adult or family member should ideally be positioned close to, and within sight of, the defendant.

'It is clearly implicit in this wording,' says Mr Neil, 'that unless there are security or other reasons for keeping a young defendant in the dock, she should sit outside it. I ask that Lesley be allowed to sit behind me in junior counsel's row, next to my solicitor.'

For the first time I focus on the row behind Mr Neil. It is occupied by a gangly youth with large specs and a sprouting of spots. He wears what looks suspiciously like a school blazer. Even with a mighty stretch of the judicial imagination, I cannot believe this is either junior counsel or solicitor.

'Work experience,' says Mr Neil. If he is trying to make this sound normal, he is failing. I stare at the boy. By now I have located the legal aid form and know that Lesley has the benefit of legal aid for a junior counsel to assist the silk.

'Welcome as the young man is,' I say, 'the public is paying for something rather more, Mr Neil.'

'My junior is briefly detained in another court. He will be here soon.'

'I'm glad to hear it.'

'And my Instructing Solicitor, who isn't paid to be here,' the subtle weight of the words shifts on his tongue, 'will attend as soon as he has finished speaking to another client in the cells. Meanwhile . . .'

We both look at the boy in the blazer who, under our gaze, squeezes uneasily at a pimple on his chin.

'So may my client sit behind me?'

I cannot tear my eyes from the boy. I suspect Lesley Brown will be better off in the dock but the law is the law. In fact, this situation rarely arises because at the Old Bailey, young defendants are most commonly indicted for group or gang crimes and anything up to seven or even eight of them are tried together. They tend to be a mixture of those just over and those just under eighteen. This means that in law some are adults and some children, but it certainly doesn't indicate who led the wrongdoing or who is the more dangerous. Often older boys of less intelligence are drawn into things by younger, brighter ones. To allow the latter to sit outside the dock could create injustice – or at least the perception of injustice. And in any event it would be impossible, with a number of defendants in custody for murder, to maintain proper security if they all sat in the body of the court. These realities are well understood by counsel and applications are few. But Mr Neil is in a different position. His client sits alone in the dock. Although she is not among the youngest who appear at the Old Bailey, she has never before been tried for any offence and has no experience of a courtroom or the process in it. Moreover, she has been deemed by the Home Office to be a victim of exploitation. This doesn't mean she is, but it is a starting point and cannot be ignored. Any member of the public can come into the gallery* and if the drug dealers for whom she had worked were to walk in, it could put additional pressure on her. I see Mr Neil is about to explain all this to me at length. I forestall him.

'I think I have the points,' I say. 'Mr Tidmarsh?'

Tidmarsh rises to his feet. When he speaks, his tone is aggrieved but not mutinous. He is a reasonable man. He concedes she has no history of violence nor of absconding, and that he could place

---

* Though open justice is central to our system, the judge does have some powers to close the public gallery – see Appendix I, YJCEA 1999 s25.

officers near the court door for extra security. 'I don't,' he says, 'see that it is absolutely necessary she sits in the dock. I suppose we could start with her in counsel's row and see how matters progress.'

Mr Neil, on a roll, presses further. 'And her mother,' he says. 'The Criminal Practice Directions stipulate a parent, guardian or other suitable supporting adult should sit with her. Her mother is in the public gallery.' He points up to where a woman leans anxiously over the wooden rail. The security officer who keeps order up there steps forward and gently asks her to sit back. She doesn't look the sort to hurl things down on me, but then her daughter doesn't look the sort to chop up a little old lady. You never can tell.

'Mr Neil, is Lesley's mother to attend court every day?'

'I'm sure she will do her best, My Lady.'

'I'm sure she will, but it can be distracting for the jury and raise speculation among them if she comes some days and not others.'

'I can speak to her about it.'

'Very well, then she may sit by her daughter today. Perhaps you would then let me know what you think is really in Lesley's best interests once the jury is empanelled.'

So the mother is brought down from the public gallery into the well of the court, and Lesley is set between mother and blazered boy. Lesley looks too firmly earth-bound to bolt but Mr Tidmarsh is taking no chances. He places a police officer at the door.

I pick up Mr Neil's list. Next on it is the intermediary.

I feel a headache coming on.

CHAPTER FOUR

INTERMEDIARIES ARE A RELATIVELY new development in the criminal courts. Originally intended to help child and other vulnerable witnesses give their evidence, their availability has been extended to defendants who – let's face it – have a very large stake in following the complexities of a trial, and in being able to communicate effectively with their counsel, the judge and jury.

I've seen plenty of intermediaries over recent years, particularly in cases involving the young. They come in all flavours from very good to very bad. The best are respectful of the needs of the courtroom as well as the child. The worst get overly close to the child and make impossible demands on the trial process – like having breaks too often. You really can't expect a witness to give evidence and a jury to follow it, if every ten minutes we have to stop. On the occasion when one intermediary required this of me, she also wanted the child to be allowed to run up and down the dock at will, and to have with him a familiar object to hold – in his case a bowie knife. Usually, though, the intermediary is a practical protection for a young defendant and a help to everyone else. So, back to Mr Neil and his application for one.

'My Lady, I need an intermediary to facilitate communication with my client, who is having difficulty following my discourse.'

If his discourse involves words like that, I'm not surprised she isn't following. 'Have you tried using simpler language, Mr Neil?'

Silly question. But I need more information, so I'll try another. Applications are usually accompanied with a report prepared by a professional – often the proposed intermediary – who has met the child and spoken to their family and school. Such a report will assess the child's ability to understand and process information, will advise what is needed to ensure the child can concentrate during the trial, and will alert the judge to any particular difficulties the child might have. It might, for example, suggest a short break every forty to forty-five minutes, and that the barristers use simple language and sentence structures. If a defendant is giving evidence, the intermediary might 'vet' any written cross-examination plan, and even intervene to ensure that questions are phrased in a way the defendant can understand. Outside the courtroom, the intermediary is expected to assist in conference to ensure that the defendant can understand advice and give instructions.

It is sometimes hard to remember that intermediaries are not part of the defence team. They are neither advocate, appropriate adult nor supporter. They are independent and owe their duty to the court.* They can be hugely helpful in ensuring the trial is fair, but they are a limited and expensive resource, and can alter the pace of a trial dramatically. If Lesley needs one, she shall have one, but does she need one? The judge must make this decision. And on what basis is this judge to decide? Certainly not on the mere say-so of the defence barrister. But his say-so *is* enough to alert me that I need more information. So I ask him if he has any sort of psychological or psychiatric report for me to see?

He shakes his head.

'Any school report?'

Another shake.

'Any anything?'

It seems not.

Mr Tidmarsh adopts a look of calculated astonishment which causes Mr Neil to wrap his silk gown about himself and pronounce,

---

* Criminal Procedure Rules 2020, rule 18.

'I have spent a deal of time with my client. In my judgement . . .' (a pause in which we are all supposed to appreciate that on this matter his judgement is preferable to anyone else's) '. . . my client loses concentration after twenty minutes.'

Does Mr Tidmarsh mutter 'after twenty minutes with you, anyone would lose concentration'?

But twenty minutes really is very short. 'Mr Neil, does she really need a break so often? Until recently she seems to have sat perfectly happily through school lessons which must have lasted two or three times that long.'

Neil looks mutinous. 'The pressures are very different when you are standing trial for murder.'

True. But before I endorse the expenditure of public money, I must be satisfied it is justified. The trial is due to start in two weeks' time. I encourage Neil to have an intermediary's report prepared before then and to make his submission again when he has it. In the hope that I can deal with the rest of his applications at the same time, I ask that any report addresses all the other matters on his list. Throughout this, behind him Lesley sits, brooding and mute, her head down, her body skewed away from her mother, away from everyone.

'Are you all right, Lesley?' Perhaps I shouldn't ask. Speaking directly to a defendant instead of through their advocate can be unwise. Defendants can say things better not said, or at least better not heard. But the courtroom, which, once the trial starts, will be stuffed like an overfull cushion, is presently almost empty. There are no jurors and few people in the public gallery. And I am concerned about the girl.

'I want to go back to the dock,' says Lesley. Her voice is mature, like her body. She seems to know what she wants, and presumably has a good reason for it, but Curtis Neil emits a squawk of protest.

'Lesley, your barrister wants you to be near him and with your mother.'

She scowls at Neil. 'But it's me on trial, not him, and I want to sit in the dock.'

'No, you don't,' he says.

'Yes, she does,' says Tidmarsh.

'No, she doesn't,' hisses Neil.

'Yes, I do,' says Lesley.

The three of them glare at each other until I bring the weight of the law down on my desktop, which makes them all turn sharply.

'Lesley, can you tell me why you would rather sit in the dock?'

She bites her lip, but she knows this is her chance and makes a visible effort. 'I feel safer there.'

'Safer in the dock?'

She nods.

I want to ask safe from whom, but what if she says 'safe from my barrister'. I study her for a moment. Something about the way she is sitting makes me uneasy. She has placed herself so that she is slumped in her seat, turning away from her mother, but her arm is pressed against that reassuring presence, so what else is she turning from? The public gallery? I scan the rows of seats up there. They are empty save for a middle-aged couple sporting T-shirts that say AUSTRALIAN AND PROUD OF IT, and an earnest youngster with a notepad. Tourists and students are common currency in the courts' galleries. Nothing alarming here. The only others are at the far end, near the little entrance door – two young men, both dressed in black hoodies, sitting silent and apparently blameless. I wouldn't look twice at them except for this – they are staring straight down at Lesley. I can't control where members of the public turn their eyes, but still I make a mental note to keep an eye on the gallery during the trial.

'Mr Neil, I intend to give you an opportunity to speak in private to Lesley about where she should sit during the trial.'

'Before you do, My Lady, may I raise the issue of Lesley's plea to Count Two on the indictment. At an earlier appearance she pleaded not guilty to both Count One murder, and Count Two doing acts tending and intended to pervert the course of justice.'

'Does she wish to change her plea to Count Two?'

'Not exactly,' says Curtis Neil. 'The charge alleges that she perverted the course of justice in three ways – by dismembering the body, purchasing and using cleaning products to conceal that dismemberment, and disposing of the body parts. The offence is, of course, made out if any one of them is proved. Lesley accepts she bought and used the cleaning products and disposed of the body parts, so she accepts guilt of the offence of perverting the course of justice. She does not accept dismembering the body so she does not accept guilt of the count as drafted. If Mr Tidmarsh will delete the allegation of dismemberment, Lesley will then plead guilty to Count Two. I assume that in these circumstances he will do so.'

'That,' says Tidmarsh, 'would be an unwise assumption. Dismemberment is the most heinous part of this allegation and I have no intention of deleting it.'

'But by accepting that she used the bleach and scattered the body parts, she is accepting guilt of Count Two. You can't try it.'

'I can,' says Tidmarsh sturdily. 'I want a verdict on that issue.'

'Well, you can't have one.'

'I can.'

'Can't.'

'Can.'

'For Heaven's sake, man. If the jurors are sure she used the bleach and scattered the body parts they will return a verdict of guilty, and you still won't know what they thought about the dismemberment!'

The two men stare angrily at each other. I cough softly. 'The test, gentlemen, is whether the disputed allegation could make a meaningful difference to sentence. Do you say it could, Mr Tidmarsh?'

'I do, My Lady. Even if the defendant were to be acquitted of the murder, the dismemberment puts her closer to the actuality of it. It is a direct and horrible act of disrespect and degradation which, if proved, no judge could ignore in sentencing.'

'If proved . . .' hisses Mr Neil.

'Precisely,' says Mr Tidmarsh. 'That is why I will seek the jury's verdict on it.'

I try again. 'Gentlemen, there is a simple solution. Mr Tidmarsh, please remove the use of cleaning agents and the disposal of body parts from Count Two and put them in a new Count Three. That will allow Lesley to plead not guilty to Count Two, the dismemberment, but guilty to Count Three, the matters which she admits. The jury can then return verdicts on Counts One and Two, and whatever those verdicts are, I will sentence her on Count Three at the end of the trial. Can you argue against that, Mr Neil?'

Neil clearly would if he could, but finds he cannot. A low growling sound comes from him, but he remains in his seat.

Problem solved.

CHAPTER FIVE

ON A MONDAY TWO weeks later, the matter is listed for trial. I had been expecting the defence back before this with their renewed application for an intermediary but when I ask about it, Curtis Neil manages to look as if he can't think what I'm talking about.

'Oh that,' he says.

'You have a report?'

'Er ... if Your Ladyship will make the usual allowances ... perhaps a break every forty-five minutes and a requirement that we all take care to avoid complex language, I won't need to trouble the court with an application at the moment. If, in due course, my client decides to give evidence, I may have to raise the matter again, but until then ...'

Reading between the lines, I see that he now has a report and it doesn't support the need for an intermediary. I suppose it says that Lesley is bright and competent for her age; that if I take sensible precautions, she will manage well enough but perhaps she will need some help if she gives evidence. Whatever it says, she has Mr Neil to protect her interests – if only she will trust him. So I agree to a ten-minute break every forty-five minutes and that we should all take care about the way we express ourselves – though some of us, I point out, always do. That deals with points two to six on his list. So, what about point seven?

'I am still reflecting on that,' he says.

'Would you like to give me a hint as to its subject matter?'

'I'd rather not, My Lady. It may come to nothing.'

'Like points two to six,' murmurs Tidmarsh. And Neil mouths

something which, if I didn't know better, I might think was 'Ha Bloody Ha'.

Time to move on.

'So, gentlemen, are we ready for trial?'

We are. Lesley is back in the seat behind her leading counsel. Presumably persuaded there by him. Barristers always seem to think it will impress the jury that a judge has allowed their client out of the dock. Given the scowl on the girl's face, I'm not so sure. But where is her mother? Mr Neil says he doesn't know. Where is her junior counsel? Her solicitor? He doesn't know that either. Still, she has him, and she has the boy from work experience, and unless I am to delay matters we must get on. The cost to the public purse of keeping everyone waiting is eye-watering. So we make a start.

The first step is to empanel a jury. They will be drawn from the group who arrived fresh at the Old Bailey that morning to answer their jury summonses. Thirty of them have been randomly selected and sent down to my court. Until today they have never met. Until this moment they may have barely focused on each other. They are an amorphous mass but from their ranks something different is about to come into being. A jury of twelve whose verdict will – one way or the other – alter Lesley Brown's life for ever. Tom Tidmarsh, at my invitation, tells the waiting panel in a sentence or two what the case is about.

'The murder of an elderly woman called Lilian Sopher. Killed in all probability by a knife wound. Hard to tell because after the killing, her body was chopped up and left in pieces around Hackney Downs.' That makes them stare. 'No eyewitnesses to the killing,' he says, 'but plenty of evidence to show that the person who got rid of the body was Lesley Brown.'

They cannot tell from the name given to them by Mr Tidmarsh whether the defendant is male or female. They certainly cannot tell that the alleged killer was only fifteen years old at the time, and even now is not yet seventeen. They turn to the dock, where a lone man in uniform sits. They frown, puzzled.

Tidmarsh continues, 'The defendant is represented by My Learned Friend, Mr Curtis Neil QC, who sits beside me.'

Neil nods stiffly to the jury panel. Forces a smile.

'His client,' says Tidmarsh, 'sits behind him. Yes, that child. That . . .'

Whatever is he going to say? That creature? That monster? Take care now, Tom. You are prosecuting, and fairness is the touchstone.

'That girl, so young the judge has allowed her to sit out of the dock and near her counsel.'

Some of the panel who had been wondering what excuses might get them out of jury service think, after all, this is interesting. Others are horrified. When my clerk begins calling their names, I release one who, almost weeping, explains that she crosses Hackney Downs every day on her way to work and cannot bear . . . cannot think how . . . Her hands are shaking. Her lower lip trembles. There are plenty of other courts in the building where she can do her jury service. It would be an unnecessary cruelty to inflict this case on her and I don't. Esme takes her off and we continue with the calling of names. The remaining members of the panel are sobered by the thought of what is to come. No one else raises an objection. The twelve seats are filled. The twelve jurors take their oath or affirmation* to bring in true verdicts in accordance with the evidence. And by midday Mr Tidmarsh has begun his opening.

It is very easy to become so absorbed in the difficulties of a defendant that one overlooks other things. Important things. Things like Lilian Sopher. Tom Tidmarsh opens his case by giving the jury copies of the now-three-count indictment and explaining that Lesley Brown has

---

* The affirmation is the same promise to tell the truth as the oath, but the promise is not made on a Holy Book.

pleaded guilty to Count Three, the cleaning up of the flat and taking the body parts to the Downs, where she disposed of them. He then asks Esme to hand out copies of a graphics bundle – a thirty-page A3 document – one between two for the jurors. Counsel already have theirs, heavily annotated and ready for duty. There is one for me and one for Lesley Brown. Tidmarsh invites us to open them at page 1, and there she is. In a photograph on the left-hand side of the page, no longer a shadow but a real person. Lilian Sopher. The picture, a close-up of her head and shoulders, had been taken in summertime, perhaps the year before she died. She is in a park. There are roses behind her. The image is sun-bleached and she smiles uncertainly into the camera, a frail figure with thinning grey hair beneath which the outline of her skull can be made out. Beneath is written her name, Lilian Jane Sopher, and the dates of her birth and of her death at not quite seventy years old. On the right-hand side of the page is another photograph. This one is of Lesley Brown. No middle name. Only the date of her birth. It shows her in the custody suite of the police station where she was taken after her arrest. It is clear and uncompromising. So is she. She looks dark and determined, brows beetling, lips tight. Different in every way from Lilian Sopher.

A palpable quiver runs through the jury as they study the two faces. Mr Tidmarsh allows them the moment. Then he begins. Pages 2–4 are of stills from the CCTV footage recorded in the little mini-market ... images of Lesley at 6 p.m. buying bleach and cleaning materials. Other cameras in the street show her going off in the direction of Lilian Sopher's home.

'You can be sure,' he tells the jury, 'that the defendant had not yet been to the house that afternoon because the CCTV footage from all the neighbouring streets has been studied and there is no sign of her. So does her visit to the shop at 6 p.m. show her before the murder, already preparing to clean up after it? If so, it is a planned and calculated killing.'

We turn more pages and find ourselves looking at stills of Lesley returning up the road. It is now 11.17 p.m. and dark. She is caught in the headlights of a passing car, dragging a heavy suitcase. Turn another page and here she is later still, with the suitcase, disappearing into the darkness of Hackney Downs.

Tom Tidmarsh describes how the following morning a 999 call from an early dog-walker brought police to the Downs. One look at what his dog had found led to a full-scale scouring of the area and photographs of what was found. It is a relief to get past these pages, and to find ourselves instead at Lilian's front door.

Her flat is the downstairs of a terraced house. Upstairs on the first and second floors there lives a family – mother, father and two children. The neighbours share a communal hallway. The photographer steps inside and shows us the hall full of ordinary things – children's bikes, coats on hooks, a shopping trolley – and things that look strangely out of place . . . police cones and tape, discarded disposable gloves, a dropped tape measure. The photographer captures it all then takes us – over the page – through the door that leads into Lilian's flat, where the first thing that meets our eyes is a jumble of cleaning products and areas of carpet and walls with dark stains and splashes on them. Blood, says Mr Tidmarsh. We do not doubt it.

'The bleach and cloths and air freshener have all been used,' continues Mr Tidmarsh, 'and scientific examination revealed Lesley Brown's fingermarks on them. Her prints are on the handle of the suitcase recovered from the park, too. So is her DNA. Samples of Lilian Sopher's DNA were obtained from her toothbrush and her hairbrush, and further tests show that the heavy bloodstaining on the walls and carpet and inside the suitcase came from her. The body parts recovered from the Downs are most certainly those of Lilian Sopher.'

There is a silence in the courtroom as we absorb all this. The horror of it. The idea of a young girl dismembering the body of an elderly woman and packing it into a suitcase. The idea of her taking body parts across London and disposing of them in the night. But the horror mustn't be allowed to displace the fact. Because while this account provides very strong evidence that the defendant was complicit in cleaning up the scene and disposing of the body . . . and while it puts her close to the scene of the killing . . . how does it prove she was the killer? Mr Tidmarsh explains.

'The case against the defendant is a circumstantial one. That means there were no eyewitnesses to the killing and certainly no one to say they saw her do it. But circumstantial evidence can be strong because it draws not on one person's account but on many different strands of evidence which, when taken together, will drive you to the irresistible conclusion it was this defendant's hand that killed the old lady.'

And then he lays on the table the final piece of his jigsaw. 'Although she denies the killing and dismemberment, she has admitted disposing of the body parts. And here is something you will want to think about . . .' he wags a telling finger at them, 'at no stage – not once – has she ever said anyone else was at the flat or that she was asked to go there by anyone else. If she didn't kill Lilian Sopher, she must know who did, and she has been given every opportunity to name that person, both in her police interviews and in her defence statement to the court. If she has never named another killer, you may conclude it is because there is no one else to name.'

By 4.30 p.m. Tom Tidmarsh has finished his opening and painted a compelling picture. Throughout it all Curtis Neil has kept his head down. Lesley Brown has solidified into a thing of stone. When the jurors look at her – as they do frequently during the Crown's address to them – their faces harden. But, in truth, they have not yet heard a word of evidence. They certainly haven't heard any evidence tested. Tomorrow that process will begin.

CHAPTER SIX

NEXT MORNING MR TIDMARSH starts calling the evidence upon which he has built his opening. He could begin with those who knew Lilian Sopher, neighbours or perhaps a relative ... something which puts flesh on the bones of the story, making the emotion real for a jury. If we are hoping for this, we will be disappointed; but if we want to understand how this prosecution was put together, the day is illuminating. Tidmarsh elects to build his edifice from the ground up. His first witness is one who can give the court a scaffold on which to hang all else that will follow. He calls the officer in charge of the CCTV material.

The man is tall and thin and dry but he knows his stuff; and by the time he has finished, so does the jury. He explains how a CCTV team works. It will begin by locating the many cameras in streets and homes, in gardens and shops in a relevant area. They will then set about recovering hundreds and hundreds of hours of footage from them. On each recording, officers must establish whether the images are relevant. To do this they must establish the correct time of recording. This isn't always easy because although all cameras show on each piece of footage a date and time of recording, this information can be wildly inaccurate. It is now common practice for an officer, at the time of seizing footage, to check the camera's clock against 'real' time, for instance on the speaking clock. This allows the officer to work out how much ahead of or behind real time the clock on the camera is, and thus to establish the real time of any particular image on the footage. In due course, an accurate sequence of events of all footage from all cameras will be created.

Once the footage has been collected, there will be a frame-by-frame examination of it. The task requires time and meticulous attention. The relevant must be sorted from the irrelevant, the positively from the possibly probative. Finally, a chronological history of what happened will be put together. It can be very powerful indeed.

In this case the endless hours of routine, painstaking police work have produced excellent results. As the officer explains, in the hours after the man and dog found the suitcase and police arrived, a search was made of the Downs and various of Lilian's body parts recovered. The areas where they were found had a reasonable footfall and detectives thought it highly unlikely they had lain there undiscovered since the previous day. This gave them a time frame. The pattern of where the various parts had been scattered helped them focus on the likely route by which the body had been brought to the place. This gave them a geographical frame. Concentrating on these features, they seized and examined footage from CCTV cameras on the likely roads at the likely time. On one of the main access routes to the area they found what they were looking for . . . images of a girl pulling a suitcase that matched the one recovered. Once they had these images to work with, they set about identifying cameras on routes that could have brought the girl to that point. It didn't take them long to find the same girl with the same suitcase emerging from a car less than quarter of a mile away. The officer plays us the footage. It is undeniably Lesley Brown getting out of the vehicle. It isn't possible to read the number plate but it is possible to see the type of car and a series of scratches on a rear door. Using this as identification, police systematically worked their way back through the various access roads to the drop-off point and found footage that, together with what was captured on an Automatic Number Plate Reader, gave them the car's registration number. From there, it was easy to identify the Prius as a minicab. They went to the cab company and from its records identified the cab driver and the booking. This took the police back across London. The cab had been ordered by phone at 22.40 the night before. The fare was to be picked up on a street corner. It took the driver thirty-five minutes to get there, but the girl was still waiting. A short statement from the driver says she got in with a large suitcase. Police efforts to trace the phone used to make the booking came to nothing – it was unregistered and pay-as-you-go, as they so often are in these cases. But the pick-up point – close to Lilian Sopher's home – gave police another area, another set of CCTV cameras to investigate. By now, however, five days had passed since the discovery of the body and they had to act quickly because private footage is often on a continuous loop, recorded over every week or so. Spurred on, they worked through twenty-four-hour shifts, and within a couple of days they had found the girl with the suitcase on a street camera timed at 22.27 on the critical evening. They checked all the CCTV in that street, and so they arrived at the little corner shop. The shopkeeper was – as he had been that night – behind his counter. And when shown the image of the girl in the footage, he immediately recalled her. Something about her, he said. Something made him remember. And yes, he still had the CCTV footage from that day . . . and yes . . . within half an hour he had located it and played it back for the police who, leaning on his counter, watched Lesley Brown making her purchases.

Useful as all this was to the investigation, it didn't take the police to the name Lilian Sopher, or to the house where she lived and died. There was nothing on the body or the scraps of clothing still adhering to it, or the suitcase, to identify her.

And so the tall, thin, dry officer comes to the end of his evidence and leaves the witness-box to be replaced by one who is short and plump and has an endearing Welsh accent. He talks to the jury as if he were about to offer them a cup of tea and a slice of honey loaf.

'We knew from the pathologist, you see, that the bits of body were all from one person, and that it was an elderly female. We were hoping she would be reported missing but you know how it can be in London . . . someone can go unmissed for a long time.' He frowns disapprovingly, as if such a thing could never happen in Mumbles. 'We wanted to circulate her description, but we didn't have much to go on. We couldn't be sure of height or age. We had a head, but,' he shakes his own, 'it was hardly in a condition to be photographed and put up on posters. Credit where credit's due, mind, it was the pathologist who suggested getting an artist to use it to make an impression of what she was like in life.'

The jury's eyes open wide at that. One of them starts to scribble a note but the officer gives her a look that says, 'Don't ask, love', and she doesn't. 'Actually,' he goes on, 'it came out better than you would think. Once we had it, we took it back to the corner shop where we knew the killer had been before she went to the victim's home and—'

Mr Neil – who has given the officer free rein till now – is suddenly on his feet. 'I would be grateful if the officer could refrain from misleading the jury. He is entirely wrong to call my client a killer. That is the very issue the jury are here to decide. He is entirely wrong to say she was on her way from the corner shop to the Sopher house. He has no idea what time she arrived there, or if she arrived at all. For all he knows she handed the cleaning materials to someone else who later handed back to her the suitcase. He has no idea . . .'

The officer flushes scarlet, poor man, and starts to give an explanation which causes a further explosion from the defence. Tom Tidmarsh thinks he had better join in and in a moment they are both at it. Life is too short for this. Mediation is required. I ask the witness to stick to the facts and to tell us what happened when he showed the sketch to the shopkeeper.

The officer is still mortified. Also unsettled. 'I have a note of what the shopkeeper said but . . ." he looks anxiously at defence counsel; somewhere in his training he has heard about hearsay evidence, '. . . but am I allowed to tell you that?'

Strictly speaking, what someone else said to the officer is hearsay and not admissible unless by agreement. The alternative would be for the shopkeeper himself to come and tell us, but sometimes the defence feels on safer ground with a police officer who is expected not to go beyond the word of his note, the content of which both sides will already know. So I ask, 'Mr Neil, is there any objection to the officer telling us the words of the shopkeeper?'

Curtis Neil, mollified at having shamed the man, shrugs. 'It's not in dispute that the shopkeeper knew the deceased and identified her. If the witness wants to read out his note of the exact words, I have no objection.'

So the officer opens his pocket book and begins. 'He – the shopkeeper – examined the drawing. Then he said, "I hope I'm wrong but I think it might be Lilian." I asked him who Lilian was and he said, "She's an old lady who lives round here. I don't know exactly where. Close enough that she sometimes comes in her carpet slippers. She came most days for a little bit of shopping – a loaf of bread, a tin of beans, milk, cat food."'

'Is that all he said?' asks Tom Tidmarsh.

'He also said, "I haven't seen her for over a week."' The officer takes another cautious look at Curtis Neil and seeing all quiet there, goes on. 'Once we had a first name, and an area, we checked various registers and lists, including the local GPs. Within twenty-four hours we had her – Lilian Sopher – full name, address, the lot.'

The prosecutor sits. The defender stands. The officer squares his shoulders within his serge uniform. I ready myself for fireworks, but none come. Neil turns to look long and hard at his client, who is staring at her hands in her lap.

'No questions,' he says. I can feel he is itching to have a go at this witness. To ask what steps have been taken to identify others who might have gone to the flat. To get the man to admit he cannot rule out others being there. But 'no questions' is all he says, and Lesley gives a small nod.

And so we come to the end of the day's evidence.

CHAPTER SEVEN

Next day, Tom Tidmarsh moves the jury's focus from Lesley to Lilian and calls to the witness-box the dead woman's sister. From the moment she enters the courtroom we are all mesmerized. We have seen, studied, the living face of Lilian captured in a photograph that day in the park. And now in front of us, here she is walking, breathing, looking about.

'Twins,' Irene Parkinson (née Sopher) tells us after she is sworn and settled. 'But I was born first and I suppose I've always had the edge. I came easily but poor Lilian had a difficult birth. A little brain damage. Only a little, you understand. She was just a bit slow. But she had the sweetest of tempers.' Her voice is quiet but clear and its wistfulness carries across the courtroom. I look at Lesley to gauge her reaction and am in time to see her glance up at the public gallery then bury her head against her mother's shoulder. I look up too, but see only the door closing, leaving rows of empty seats. When I turn back, Lesley's mother is tugging at Curtis Neil's gown. There is a hurried conversation. Some gesticulating. I ask the witness to pause. After all, someone from the defence side needs to listen to her evidence.

'Mr Neil,' I say, 'is there a problem?'

The silk is whispering urgently to his client. She is shaking her head. He seems to be querying something but she won't answer him. He gets to his feet.

'My Lady, I'm afraid Lesley is feeling unwell. I wonder if she might leave the courtroom until she has recovered?'

'Is she actually ill, Mr Neil, or only distressed?'

'I'm not a doctor, My Lady.'

'Well, do you want me to call one?'

'One what?'

If Mr Neil is being deliberately obtuse he is about to get the sharp edge of my tongue, but Lesley really does look rather green and nothing delays a trial like a defendant vomiting in counsel's row.

'She is quite content for the evidence to continue in her absence,' says Mr Neil.

I don't ask if he has checked this with her. It would be cruel to interrupt Irene now, and if Neil is happy for us to continue in the absence of his client, who am I to argue. So after Lesley is helped back to the dock and through the door that leads down to the cells, we get back to the witness.

'Mrs Parkinson, I'm sorry for the delay. You were telling us about you and your sister.'

She picks up the thread. 'I left home to marry when I was twenty but Lilian remained with our parents. Our dad died first but she stayed on with Mum. She never lived alone until after Mum's death. Then we sold the house and the Council found Lilian her own place. It was a ground floor in a little terraced house. Very small, but she loved it. She was very proud of it.'

'And once Lilian moved there, how often did you visit her?' asks Mr Tidmarsh.

Irene puts her hand to her mouth but can't conceal how her face is crumpling. Her eyes are damp now. Esme hands her the box of tissues.

'Take a moment,' I say. 'There's no rush.'

She draws a breath and steadies herself. 'I live north of London but there's a good train service into town. Until a few months ago I came down every week to see her. But then . . .'

The pause hangs in the air from where Mr Tidmarsh deftly collects it. 'Then?'

She sighs. 'Then she kept saying she was busy or that she was going out with friends. At first I was pleased that she was meeting people. I wanted her to have the best life she could. But after a few weeks of this I began to think she just didn't want to see me and . . .'

'You were upset with her?'

'I stopped phoning so often. I stopped suggesting I would visit. And now . . .' She shakes her head. Because now it is too late.

'I wonder,' says Mr Tidmarsh, 'if you would look at some photos of Lilian's flat.' And to Esme he says, 'The graphics bundle, please, exhibit 1.'

When the witness has the document he asks her to turn to page 11. She does and gives an audible gasp. 'But . . .' she says. There is a pause while she organizes her thoughts. 'But it never looked like this.'

We all have the bundle open at page 11, where Lilian's living room is shown. It is not that of someone proud to call it home. The sofa has been used as a bed. There is a greasy and coverless duvet thrown carelessly over it. There are jeans and T-shirts discarded around it, and a pair of trainers too. The little round dining table is covered with half-eaten takeaways and beer cans. A tiny low coffee table has things on it – a pair of tiny scales, small clear bags, a scattering of white powder.

'Is this how your sister kept her home?' asks Tidmarsh.

'No,' says Irene shortly. 'And obviously those aren't her clothes.'

'Do you know whose they are?'

She shakes her head. 'As far as I knew, Lilian lived alone. Apart from Oscar.'

'Oscar? Who's Oscar?'

Before she can answer, someone on the jury says, loud enough to be heard, 'The cat.' And I guess we've all been expecting Oscar ever since we heard that Lilian bought cat food at the corner shop.

'The cat,' confirms Irene Parkinson. 'But . . .' she stares at the pictures, her face creased in puzzlement, '. . . but where's Oscar's basket? It was always there beside the television. And . . .' She is turning the pages now, wincing at the horror of stains in the bathroom. It's the kitchen she is looking for. And when she finds it she stares at each image in turn, then shakes her head. 'And where are Oscar's bowls?'

'Are you sure about Oscar?'

Irene looks at Tidmarsh indignantly. 'There's a picture of him in my sister's bedroom.' She takes us back through the pages, and there, on the bedside table, is a framed photograph of a heavy old cat, happily sleeping out his days in Lilian's lap.

Poor Oscar is gone, but when and where and how we don't know. Cats die, as we all do. When Tom Tidmarsh sits down, Curtis Neil decides to let well alone and restricts himself to only one matter in cross-examination. It is, however, a telling one.

'Mrs Parkinson,' he says, 'you noticed a change in your sister's behaviour and now you see a change in her living conditions too?'

She nods.

'But the change you noticed began some time before her death?'

'Months before.'

The barrister is implying that all this . . . whatever led to Lilian's death . . . started long before there is anything to say Lesley was at the house. Of course, we don't know when Lesley did first go to the house. Or how often she went. But there is certainly no *evidence* that she was there before the night she took the body, and now there is evidence of the elderly lady changing some time before that.

CHAPTER EIGHT

LILIAN'S SISTER HAS BROUGHT the case to life. At least, she has brought into the courtroom the reality of the death. Tom Tidmarsh wants to keep that reality before us, and his next witnesses are well placed to do that. They are the neighbours from upstairs. First in the witness-box is Aakil Kapoor. Lesley has recovered enough to return for this evidence, but she looks very unhappy. She has placed herself on the other side of her mother and further from her counsel.

Mr Kapoor takes the oath on the Gita. He looks at the dock, sees there is no defendant there, asks something of Esme. She whispers back, and he looks over to where Lesley sits. When Tom Tidmarsh claims his attention, he confirms his name and that he lives with his wife and two children on the floors above Lilian Sopher's flat. He looks to be a firm and sensible man but he is clearly upset.

'I want to say something,' he says. He is speaking to the court, but his focus is all on Lesley, who shrinks under his gaze. 'I want to tell you that Lilian was a lovely lady. I want to make that point because what happened to her was not lovely.'

Tom Tidmarsh nods. 'We understand,' he says. And gently he takes Mr Kapoor back to the content of his witness statement, which says this:

I have been told by police that the dismembered body of my neighbour Lilian Sopher has been found. I have been asked to describe how Lilian lived and if I know any of what led up to her death. I can say that until six weeks ago I had no concerns for Lilian. She was elderly and sometimes a little confused, but she was a lovely lady. She was always friendly and kind to my children. In fact she was kind to everyone. I can think of no one who would have wanted to hurt her in any way. But six weeks ago I began to notice a change. She appeared nervous. She did not go out as she had before, and when I did see her, she seemed to avoid me. I noticed that she was always wearing the same clothes and her hair was unbrushed. These things were very different from how she had been before.

'So,' says Mr Tidmarsh, 'Lilian changed. Can you tell us why?'

'It is as I said in my statement. I believe it had to do with the boys,' says Aakil Kapoor. 'Not boys. Young men. I saw three of them coming and going. They were there at all hours. They played loud music during the night. I went to complain – they were keeping the children awake, you see . . .'

'And did you speak to any of these young men?'

'I spoke to one of them.'

'Can you describe him?'

'White, aged about twenty-two or twenty-three.'

'Height?'

'I don't know. He was tall. And he was very thin.'

'Facial hair?'

'Yes. But as if he hadn't bothered to shave rather than that he had grown a beard.'

'The other two?'

'Shorter. One skinny, the other just average build.'

'Did you see the faces of either of these other two?'

'No.'

'Can you say if they were male or female?'

The question takes us all by surprise, including the witness. But Tidmarsh would dearly like to show Lesley had been to the flat before the fateful night. Or at least that she might have been there.

Aakil Kapoor gives the question careful thought. 'I assumed they were male,' he says at last, 'but since I didn't see their faces, I guess I can't be sure.'

This is as much as Mr Tidmarsh can hope for. He moves on. 'You spoke to one of the three. Tell us about that.'

'I knocked on Lilian's door. This man opened it. I tried to explain about the noise. About the children.'

'What did he say?'

'He told me to . . .' He flushes. 'Am I allowed to use bad language?'

'We need you to tell us exactly what he said.'

'Well, then. He told me to fuck off. He shut the door on me. There was something about him . . . I didn't knock again. I watched out for Lilian and after a few days I managed to catch her in the hallway. I tried to explain to her. But she didn't seem to understand. I asked who these men were, but she just seemed . . . I don't know . . . bewildered.'

'And is there anything else?' asks Mr Tidmarsh.

He knows there is, of course. He must know – as Curtis Neil and I know – there are another two pages in Mr Kapoor's statement about the people who rang Lilian's doorbell all through the night. Some came in, some only stood on the doorstep and spoke to the young men. He tells us about them.

'Did you report the matter to anyone?'

He lifts his shoulders, extends his hands in a helpless shrug. 'I called the Council. They asked if I wanted to be rehoused. I said no, I just wanted this behaviour to end. To end,' he says, 'but not like this.'

'Is there anything else you can tell us?'

He stops to reflect. 'I don't think so,' he says. 'I was at work all day. My wife might be able to say more.'

Curtis Neil stands. Again he has only one question in cross-examination. Again it is a good one. 'Mr Kapoor,' he says, 'the idea that one of the three men was a woman never entered your head, did it, until Mr Tidmarsh put it there?'

After lunch his wife gives evidence. Nita Kapoor is younger than her husband. She is a sweet-faced woman anxious to help. Not the sort likely to cause the court problems, you might think. But think again, because you never can tell. She is a little nervous, and Mr Tidmarsh sets out to settle her with what he believes is an easy question.

'Mrs Kapoor, I want to ask you about the last time you saw Lilian Sopher. It was the day before her remains were discovered on Hackney Downs, I think.'

This should be uncontroversial because it is how Mrs Kapoor's witness statement begins, so it's a surprise when she says, 'No.'

'No?'

'No.'

'Well, when did you last see her?'

'Two days before her body was found.'

'Are you sure about that?'

'Absolutely sure,' she says. 'I was told her body was found early on the Tuesday morning. I last saw her on Sunday morning when I was taking the children to the park.'

'You did not see her after Sunday morning?'

'I did not.'

'Are you sure?'

'I am.'

He hesitates. 'And if your statement says different?'

'Then the police officer who took my statement must have written it down wrong.' She pauses. 'He was . . . impatient.'

'Did you check the statement before signing it?'

'He told me to read it through but his handwriting was dreadful and I was upset. Perhaps I missed something. But, whatever the statement says, I last saw Lilian on the Sunday morning.'

Tom Tidmarsh frowns. He can hardly cross-examine his own witness, but he would rather have Lilian positively alive on the Monday. The closer he gets the death to the removal of the body from the house that Monday evening, the closer he gets Lesley to the killing. This unexpected evidence is a blow but there's nothing he can do about it, so he presses on.

'How well did you know Lilian Sopher?'

'She was my neighbour. A good neighbour. She was nice to my children. They loved her and Oscar.' She shakes her head. 'Who would do these terrible things to an old lady and a cat?'

And with these words, Nita Kapoor innocently delivers a second blow. This time, in fact, she alarms both barristers. Neither of them knows what she is about to say. There's not a word about Oscar's fate in her statement. The two barristers look at each other, their eyes narrowed. Something terrible has happened to Oscar and the witness knows it but they do not. It may be important to the case. But it may be inadmissible. If Nita Kapoor blurts out something inadmissible – especially if it is prejudicial to the defence – it might derail the trial, force me to discharge the jury, lead to a retrial. Witnesses might have to give their evidence all over again. It could cause a deal of grief for everyone, and a lot of costs on the public purse. Much hangs on the look that is currently passing between Tidmarsh and Neil.

The safe course would be to ask Mrs Kapoor to stop, and for an officer to take a further statement from her to find out what she knows. But any further statement must then be served on all parties and instructions will have to be taken, and there may be submissions and I will have to give a ruling which may be later examined in the Court of Appeal. A lot of 'mights' and 'maybes'. Possibly a waste of a lot of time. Is it easier just to ask her and see what emerges? But . . . both barristers look at the jurors, who are sitting forward in their seats, agawp to know what happened to Oscar. Nothing catches the heart of a jury like a sweet old cat – unless it's a sweet old dog. Are the barristers thinking what I am thinking? If the jurors don't hear the fate of the cat, they will send a note. If they don't get an answer, they will speculate. Tidmarsh whispers something to Neil. Neil turns to Lesley. Is he asking if she knows anything about the cat? She looks at him, her eyes large. But she shakes her head, and to a further query – perhaps 'are you really sure about this?' – she shakes her head again, more firmly this time. So Mr Neil murmurs his assent, and the prosecutor turns back to his witness.

'Mrs Kapoor, you mentioned the cat. Oscar?'

'Yes,' she says. 'Poor Oscar. The children found him on the kerb outside the house. They were horrified. We all were.'

'When was this?'

'It was on that same Sunday. When we returned from the park.'

'And what had happened to Oscar?'

She closes her eyes and when she speaks her voice is low. 'I thought at first he had been hit by a car. There was nothing I could do to help him. I knocked on Lilian's door but she didn't answer, and in the end I thought I could not leave him lying there. So I got a little shovel and a sack to put him in. It was only when I was moving him that I saw what had killed him. His head was smashed in. Really smashed. The skull quite crushed on one side. Tell me,' she says to the barrister, 'how a car could do that?'

When Nita leaves the witness-box the case looks subtly different from how it had looked before. Lilian was alive and apparently well when the Kapoors left for the park on Sunday morning. Oscar was dead when they returned. At that time Lilian did not answer her door. No one, it now seems, saw her alive after that.

CHAPTER NINE

THE FOURTH DAY OF the trial, and Tom Tidmarsh has indicated that today he will take us deeper into the events at Lilian's flat and what had been going on there prior to the time of her death. So far – when you think of everything that can go wrong in a murder trial – things are running relatively smoothly. I am still keeping an eye on the public gallery to make sure no one up there misbehaves. And I am getting concerned about what seems to be the unhappy relationship between the defendant and her leading counsel. Still, nothing has happened to require my ruling or intervention. I have been telling myself that things could be a lot worse. And when I walk into court that next morning, they are.

Lesley is back with Curtis Neil but they sit there alone. No mother, no junior, no solicitor. Even the boy with the blazer seems to have had all the work experience he can take. And I can see, even across the courtroom, that things are not well between the girl and her barrister.

As I get to my chair and Esme pulls it back so I can sit, Lesley puts up her hand and says, 'Please, please can I sit in the dock?'

'No,' says Curtis Neil.

'I think she is talking to me, Mr Neil, not you.'

Lesley is very pale, Neil is very red, and I am in no mood to deal with tantrums. This morning I have discovered a leak under my bath, signs of a mouse in a wardrobe, and the milk had turned before I could make tea. Although Curtis Neil can't be expected to know about leaks and spoiled milk, he picks up that the judicial breast is not a happy one, and that its unhappiness is about to be unpacked on him.

'I mean,' he says, 'it will look so odd to the jury.'

'You should have thought of that before you persuaded me to let her sit with you.'

'It was so she could be with her mother and my junior and—'

'And on that point,' I interrupt, 'where exactly . . .?'

'I have no idea,' he snaps. 'Before Your Ladyship asks, I have no idea where they are.'

'Not any of them?'

'No.'

And after all, it is hardly his fault. He has got himself to court on time. And he is having to manage everything alone. There's not much I can do about the mother, but there is about the junior.

'Mr Neil, if your junior is too busy to appear in this trial, he should have returned the brief to another barrister.'

'I can assure Your Ladyship that my junior is working diligently on the case . . .'

'But not in my courtroom.'

'No. Not in your courtroom. But he is working on it every day after he has finished in another courtroom, where his previous trial is badly overrunning through no fault of his. Meanwhile he is helping me each evening, preparing complex cross-examination and researching points of law.'

I stop myself from saying that so far I've only heard a modicum of cross-examination and no points of law at all. But if his junior is stuck in another court, there's not a lot to be gained without disrupting another judge. Cases do sometimes overrun and counsel is rarely to blame.

Mr Neil reads the runes. 'My Lady, I am perfectly able to deal with this morning's evidence without assistance from my junior or solicitor or anyone else. Lesley will manage this morning without her mother. Shall we just get on with things?'

'Getting on with things' is a subject dear to the heart of most judges, including this one. I would yield, but there is Lesley, looking increasingly desperate. Should I try to find out why she is so distressed? The relationship between her and Neil is clearly teetering. But he is good at his job, and at the moment he is all she has. If I topple the edifice, what then? I might be left with an unrepresented child defendant facing a charge of murder and the risk of life imprisonment.* While I hesitate, the door of the court opens and Lesley's mother walks in. The entire courtroom turns to stare at her. She grows flustered and stops. What I ought to do is thank her for attending and invite her to sit beside her daughter and make sure Lesley is all right. What I actually do – Lord forgive me – is entirely other.

'You're late,' I snap at her.

She puts a hand to her chest as if I have punched her there. 'I'm sorry.'

'I'm sure you are, but why are you late?'

For a moment she doesn't reply. For a moment I think it is because she has no answer, but – be patient, Judge, and you will find that she has plenty of answers. So many, in fact, that she needs time to arrange them in her head. When she speaks, hesitatingly at first then with an increasing need to explain herself, it turns out she does two cleaning jobs before she comes to court . . . in offices . . . they are nice people and make allowances for her but they do need the place clean. She leaves her eight-year-old son and thirteen-year-old daughter at home. She should be back in good time to get them to school but her train was cancelled. When she got home her son had been sick. She thought he had a slight fever. He can get very poorly very quickly if she doesn't keep an eye on him. He has special needs

---

* Although for a person of Lesley's age it is called 'detention during HM's pleasure', it is an indeterminate sentence with no fixed release date, the direct equivalent of a life sentence for an adult.

and goes to a special school where they understand him and he is OK there, but how could she send him when he wasn't well. And her other daughter is only thirteen and it didn't seem right to leave her with a sick child. And she knew Lesley needed her, but ... and so she had to find a neighbour ... she has very good neighbours ... and she is sorry she sometimes has to leave court early but she has another job cleaning a shop at the end of the day because it is difficult to make ends meet, especially now Lesley isn't ... Lesley used to have a job too. Her mother had thought it was in a market where they kept her for long hours but paid exceptionally well ... but now she wonders ... wonders ...

When you see what some people are coping with, a leak under the bath doesn't seem so very bad after all.

'Sit down,' I say. 'Get your breath back. When you're ready, we'll get on.'

CHAPTER TEN

LESLEY IS CLEARLY GLAD to have her mother by her side, and though she still looks very uncomfortable, she settles down. Esme brings the jury into court and Tom Tidmarsh calls his next witness. Detective Sergeant Crabbe is a big man with an overly sharp tie and the sort of confidence that makes people like Curtis Neil want to knock it out of him. He takes the oath in a loud voice, identifies himself by name, rank and number and explains that he dealt with various aspects of the investigation, including the searches of the house and the arrest of the defendant. He turns to Tom Tidmarsh.

'Where would you like me to begin, Sir?'

Tom Tidmarsh is not used to being led by his witnesses. 'Um . . .' he says.

'Very well, Sir. I'll start with the flat, shall I?' And off he sets. Tidmarsh can barely ask a question before the answer comes shooting back.

Was he present at—?

Yes, he attended the flat when it was first identified, and was present throughout the searches of it. It was he who directed the photographer's attention to areas of interest. It was he who noted and caused to be photographed the scene in the bathroom that everyone agrees is where the body was dismembered – the heavy bloodstains, the gobbets of flesh in the U-bends of sink and toilet, the chips of bone and tendon. As for the living room and kitchen, yes, he saw all those features visible in the photographs and can explain them all to the jury.

You might have thought nothing would stop Detective Sergeant

Crabbe, but Curtis Neil intends to have a go. At the suggestion that the officer can explain the chaos in the living areas, the barrister shoots to his feet and says, 'No, you can't. You may be able to say what the scene is consistent with, but you cannot say what was actually going on.'

Curtis Neil has a point and I am about to warn the officer to take care but he is too quick for both of us.

'When you have been to as many drug houses as I have,' he says, 'you know one when you see one.'

The jury enjoys this. So does Mr Tidmarsh. But I have to keep control of the court.

'That may be, Detective Sergeant Crabbe, but you will confine yourself please to what you observed, and what your experience tells you it is consistent with.' I make the mistake of thinking the officer's nod is a respectful one.

'Very well, Ma'am.' Pronounced to rhyme with 'alarm'. He pulls out his pocket book but barely needs to consult it. 'I saw evidence . . .' a pause, a stress, '*consistent with* a number of people living at the address, or at least sleeping there. In the bedroom was a flannel nightdress . . .' he gives Neil a long look, '*consistent with* an elderly lady occupying the room. In the living room was bedding on the sofa and chair *consistent with* at least two people having slept there. A pair of denim jeans and trainers and a T-shirt, the sizes and styles suggesting . . . no, I correct myself, *consistent with* at least one of them being young and probably male, though of course females can wear male clothing. The size of the trainers is the same as those worn by the defendant. Not *consistent with*,' he says, 'just plain fact.'

A vein throbs in Curtis Neil's neck but he says nothing.

'In the kitchen and on the table in the living room were the remains of a lot of takeaway meals. Also thirteen empty beer cans and one almost-empty whisky bottle. On the coffee table a cannabis joint and a roach clip, together with two pipes for crack cocaine and a syringe. Near them a small set of digital scales and fifteen small clear plastic self-sealing bags. While I cannot say what had been going on there, I can say this was all entirely *consistent with* the use of and the dealing in drugs.'

'Thank you,' says Mr Tidmarsh. And why not. He has reason to be grateful to the detective, who has mastered the art of the lingering emphasis and the subtle pause. 'Now, officer, we know that until shortly before her death, Lilian Sopher lived alone at this address. Taking everything into account, does your *long experience . . .*' Mr Tidmarsh adopts both emphasis and pause, 'suggest an explanation consistent with what you found in the flat?'

'It certainly does,' says the detective. 'It is just what I would expect to see if this lady had been the victim of "cuckooing".'

'And could you explain the concept of "cuckooing" to the jury?'

'I could, Sir. Cuckoos lay their eggs in the nest of another bird and take it over. Drug gangs take over someone's home and then use it to store and deal drugs there. They pick on vulnerable people. They terrify their victims into submission. They target the elderly, the mentally ill, those with no one near by to help. Such victims can become prisoners in their own home, sometimes in one room of their home.'

A sudden movement from Lesley draws my eye to her. She is looking up at the public gallery, scanning the rows. The same two men I had seen before are back. As before they are doing nothing amiss, only meeting her gaze. But this seems enough to overwhelm her. The jurors, concentrating on the officer's words, his description of victims of 'cuckooing' which so closely describes Lilian Sopher, don't appear to notice. Tom Tidmarsh, satisfied, has sat down. It is Curtis Neil's turn to cross-examine. He glances at his client, then turns away from her to the witness. It is at this moment that Lesley, managing to tear her gaze from the men in the public gallery, puts her head down on the desk in front of her and starts to sob. They are the tears of an exhausted child.

'Let's take a break,' I say. 'Now.'

Esme is used to bringing down the curtain on unscripted drama. Before the jury knows what is happening, she has them out of court.

'Mr Neil, what is going on?'

He shakes his head.

'Do you want some time to talk to Lesley?'

'I'm not sure that will help.'

'In what sense?'

'In the sense that though I will talk to her, I don't think she will talk to *me*.'

In the silence that follows I feel rather than see the eyes of two men in the public gallery on me, on Lesley and on her mother. I need to get to the bottom of this but how can I if the girl won't tell her counsel what's going on? She is sitting very still now. You might think still is still, but it isn't. There is a different sort of stillness that happens when you try to think yourself out of a place because you cannot bear to be there. Lesley is slipping away from us. She either won't or can't participate in her trial. She is in danger of going to prison for a big chunk of the rest of her life. And perhaps she deserves to. But not until her guilt is proved after a fair and thorough examination of the evidence. And it seems that at the moment she just won't let her leading counsel do that. I have seen her lose concentration, feel ill and burst into tears. I just can't let this go on. Curtis Neil clearly cannot relate to his client. That leaves one person I may be able to turn to for help.

'Mr Neil, where is your junior?'

But before Neil can answer, like a *deus ex machina*, a voice says, 'I'm here, My Lady.' And here, indeed, he is.

Ben Guardino. Young, olive-skinned, he isn't a tall man but he has a presence that makes you look at him, a voice that makes you listen. 'I'm so sorry to have been absent from the case. There were . . . unforeseen problems in another matter.'

'There are unforeseen problems in this one too.'

He is obviously used to dealing with tetchy judges. 'I am entirely at your disposal now, My Lady.'

'It isn't me who needs your services, Mr Guardino. It's your client.'

He bows his head. 'Would Your Ladyship rise for a short while? If I had twenty minutes with Lesley, we might find a way forward.'

I rather think that what is needed isn't a way forward but a way back – a reverse gear to get us out of the cul-de-sac into which we have wandered. But I am running out of options. So I rise and leave Guardino to the field.

CHAPTER ELEVEN

As she leads me back to my room Esme says, 'What's up?'

'I'm not sure. Something in the public gallery, I think.'

Esme has been around a long time. She knows what's what. 'The two in black?' she says.

'Maybe. Let's see.'

After twenty minutes a message reaches me. Mr Guardino would like another five if Her Ladyship would indulge him. Her Ladyship does. It is longer than that before he is ready but Her Ladyship exercises patience. After all, what else is she to do? At last I get a note. It is from Ben Guardino.

> My Lady, you may recall point seven on Mr Neil's list. I need to raise that matter now. In order to do so, we would be grateful if the public gallery could remain closed while we put the issue before the court. Mr Tidmarsh is aware of this note and has no objection to my request.

So when we sit again, the public gallery remains closed. On one side of the court are Tidmarsh, his officers and a lawyer from the CPS. On the other, Neil, Guardino, Lesley and her mother. There is no one else present except for a dock officer and my staff.

'Gentlemen,' I say to counsel, 'I have done as you requested and closed the public gallery. However, the principles that govern criminal courts require me to open it unless there is good reason to do otherwise.'

It is Ben Guardino who gets to his feet, not Curtis Neil. 'We entirely understand, My Lady. And we are grateful.'

'Mr Tidmarsh?' The prosecutor only looks uneasy.

But it's a wise judge who knows when not to push her luck, so I simply say, 'This court, for the moment, is in Chambers.'

Tom Tidmarsh is, of course, right to look uneasy. I am doing something which, though not uncommon, is a departure from the general rule. That rule says it's a principle of our common law[*] that all criminal proceedings take place in open court unless doing so would interfere with the proper administration of justice. Although courts do have power to order that the public be excluded, any derogation from the principles of open justice can only be justified where the public's presence would frustrate or render impracticable the administration of that justice.[†]

Over the years various statutes have permitted the exclusion of the public (though not always the press) in specific circumstances. These include where a child or vulnerable adult gives evidence of a sexual offence[‡] or during evidence which would, if published, be prejudicial to national safety.[§][¶]

---

[*] The common law is the part of our law which derives from custom and earlier court cases and decisions rather than statutes.
[†] Official Secrets Act 1920 section 8(4); Official Secrets Act 1989 section 11(4).
[‡] Youth Justice and Criminal Evidence Act 1999 section 25.
[§] The European Convention on Human Rights article 6(1) might be thought broader than our domestic law. It says, 'In the determination . . . of any criminal charge against him, everyone is entitled to a fair and public hearing . . . Judgment shall be pronounced publicly but the press and public may be excluded from all or part of the trial in the interests of morals, public order or national security in a democratic society, where the interests of juveniles or the protection of the private life of the parties so require, or to the extent strictly necessary in the opinion of the court in special circumstances where publicity would prejudice the interests of justice.'
[¶] AG v. Leveller Magazine Ltd [1979] AC 440; Re Times Newspapers Ltd [2009] 1WLR 1015.

Open justice is entrenched in our system. Exceptions are rare and must be necessary and proportionate. Only the minimum departure from it will be countenanced. But – and here is the point – however important the principle of open justice, it must give way to the more fundamental principle that the court's purpose is to do justice to the parties and the facts.* So I can exclude the public and sit 'in camera' or 'in Chambers' but only if I really must in order to administer justice.†

'All right,' I say, 'who is going to tell me what's happening? Mr Neil?'

Curtis Neil gets to his feet. 'My Lady, we think it preferable for my junior to argue this point. Lesley has found it easier to . . .' he searches for the right word, '. . . to work with Mr Guardino.'

Of course she has. He is younger and more sympathetic. He is almost certainly a better listener. But he doesn't have the experience or the proven track record of a QC. You don't get that accolade for nothing. Lesley has been given legal aid for 'a silk', and the public is paying one but . . . Curtis Neil may not be able to communicate effectively with his client, but he has found the route to me. He smiles ruefully. 'Sometimes, My Lady, a different approach is required. Mr Guardino and I are working together on the problems thrown up by this . . . unusual situation.'

So Neil is wiser than I had given him credit for. He and Guardino have found a way of getting through this and I will do no good by making it more difficult for them. I content myself with a nod and Lesley's junior counsel gets to his feet.

'We have a problem,' he says with disarming frankness, 'but I'm

---

* Guardian News and Media Ltd v. AB [2014] EWCA Crim (B1).
† I can't do it just to save someone from embarrassment, reputational or financial damage or to conceal facts it might be better to keep private. R v. Malvern Justices *ex parte* Evans; R v. Evesham Justices *ex parte* McDonagh (1988), 87 Cr.App.R.19; R v. Dover Justices *ex parte* Dover DC [1992] Cr.L.R.371 DC.

hopeful we can find an answer. It is common ground between all parties that Lesley was at one point involved with a drug gang. We ask the court to act upon the basis – at least for the purposes of this discussion – that she was driven to those actions initially by a desire to help her family. But that when she tried to withdraw, she was coerced into continuing by gang members who threatened to harm her mother and siblings if she stopped working for them.'

So that was it. Or might be. If it is true. A child, seeing her mother desperate to keep the family together, doing three jobs a day and trying to care for a little boy with physical and mental difficulties, thinks she has found a way to make money to help her mother. And ends up trapped. Do I accept this or not? The first question is whether the Crown accepts it.

'Mr Tidmarsh?'

The prosecutor gets to his feet. He is wary. 'Before I commit the Crown to a position on this point, I would like to hear what Mr Guardino has to say.'

Guardino nods. 'There has been a formal finding by the Home Office that Lesley was a victim of human trafficking and exploited by this gang. I entirely accept that is not a defence to murder. We do not advance it as such. I only ask Mr Tidmarsh to accept it for the purposes of what I am about to ask the court.'

The defence junior checks that his prosecutor is mollified. He is.

Guardino continues, 'Since the beginning of the trial, Lesley has been aware of two people in the public gallery whom she believes are linked to the gang. She worries because her mother has to come to court and leave it each day. She worries that if in the course of the trial she says anything that upsets or offends them, they will take revenge on her family. She is horrified that she has brought this danger to their door.'

And so she should be. But my job isn't to make moral judgements. It is to make sure this girl gets a fair trial.

'Mr Guardino, let me be clear about the issues in the case. Am I to understand that Lesley's defence to murder and dismemberment is that the gang carried out these acts and she was recruited only to dispose of the body?'

'Yes.'

'And that she knows the identity of those responsible but is too frightened – either for herself or her family – to say who they are?'

Again, 'Yes.'

'And that if I make a ruling that ensures these people cannot hear what she says, she might bring herself to name them?'

He hesitates. I can see he wants to say yes for a third time, but in the end he shakes his head. 'I cannot go that far, My Lady. If she named them, her revelation would inevitably come out, and she is very frightened of the consequences that might follow. As her lawyers, we can point out the advantages of her cooperating with police . . . but we can do no more.'

No wonder Curtis Neil has been having trouble with this girl – this girl who, if what I'm hearing is true – must make decisions no child should have to make. But Ben Guardino knows his job.

'My Lady, as her lawyers, Mr Neil and I must ensure she has the best opportunity to present her defence. Our anxiety is that her fears are preventing this from happening.'

'How?'

'What if she is inhibited from giving us proper instructions? What if she feels unable to get into the witness-box and give her evidence? What then?'

What, indeed. 'And you want me to . . .?'

'We want you to close the public gallery so that she does not have the pressure of seeing those two men watching her.'

I pause, trying to take in the situation. It's a nasty one. I can think of all sorts of law to describe it, but in plain English, it's a mess and I say so.

'My Lady,' Mr Tidmarsh is on his feet now, 'we for the Crown are not unsympathetic to Lesley's fears. And though it is our case that she is the killer, we would certainly like to identify those behind the drug dealing. But no one in the public gallery has behaved improperly. There is no evidence of anyone threatening the defendant or her family. Even if her fears are genuine, they may not be justified. There is certainly nothing to justify the exclusion of the entire public . . . At most, Your Ladyship might consider excluding only those two men.'

'But then they would know she had pointed them out,' says Mr Guardino, not unreasonably.

'Still,' insists Mr Tidmarsh, 'Your Ladyship cannot act upon unsupported assertion. You must have some evidence of impropriety or . . .' He leaves the sentence unfinished.

And this is why I called the situation a mess. On the one hand, if Lesley's fears are real, even if unjustified, and they deter her from taking part in her own defence, how is the trial fair? On the other hand, I cannot exclude the public without an evidence-based reason for doing so.

There must be something in my armoury I can draw on here. I must have come across something similar before. Or something I could adapt. After all, Tom Tidmarsh is right. I don't need to exclude the whole public, I don't even need to formally exclude the two men if I can find another way to deter them from coming into the public gallery. If Lesley has got herself involved with dangerous people, I can't protect her or her family. But that isn't what I am paid to do. My job is to put her mind at rest if I can, so that she has confidence in the process that is trying her. And suddenly I have an idea . . .

'Mr Tidmarsh, Mr Guardino, what if I open the public gallery but require those coming in to provide identification and an address? And perhaps the prosecution would be kind enough to send a police officer to sit up there. If genuine visitors don't wish to provide these details, there are plenty of other courtrooms where they can go. But these measures might be enough to encourage any less-than-genuine visitor to move on.'

The defence team put their heads together. A hurried discussion. And Mr Guardino says, 'We are grateful for the suggestion and would like to try it.'

Mr Tidmarsh looks to his team – the CPS lawyer, the senior officer in the case – and he too nods. A policeman is sent upstairs. Security are given instructions and equip themselves with clipboards. The gallery is opened. There is a pause, voices from the corridor beyond. One by one, people come in. If they look puzzled, they don't seem upset. When half a dozen or so have entered, we hear a short disturbance outside the door. It grows. It fades away. A security officer puts his head round the door and gives me a thumbs up. He takes his watchful seat. There is no sign of the men in black. I draw a sigh of relief.

'Gentlemen, I think we are ready to resume.'

Curtis Neil says, 'My Lady, would there be any objection if Mr Guardino cross-examined the remaining prosecution witnesses?'

'No objection from me, Mr Neil. It is a matter for you how you organize these matters. But . . .'

Curtis Neil reads my mind and smiles darkly. 'If Your Ladyship is concerned Mr Guardino has been distracted by another case, you can take it from me he is more than able to take over in this one.'

There is nothing more to be said except, 'Bring in the jury, please, Esme.'

CHAPTER TWELVE

THE JURORS ARE IN their seats and DS Crabbe is back in the witness-box. He looks aggrieved when Ben Guardino stands up to cross-examine him, as if he is worthy of something more than a junior.

'Good morning, officer,' says Guardino.

The DS looks pointedly at the clock which shows one minute past midday. 'Good afternoon, Sir.'

Ben Guardino smiles cheerfully. 'You're right,' he says. 'We've lost a bit of time this morning, but let's make up for it now. Shall we talk about the exhibits you found in the living room and kitchen?'

'If you like, Sir.'

'Well, let's, then. The jeans and T-shirts, and the trainers. The cans of beer and the takeaway dishes. Were they all sent to a laboratory?'

'Of course.'

'To be examined for fingermarks and DNA?'

'The scientists will have done their best.'

'And their best will no doubt have been excellent.'

DS Crabbe doesn't deign to answer.

'And naturally the prosecution will have compared the results of their excellent scientific work with the prints and DNA of my client?'

'Naturally.'

'And you can confirm, of course, that there is no match.'

The officer gives a stiff nod.

'Would you be kind enough, officer, to give an audible answer?'

says Ben Guardino sweetly. 'For the record, you understand. So to be clear, there is no scintilla of evidence that Lesley Brown ever wore any of those clothes or footwear, nor that she ate any of the food, nor that she drank any of the alcohol found in Lilian Sopher's flat.'

'That's right, Sir.' A pause. A crafty look. 'But there is evidence that she drank from a bottle of water found in the kitchen. DNA matching hers was found on the plastic rim.'

Guardino is unfazed. 'Ah, yes. That would the bottle of water she bought at the corner shop at the same time she bought the bleach?'

Crabbe restrains himself from saying that cutting up bodies is thirsty work and settles for, 'Possibly. But possibly not. There were two bottles of water. One was bought on the day Lilian Sopher was killed, the Monday. One was clearly bought on an earlier occasion.'

The jury sits up at this. So do I. We know nothing about a second bottle of water. Have we missed something? If we have, Ben Guardino hasn't. 'Of course,' he says smoothly. 'There were two bottles of water in the kitchen. One bore Lesley's DNA on the rim. The other did not. It looks rather as if she drank directly from one bottle but not the other. The big question is when. If it was on the occasion when she removed the body parts, it takes your case no further. But if it was on an earlier occasion . . . well, that would look very bad indeed for young Lesley, wouldn't it?'

The officer nods.

'Because that would mean she had been there before and been part of the whole history of what seems to have been cuckooing in the flat.'

'Yes,' says Crabbe.

'Which she denies. Of course, you know she denies being there on an earlier occasion.'

'Defendants often deny things.'

Guardino seems to think about this, giving it all the respect he would accord to a rational comment. Finally he asks as in a spirit of genuine enquiry, 'So do you have any evidence to show she was there and drinking from a bottle of water on an earlier occasion?'

'No, Sir, I haven't. No one can tell when DNA got onto an object.' He manages to make it sound as if Lesley Brown has pulled a fast one on him and on the jury.

'Well, now,' says Guardino, 'that is very fair of you. Very fair indeed.'

It certainly isn't. And the officer knows it. He stirs uneasily.

'No evidence of Lesley at the flat in the previous weeks,' Guardino's tone is musing, 'but plenty to show others were. Mr Kapoor saw three of them. Drugs were apparently being sold from the premises. The remains of food and alcohol consistent with a number of people being there apart from the deceased. Someone killed the cat no later than the Sunday before Miss Sopher's body was found.'

'Obviously,' says DS Crabbe.

'As you say. The facts are obvious. But what I'm wondering is why, if the cat was killed on the previous Sunday, you are so sure Lilian wasn't killed until the Monday – because that is what you told the jury a moment ago, isn't it?'

'It is, Sir,' says Crabbe, standing up very straight. 'The old lady must have been killed on the Monday, because she was seen by her neighbour Mrs Kapoor that day.'

'Now there,' Guardino's voice is gentle, 'there I fear you are wrong.'

'Look,' Crabbe loses what he has left of cool, 'I took the statement from Mrs Kapoor. And the statement says it was the Monday.'

'Oh,' says Guardino. 'It was you who took the statement, was it? Well, you're right about what the statement says, but . . .' He allows a pregnant pause. Everyone in the courtroom knows what's coming – except DS Crabbe. 'But it's not what Mrs Kapoor says. Has no one told you that, Mr Crabbe?'

Of course they haven't. It is forbidden for a witness to be told what another has said. And though Ben Guardino has done just that, he has made a valuable point for the defence. I wait for him to sit down, but he doesn't. 'Do you have more questions for this officer?' I ask.

'I do, My Lady, but I wonder if we might have a short break first. I would like to take brief instructions from Lesley.'

CHAPTER THIRTEEN

'Fifteen minutes,' I tell Esme, 'then we sit again.'

She nods. 'How does a kid like that end up doing what she did?'

I point out we don't yet know what she did.

'We know enough,' she sighs. 'What sort of world do we live in where youngsters like her fall into the hands of gangs?'

'I suppose it's always been like that.'

She fixes me with a wondering eye. 'You think?'

Actually, I don't know what I think. Have children always been used by criminals? Have they always been drawn into gangs?

Once I am alone, I turn to the computer – the Old Bailey online archives are familiar to the machine now. I have only to type in the first letters and it helpfully flags up the web page. I'm sure I'm right about gangs preying on children – after all, I know my *Oliver Twist* as well as the next judge. It is a surprise, then, when no combination of 'child', 'gang' or the like produces the result I'm seeking. There are children aplenty. There are gangs too. But none that explore how the former have been exploited by the latter. Still, if Dickens wrote about it . . . I try a different tack. In a general search engine I type 'nineteenth century' and 'child criminals'. Up pops a report published in 1816 by the Committee for Investigating the Alarming Increase in Juvenile Delinquency in the Metropolis. It makes fascinating reading. It concluded that thousands of boys in the metropolis aged under seventeen were daily engaged in the commission of crime. It noted their association with 'professed thieves of mature age, and with girls who subsist by prostitution'. It described how 'these unfortunate lads' were organized into gangs and how they planned their enterprises and afterwards divided the plunder. There was a careful analysis of the causes of all this, listed as 'the improper conduct of parents, the want of education and suitable employment'. It also noted the violation of the Sabbath and the habit of gambling in the streets. The Committee concluded that the problem was made much worse by the severity of the criminal code, the defective state of the police and the system of prison discipline. Save for the matter of the Sabbath and the street gambling, this could have been written today. In explaining how youngsters were moving deeper and deeper into crime, the report described boys doomed to mix in prison with experienced criminals until they were enlisted into their service. It's perhaps of interest that the report concluded that nothing Parliament could do by legislation would improve upon the efforts of the public in putting an end to this.

So Lesley sits in a long and dishonourable line of child victims who have been exposed to criminality and joined it. I'm still mulling over this when Esme comes to take me back to court.

In the witness-box DS Crabbe stares belligerently at Ben Guardino, who only smiles. 'Officer, I think you were the one who arrested Lesley? The jury may be wondering how you traced her.'

I'm sure they are, but I'm surprised Guardino has asked about it because the answer – that her fingermarks were on record following her arrest for drug dealing – will reveal the fact that she had been in trouble before. The Crown would not be permitted to put this before the court without my permission,* but it is always open for a defendant to tell the jury about her own bad character . . . if she wants to. So when defence counsel says, 'It didn't take you long to identify my

---

* They must make what is called 'a bad character application' in order to put before the jury previous misconduct by a defendant.

client as the girl in the CCTV images,' DS Crabbe can hardly believe his luck.

'It did not.'

'Because you were able to trace her from her fingermarks on the suitcase.'

'Yes.'

'And that was because her fingermarks were on record. Because she had been in trouble with the police before.'

'Yes.'

'The offence for which she had previously been arrested was possession of crack cocaine with intent to supply, wasn't it?'

'It certainly was. She had been dealing in drugs. Cuckooing would have been part of her stock-in-trade.' And then, in case the jurors have missed the point, 'Cuckooing is just the thing that happened to Miss Sopher.'

'Are you sure Lesley Brown had on that earlier occasion – the one that led to her fingermarks being recorded – been dealing in drugs?'

'Of course.'

'No doubt?'

'None.'

'And yet the CPS dropped the case against her. There was no conviction because there was no prosecution.' Ben Guardino affects to look puzzled. 'Why would the CPS do that, officer?'

A hesitation. 'You'd have to ask them.'

'Oh, but surely you know. Let me see if I can help you. Was it because they were satisfied that she was herself a victim of a drug gang? Didn't the Home Office make a finding that she was manipulated and exploited by criminals into criminal activity?'

Too late, Crabbe sees where he has been led. His chin juts forward. 'There's no accounting for the Home Office.'

'Well, the CPS seems to take account of it. They abandoned the prosecution on the basis that she had been used and exploited and shouldn't be held responsible. Wasn't that it? Just as she was used and exploited to dispose of the body that someone else killed.'

But before DS Crabbe can tell Ben Guardino what he thinks of this, the barrister sits down and prosecuting counsel thanks his witness and turns away. It is an angry and disappointed Crabbe who leaves the witness-box.

CHAPTER FOURTEEN

We are almost at the end of the prosecution case. All that is left are matters not in dispute ... matters that both sides intend to reduce to writing and give the jury as a series of agreed facts. Among them are the conclusions in the pathologist's report. The state of the body made examination difficult. Not every part was recovered. There are foxes and dogs on the Downs. There are birds with sharp beaks. And the use of a knife to dismember and chop made identification of the fatal injury difficult. The skull showed no trauma from a blunt object, but that Lilian had been killed rather than died a natural death is an obvious inference from what was subsequently done to her body.

I am hoping that counsel have already drafted the document of Agreed Facts to be handed out to the jury and read into the record, and that the Crown can close its case today. However, counsel seem to have a different plan.

They are in earnest conversation, then Tom Tidmarsh nods, makes a note and turns to me. 'My Lady, might I delay closing my case until tomorrow?' And seeing me hesitate, he adds, 'I wouldn't ask if it weren't important.'

Of course, if it's important, I must give him the time he needs.

As it turns out, once the jury is sent away for the day, it isn't Tidmarsh who needs the time but Guardino.

'It's entirely my responsibility, My Lady,' he says. 'I apologize. Particularly since what has now occurred to me might have done so earlier. I recognize that I am causing inconvenience, but I really would like the opportunity to cross-examine the pathologist.'

I fail to stifle a sigh of impatience. 'But I thought his evidence was agreed. Do you have something to put to him? Do you have an expert report of your own on which to challenge his views? Because if you have, it certainly hasn't been uploaded to the Digital Case System.'

He shakes his head. 'No report, My Lady. Just an idea. I am perfectly happy to share it with My Learned Friend. Indeed, I'm happy for the pathologist to be told in advance what I wish to ask so he can give it some thought. But . . .'

Lesley is watching the discussion unfold with a sense of engagement I haven't seen in her before. And after all, this is her trial, her life. And Lilian's death. Surely I can spare the two of them the time to ensure everything is done properly. Surely I must. So we rise, and during the night I wake once, twice, a third time, always wondering what has happened – and what will happen tomorrow.

The pathologist has given evidence in my court many times before. He is sound, and fair, and can explain difficult concepts in easy terms. Although he is usually instructed by the Crown, he is equally happy to act for the defence. Neither of them is his master. He owes his duty only to the court and to the truth.

He has come along at short notice and – is it my imagination or is there still an odour of the dissecting room about him? Tidmarsh sets the scene.

'Doctor, when you were asked to carry out the post-mortem, were you told by the prosecution the facts already established?'

'That is the way it is always done. I have a note . . .' He opens his papers. 'I was told that on the Tuesday morning, following a 999 call from a member of the public, police recovered body parts from Hackney Downs. And that it was believed they or some of them were those of an elderly Caucasian lady who had not been seen since the previous morning.'

'Armed with that information, what did you do?'

'I examined the recovered body parts. They were incomplete but I was satisfied that what I had came from one body, a female beyond middle age. Given the way in which it had been cut up, it was impossible to positively identify any fatal wound but it was likely that death was inflicted with a knife.'

'Were you asked to give a time of death?'

The pathologist gives a small shake of his head. 'I'm afraid it isn't how they do it on television. You can very rarely give an accurate time of death from the body alone, still less when it has been treated as this one had.'

'You were told the female was last seen on Monday morning. Did you question that?'

'As I say, establishing time of death in a case like this is extremely difficult. You can look for things like rigor mortis and livor mortis – the stiffening of the limbs after death and the discolouration of the skin due to pooling of blood which is no longer being pumped around the body. With only dissected segments to work with ... well, it is quite impossible beyond saying the body hadn't putrefied to any great extent. So not many days.'

Tom Tidmarsh sits and Ben Guardino gets to his feet. He asks if the pathologist could explain the concept of putrefaction.

The doctor looks at the jury. Twelve pairs of eyes meet his. The courtroom falls very silent. 'The moment you die,' he says, 'the body begins to break down. Bacteria invade. Decomposition is under way. But its speed depends on many factors, both internal and external. These include age, condition of body, cause of death, the ambient temperature, moisture and air and light exposure.'

'The body had putrefied to some extent?'

'Yes. The first signs are usually a greenish discolouration on the outer skin of the abdominal wall and under the surface of the liver, and these are thought to appear around eighteen hours after death.

The liver was not recovered. I suspect that some of the material found in the lavatory pipes represented an attempt to dispose of the soft organs. However, the trunk of the body was examined and there were clear signs of the discolouration I mentioned.'

'Clear signs? Suggesting a period after death of more than eighteen hours?'

The doctor pauses. 'There are many imponderables in this case. The remains had been outside on a cool night for some hours, which might delay some aspects of the process. Before that they must be supposed to have been in the flat, but I have no idea of the temperature and conditions there, nor at what stage after death the dismemberment took place. The extensive bloodstaining of the premises in the photographs I was shown suggest it could have been relatively soon after she died.'

'Let's approach it another way. At what time was the torso brought to the mortuary and put into storage that might have inhibited further decomposition?'

The doctor consults his records. 'At 11.20 on the Tuesday morning.'

Ben Guardino controls the smile that tugs at the corner of his mouth. 'So death must almost certainly have occurred before 6 p.m. on the Monday evening.'

'Oh yes,' says the doctor. 'Bearing in mind what I saw, I should certainly say before 6 p.m.'

'Could the killing have taken place on the Sunday morning?'

Again the doctor stops to think. 'In my judgement it could have taken place any time from the early hours of Sunday to perhaps mid-afternoon on Monday. Beyond that I am not prepared to go.'

But Guardino doesn't need to take him beyond that. The idea that Lesley bought the cleaning materials in advance of the killing and in preparation for carrying it out cannot be right. Even more importantly, there is no evidence Lesley was ever at the flat before 6 p.m.

on the Monday. And if she wasn't, she could not be the killer. I don't know if the doctor realizes the significance of his words, but the rest of us do.

Ben Guardino has one last question. 'You said you thought the dissection was likely to have taken place relatively soon after death? How long would it take someone to do that?'

The pathologist hesitates. 'You use the word dissection but this was really no more than a . . . well, a chopping-up. It was not done with care or with any thought to precision. Unless you know where to cut – as clearly the person who did this, did not – it requires a lot of brute strength. It would take a significant number of hours.'

'And it would be a . . .' Guardino pauses, 'a messy business.'

'Very.'

I cannot be the only one thinking of the short statement from the cab driver who collected Lesley and drove her to Hackney. Surely if she had been covered in blood, he would have said so?

And just like that . . . in the course of three or four minutes in the courtroom . . . the case turns.

Is the surprise that a matter of this importance did not come to light before now? Or is the surprise that it finally has?

CHAPTER FIFTEEN

EVEN BEFORE THE PATHOLOGIST leaves the witness-box, I receive two jury notes. One politely enquires, 'Is there any evidence Lesley was at the house at any time before 6 p.m. on the Monday evening?' The other, more brutally, says, 'There's no evidence the defendant was at the house at the time when the lady must have been killed and cut up.' The procedure for dealing with jury notes is simple. The jury leaves court while counsel and I consider the queries or points raised.* When they have gone off for yet another cup from the bottomless coffee pot, I turn to counsel.

'Mr Tidmarsh, Mr Guardino, this is an unexpected turn of events.'

'It is, My Lady,' says Ben Guardino, as if it weren't his fresh eye that has brought us to it. 'I'd like the chance to reflect on whether I should now be making an application that the court directs acquittals on Count One murder and Count Two dismemberment – on the basis that no reasonable jury, properly directed, could convict on them.'

The application he is describing is one that usually takes place at the close of the Crown's case and before the defence begins, and is accordingly called 'a half-time submission'. But in fact it can be made at any time the defence believes a stage is reached where a jury just couldn't properly convict.

Tom Tidmarsh gets to his feet. His face betrays nothing but its usual courtesy. 'I wonder,' he says, 'if Your Ladyship would rise for

---

* Unless the note indicates 'voting numbers' on whether a defendant is guilty or not guilty, in which case the judge keeps the note strictly to herself.

twenty minutes. I would like to talk to My Learned Friend, and those who instruct me.'

So off I go to get a coffee of my own. Possibly a chocolate biscuit, too. Back in my room, my fellow judge G puts her head round the door and asks how things are going.

I tell her what has happened. I tell her it's possible – in the light of developments – the Crown will drop its case on murder and dismemberment, but if they don't I might accede to Mr Guardino's application to stop those two counts. Even if I don't, I am confident the jury will acquit Lesley of them. I am expecting G to express surprise, interest . . . but she only nods comfortably.

'Things have a way of working out,' she says as she sets off back to another courtroom, another case.

Although I do not expect to sentence Lesley on Counts One and Two, I will have to sentence her for the matter to which she pleaded guilty, Count Three. I start to make a rough draft of what I might say. I sketch out something like this:

> Lesley Brown, you have been acquitted of the murder of Lilian Sopher and the dismemberment of her body. Those were very terrible crimes, and no one has been brought to book for them, partly because of your actions. You have pleaded guilty to acts designed to conceal those offences and therefore to protect the people who committed them. You bought and used cleaning materials to remove traces of what had happened. You carried the victim's dismembered remains to a public place, where you disposed of them.
>
> The Court of Appeal Criminal Division has repeatedly said that conduct intended to pervert the course of justice almost invariably calls for a custodial sentence. In assessing the gravity of your offence, I have considered not only the seriousness of the underlying offence, the nature of your conduct and the

consequences to justice, but the additional grief you have caused to all those who cared about Lilian Sopher. I am sure you knew what had been happening in Lilian's flat, what the cleaning products were for, and what was in the suitcase.

The starting point for an adult who committed such an offence would be seven years' imprisonment. But a starting point isn't a finishing point. I must take into account any aggravating feature beyond the offence itself. I note that it was committed against a background of what is called 'cuckooing', a cruel practice that preys on the weak and which is used to facilitate the supply of drugs. This serious factor increases your sentence from the starting point of seven to one of eight years. I must then look at mitigating features. You have no previous convictions, but I cannot give you credit for being of good character, because it is common ground that you had been dealing in class A drugs. I do however accept that your choice to become involved with drug gangs began out of a desire to make money to help your struggling mother and younger siblings. I also accept that your continued involvement was, in the end, less than willing. It is clear you felt under considerable pressure to comply with the increasing demands of the gang, and that you feared if you didn't your family would suffer. I take all of this into account. However, you could have gone for help to the authorities and you chose not to. You put your own fears ahead of what you must have known was right. You made criminally bad judgements. Perhaps your most significant mitigation lies in your youth. You had to make decisions that would challenge anyone of your age – at the time only fifteen. The law requires me to make a significant reduction in sentence for your youth, and for what I accept is your remorse, and also because I believe you are capable of change. Accordingly, the sentence of eight years is reduced to five years. Next, the law requires me to give further credit for your plea of guilty. For a guilty plea entered at the first opportunity, the law allows one third off. For a plea at trial, one tenth off. You pleaded shortly before trial but I accept you would have done so earlier, but for the format of the original Count Two and the advice of your counsel. So I am prepared to increase the discount to 25 per cent. It follows that the sentence will be one of three years four months in a Young Offenders Institution. Of this you will likely serve one half. Time already served on remand will – as always – count towards the sentence.

CHAPTER SIXTEEN

IF THIS IS, IN the end, what happens, will justice have been done? Certainly not for Lilian, nor for her sister, nor even for poor Oscar. The drug dealers, the killers, are still out there. They are still bullying and terrifying the weak and helpless, still exploiting the young and vulnerable.

And for Lesley? Such justice as the courtroom can offer, she has had. But what justice was there in leaving her – a child of fourteen, fifteen – to watch her mother struggling to hold down three jobs and care for two daughters and a disabled son? This cannot excuse Lesley. She is a bright girl and made her own bad choices. But how much better might it have been if, instead of giving her the protections of the law after she had taken these steps, we had done something to protect her before that? Should a child ever have to make the sort of moral – or in her case immoral – decisions that she did?

And for her and her family it isn't over yet. Her mother and siblings will almost certainly have to move away from the area, and when she is released from custody she will presumably join them. Together they must try to start new lives. But Lesley, I suspect, will be looking over her shoulder for many years to come. She will have to live with what she did to the body of Lilian Sopher, and the grief she has brought upon so many, including her own family. She has done what she cannot undo.

Yet Lesley is only one of many children who, trying to navigate the world we have created for them, have lost their way. Are we failing them? Has it always been thus? So often I have been able to go back to the Old Bailey archives and see how present cases compare with past ones. Often I can see that, for all the efforts we have made, the same problems beset our society now as then. This time, this case, has been no different. Not really. In the nineteenth century, London – and by extension I suppose other parts of the country too – was struggling with disaffected youth engaged in endless criminality. That has not changed. I can't compare numbers, but in the early nineteenth century what led young people to offend barely warranted a mention in the trials themselves. It took concerned citizens like those in the Committee mentioned above to examine the state of juvenile delinquency and its causes. At least now in our criminal justice system and our Parliament we recognize the problem. And whereas in both past and present, decent members of society have striven to understand and combat the root causes of the problem, now at least we formally recognize how children can become victims of the gangs in which they function.

The careful research done by that long-ago Committee, and its analysis of the underlying causes, bear some thought. Secure and loving homes, opportunities for education and employment, play an important part. Guidance to good works better than stricture. And of one thing we can be sure – merely increasing sentences is unlikely to work any better now than it did then, when the courts had available to them the death sentence for even relatively minor offending. That historical report is redolent with a belief that young people are not inherently bad; that it is our job to bring out their good. Who wants to disagree with that?

3: The Quality of Mercy

IN A NEAT LITTLE *flat on the third floor of a block in North London the Overtons have finished their supper. The heavy smell of sausages and mash still hangs in the air but now they have settled in front of the television. The sound is turned up because Mr Overton, in his seventies, is hard of hearing. But Mrs Overton can catch the sounds from the other side of the wall.*

'They're at it again,' she says.

Her husband scowls. 'You mean he's at it.'

'You're right,' she says. 'Just him. Shouting.'

'Won't be long before she's screaming. Then she'll be crying.'

'She can't help it, poor thing. You'd be screaming and crying if you had to live with that man.'

'I don't know why she stays.'

Through the wall comes the muffled roar of someone in a fury. Mrs Overton sighs. 'I'll turn the TV up, shall I? We don't want to be listening to him for the next two hours.' She heaves herself to her feet. As she does so, the voice from next door is cut off. It happens quite suddenly, in mid-bellow. 'Well, there's a funny thing,' she says. 'He's stopped.'

'Perhaps he's thought better of it,' says Mr Overton.

'He never has before.' She doesn't know what to think. But she knows what she fears, what she has feared for a long time; that one day Rodney Marsh will do for that little wife of his. After a moment she pads in slippered feet to the front door, and looks along the covered balcony. The door of Marsh's flat is open

a crack. Someone is standing there in the shadows, hesitating. But even as she stares, the crack closes and the line of light disappears.

From inside, Mr Overton calls, 'Is everything all right?'

And she does not know how to answer.

CHAPTER ONE

KATRINA ROBERTS, COUNSEL FOR the Crown, is opening her case to an Old Bailey jury. Compared to her opponent, Colin Merchant, who sits further down counsel's row, she is a slight figure but a determined one. Her dark hair peeps out around the edge of her wig. Her face is a mask of concentration. She knows this is her big day. She has been a barrister for a mere twelve years, and is still a 'junior' but here she is, entrusted by the Crown Prosecution Service to handle a murder. It is only a 'domestic' with one defendant. But still. Of course, the CPS likes to encourage the young and able. And Miss Roberts is able. She has a reputation for getting the job done. Or perhaps it's the defendant in the dock who has brought Miss Roberts this chance. Does the CPS think that in prosecuting a bewildered, prematurely aged woman, tiny between two dock officers, it looks better to have a female prosecutor? Or is it only that the CPS faces budgetary cuts, and junior counsel come cheaper than silks?*

Whatever the reason, Katrina Roberts is on her feet, addressing the jury.

'The facts are clear,' she says.

I certainly hope so because I'm the judge drafted in at short notice to sit on the case. Two other trials in the building are overrunning. A third is on hold while Covid rips through it. Cases that should

---

* All barristers – however long in the tooth – are 'juniors' unless and until they are appointed QCs (now KCs). Juniors wear 'stuff' gowns while QCs wear silk ones (hence they are called 'silks').

have started, are stuck in the queue. The list office has juggled the remaining courtrooms, judges, defendants in custody, witnesses. Various solutions have been mooted. The one that offered the least collateral damage was the one where my two-week holiday was sacrificed. Judges lose holidays all the time. It goes with the territory.

Old Bailey trials usually begin on a Monday but by the time my fate has been decided and I have been summoned back from the airport . . . by the time I have unpacked T-shirts, repacked stiff white ones and trudged into town, it is Wednesday morning. There are two people waiting for me – the list officer and my usher, Esme. I expect the list officer wants to apologize and to thank me for returning . . . but now I look more carefully I see about him a sense of urgency, as if he is about to warn of fire on the fourth floor or snakes in the sanitation. 'How long will this take?' he demands.

'Dear man,' I say, 'if I look blank, it's because I am. I have no clue what you are talking about.'

'The trial,' he says. 'How long will it take? Please tell me you can do it by Monday week. And if you can't, tell me where I will put the seven-defendant murder with vulnerable witnesses and press interest due to start then.'

'But Monday week . . . that gives me only eight days! To do a murder trial!'

'Judge can't rush these things,' says Esme. 'They take as long as they take.'

The list officer makes an effort to restrain himself. Probably because another murder in the building will only make his backlog worse. But I can see his blood pressure rising.

'I'll do my best,' I say soothingly. Though, knowing nothing about the case I have come to try, I have no idea what my best might be.

When he has gone, Esme says, 'Well, I wasn't expecting to see you again till the other side of the Pyrenees. They're waiting for you in court, but they can wait a bit longer. So can the list office. I've made you a coffee. French.'

This is why I love Esme.

Fifteen minutes later I take my seat on the Bench to try a matter about which I know next to nothing. I don't like to be unprepared, so now I listen very carefully to Miss Roberts.

'The facts are clear,' she says again.

She is much younger than I was when I first did her job. In the many years which have passed since then, I have learned a thing or two – among them, that nothing is as clear as Miss Roberts seems to think. Especially in prosecuting murder. Still, she appears to be on firm ground. The deceased, I discover, was found in the living room of the flat where he lived with his wife. Miss Roberts does not call him the deceased but rather gives him the name he bore in life – Rodney Marsh. Conversely, she does not give his wife her name – which is Mercy Marsh – but calls her 'the defendant'. These are old tricks to make him more and her less real.

'Justice for Rodney,' Miss Roberts tells the jurors, 'is in your hands.' And this is true. But then, so is justice for Mercy.

So far Miss Roberts is doing rather well. The jurors are paying close attention. She picks up the story with the summoning of police. Neighbours heard shouts and thuds. They dialled 999. Miss Roberts does not dwell on the fact that an hour passed before a young officer came. Nor the fact that he came alone because his partner had gone off duty after eating a dubious burger. Nor that he was barely a year into the job. He had dealt with 'domestics' before and knew the form. He was to see if either party wanted to make a formal complaint. They rarely did.

The young officer had gone confidently up to the front door – Miss Roberts shows us the recording from his 'body-worn camera' – and knocked on it. The door had swung open. All these months later in the alien territory of the Central Criminal Court we watch the footage and feel his confidence evaporate. He had called out. The film carries audio recording and his voice now wavers across Court 9. The open door and the silence had clearly unnerved him. He walked in, cautiously. To his right, a cupboard; to his left, a bathroom. Then down the passageway to the living room. He stood in the half-open doorway. On the grainy film we see what he saw – a wall, a gas appliance set neatly into it, and on the floor, folded like a foetus, what remained of Rodney Marsh.

The officer, maybe not understanding what he was looking at, moved forward. There was a moment of realization. A sudden stopping. Perhaps he had never dealt with a dead body before, because his shock is palpable. He staggered back. It is only then that we see Mrs Marsh step out of the shadows and walk towards him. He stood there waiting for whatever she would do next. We wait too. She put her hand into the pocket of her cardigan and pulled something out and held it towards him. We recoil with him. But . . .

'Here,' she said.

And he took the proffered tissue and wiped his face.

'Are you all right?' she said.

In a strangled voice he told her he was. Which is more than could be said for the man on the floor.

In the photographic bundle, the body has been pixelated but Miss Roberts won't spare the jury any detail. She explains that Rodney Marsh's hands were over his head as if to ward off attack. That an attack had been carried out, and with a weapon, is clear because the backs of his hands were bloodied and broken. Victims of violence, she says, often suffer these 'defence injuries' – the result of trying to protect vulnerable parts of their bodies. But Mr Marsh's hands hadn't saved him. His skull was smashed in.

'Not just smashed,' says Miss Roberts. She pauses, watches the twelve pairs of eyes widen. She picks her moment. 'Smashed,' she says, 'like an eggshell.'

Someone on the jury gives a deep sigh and Miss Roberts capitalizes on it. 'Fractures,' she says, 'to both sides of his head and to the top of the skull and its base. More fractures within the face. The pathologist will say such damage requires great force and a significant number of blows. At least six, possibly more.'

She waits while the jury digests this. One of them, it seems, would rather not because when Miss Roberts says, 'Take the skull behind the right ear,' someone murmurs, 'Do I have to?' I sympathize. Dead is dead. Does it matter whether death was caused by three blows or six? But Miss Roberts thinks it does and she has the floor. We are all captive while she tells us the skull behind the ear was in pieces. We have no choice but to follow her along the two long fractures across the head. We must picture a hinge fracture so huge, the back of the skull could be separated from the front. We all now feel we have gone as far as we can reasonably be expected to go with Miss Roberts. Perhaps she senses this because she moves on from the injuries to their cause.

'This level of damage is typical of road traffic accidents, but here it was inflicted by a single hand holding . . .' she pauses for effect, '. . . a poker.'

A poker? I'd thought that after they banned coal fires, pokers were things of the past. After all, what can you poke now? I study the photographs of the Marsh's living room. A little hearth with, set in it, a modern gas appliance – the sort that allows you to turn a knob for licking flames or glow. No chimney here, nor poker needed. But poker there was, and now Miss Roberts produces it with such flourish as can be managed when the thing is skewered to the bottom of an evidence box. She gives it to Esme who passes it first to me, then to the jurors. In turn we gaze. It seems to be designed for ornament, but is certainly capable of caving in the head of a man. The blood and hair along its length prove that. When the jurors have inspected it, Miss Roberts takes it and holds it aloft. 'A wicked weapon,' she says, 'and the hand that wielded it?' The interrogatory hangs above her beside the poker. She looks straight at the dock and the woman sitting there. 'The hand was that of Rodney Marsh's own wife. The defendant.'

We all look at the dock. The jury and I are, of course, well aware of Mrs Marsh but perhaps we haven't focused on her properly before. Or if we have, perhaps not in the way we do now. Because now we are being required to picture this slight pale woman, breathing so hard that I can see, across the courtroom, her chest rise and fall, fetching her husband crack after crack on the head. She is an unlikely killer. She sits in the dock dwarfed by the officers around her. She sees or perhaps feels the eyes on her and tenses as if she would run or hide if she could, but she can't so she puts her head down and rounds her shoulders against our collective gaze. In this position she cannot see Mr Merchant – or his sympathetic look, or his firm nod. It doesn't matter, because look and nod aren't meant for her. They are meant for the jury. They say, 'Neither I nor my client have anything to fear from Miss Roberts.' Though how there can be nothing to fear in the face of such strong evidence beats me.

But Colin Merchant QC has decades of experience in murder trials, while Miss Roberts is still a junior. She tries a withering look on him, but he is not withered. She resumes her opening. Now she thrusts at us 'severe damage to axons', now 'such bruising, bleeding and swelling that the brain was forced into the top of the spinal cord'. Even Mr Merchant looks away at this one.

She turns next to the investigation and tells us, 'As well as the neighbours who dialled 999, and the PC who attended the scene, you will hear from the forensic scientists who examined the poker for fingermarks.' She lowers her voice as if to impart a secret. 'There were none save for those of the defendant and her victim.'

Shall I interrupt her to point out that the deceased is not the defendant's victim unless and until the jury's verdict declares it so? Should I remind her that it is not prosecuting counsel's job to whip up unthinking feeling in the jury? Shall I stop her now before she goes so far over the top that she slithers down the other side? But I know so little about the case. I can't be sure where she is going. So I hold my peace and wait.

Disappointingly for Miss Roberts, after Mrs Marsh asked the PC if he was all right (no point in asking if her husband was, since he clearly wasn't), she said nothing more. More excitingly for the Crown, forensic samples from the poker yielded DNA from both Marshes and no third person. But surely there is ambit here – and surely Miss Roberts has considered it – for a cunning defendant to suggest that a third party wearing gloves had wielded the weapon? No. Mrs Marsh has no such cunning. When interviewed at the police station, she had said 'it was me' before retreating again into silence. Still, 'it was me' is a confession of sorts and in her opening, Miss Roberts makes what she can of it. As she fills in the evidential landscape, the picture from the defence perspective is so bleak that I tap into my computer's Digital Case System to see what defence is actually being advanced. Miss Roberts is ahead of me.

'There is no doubt,' she says, 'that the defendant killed her husband. There is no doubt, because she accepts it. However, she will suggest to you that what she did was not unlawful because, she will say, she acted in lawful self-defence.' She pauses to allow her hearers to absorb this before saying, 'You, members of the jury, may well wonder how someone who stoved in her husband's head could be acting lawfully. The law is, of course, a matter for the Learned Judge.' She barely nods in my direction, as if neither the law nor I are of much interest to her. It is clear I am a bit player on Miss Roberts's stage. 'But I know Her Ladyship won't mind if I trespass on her territory, just to set before you the law on self-defence.'

Now here she is in error. Her Ladyship will mind. Because if she gets the law wrong I'll have the devil's own job to put it right without prejudicing one side or the other.

'Matters of law,' I murmur, trying for and failing to find sweetness of tone, 'are, as you observe, for me, Miss Roberts. If you and Mr Merchant wish me to give the jury a direction on self-defence at this stage, you have only to ask.'

She frowns, turns from the jury to me, opens her mouth to argue. But I am too long in the tooth for her.

'Members of the jury,' I say, 'you and I try this case together. The twelve of you will make all decisions of fact. I will make all decisions of law. Why don't you take this opportunity to have a cup of coffee while I resolve this one.'

And while Esme leads them firmly out, I turn back to the barristers.

'Miss Roberts, you haven't appeared in front of me before. If you had, you would know that while I am happy for counsel to foreshadow relevant matters of law, I like to know about it before they do. Just in case. I'm sure you understand.'

Miss Roberts doesn't, apparently, understand. 'In case of what?' she says.

'Well . . . just in case you get the law wrong.'

She looks at me as if I'm mad. I am hardly – says her expression – likely to get the law of self-defence wrong.

'Do you have a copy of what you intend to say to the jury about the law? It's not in your opening note.'

She passes a sheet of paper to the clerk, who passes it to me. I read. Disappointingly, she has it exactly right. 'I know that in future, Miss Roberts, you will put matters of law in front of me before you put them in front of the jury.'

'I'll be sure to do that, My Lady,' she says. Her tone is icy. There follows a silence in which we look at each other. 'May I get on with my opening now, My Lady?'

'Not,' I say tersely, 'until the jury has had its coffee.' This is no way to start a murder trial. Unhappiness between judge and barrister helps no one. I soften my tone. 'I expect counsel could do with a short break too.'

On the way back to my room I pass the list officer. 'What,' he demands, 'are you doing out of court? Why aren't you getting on with your trial? I need your courtroom by Monday week. Seven defendants. Vulnerable witnesses. Press interest. Please, please finish by then.'

CHAPTER TWO

BACK IN MY ROOM, while we wait for the jury to refresh themselves, Esme says, 'Miss Roberts fancies herself quite the lawyer.'

'I suppose the CPS must fancy her too, to entrust her with murder...'

'Oh, she's clever enough, but she's not ... not what I would call wise.'

'And is Mr Merchant wise?'

'That,' says Esme, 'remains to be seen.'

While Esme puts on the kettle, there is time to pause and reflect on the process with which Mr Merchant and Miss Roberts are struggling – the Crown Court trial. It is a curious thing. Out in the real world things happen. Lives are lived, lives are ended. Events. In here, in the courtroom, we force those events into a framework of law. Take Mercy Marsh. She has, on her own admission, hit her husband over the head with a poker. Repeatedly. In a moment – or a series of moments – she has killed him. But neither this, nor any killing I have come across, exists only in the moment. There is a 'before'. There is a 'leading up to'. The moments have a making. Some killings are a long time in the making, some not. Some have their making in the relationship between killer and killed, some between killer and something entirely other. Usually the trial process explores 'the making'. The prosecution tries to show motive, the defence tries to show ... well ... a defence.

Some defences are simple. The simplest – the basic vanilla – is alibi. It is a defendant saying, 'It wasn't me. It couldn't have been because at the time I was fifty miles away. See, members of the jury, the receipt from the hotel where I was staying.' 'Not me' may come in flavours or with sprinkles and toppings but it is essentially 'not my hand that held the hammer ... the knife ... the poker'.

There are, however, many other defences available – many ways in which counsel like Mr Merchant might seek to prevent the prosecution proving murder. To succeed, the Crown must make the jury sure not only that the defendant did (or was party to doing) the act of killing, but also that at the same time, he – or she – intended to kill or at least to cause really serious injury. Over the years this has led to the evolution of various defences, including accident ('I never meant to hit him'), lack of intent ('I meant to hit him but I never meant to really hurt him'), self-defence ('I only meant to hit and hurt him to stop him hitting and hurting me'), diminished responsibility ('I have a mental condition that reduces my responsibility for hitting and wanting to hurt him') and loss of control ('he did or said something that made me snap and so would you have snapped in my position').

Each defence has strict rules, and courts can spend hours, days, even weeks, exploring on which side of a particular line of a particular rule a defendant falls. Yet in real life, killers are rarely occupied in analysis of the law. How many killers know, as they lunge out, whether they have actually lost their self-control or are only very angry? How many know in the bleakness of depression whether the technicality of their mental illness will give them a defence? The hand closes on the weapon. The muscles contract. In the brain a signal is given. The body responds. It is done, often in seconds. It is only later, in the courtroom, that the lawyers set about unravelling it all.

As to those lawyers, in a criminal trial they, poor things, are stuck with the law and a defendant. Defence counsel are allowed to construct a defence from their client's instructions, but they aren't allowed to invent those instructions. They mustn't make up a story. The account must come from the defendant.

I can only assume that Mercy Marsh's account leaves her lawyers with nothing to argue but 'self-defence'. If there were a choice, it certainly isn't the defence they would choose. No wonder Miss Roberts is so confident. This becomes very clear when, back in the courtroom, she resumes her opening address. The jurors are fortified with coffee – and are all attention.

'It is possible,' she says to them, 'to use force, even fatal force, lawfully. But only . . .' she gives the word its full weight, 'only if the defendant believed she had to because she was under actual or imminent attack. This,' now she raises a didactic finger, 'is the subjective test. It relates to what was going on in the defendant's own mind.'

I wait for Miss Roberts to explain that what was going on in Mrs Marsh's mind may, perhaps must, depend in part on what had happened previously between her and her husband. That is the law and it is certainly what Miss Roberts has in her note, but she doesn't now say it. She is, it seems, done with the subjective and turns to the objective.

'And even, members of the jury, if the defendant subjectively believed this, self-defence is still only available IF,' she capitalizes the word, 'the amount of force she used was objectively reasonable in the circumstances as she believed them to be. This,' a second finger joins the first, 'is what we call the objective test. The Crown says the defendant passes neither the subjective nor the objective test and was not acting in lawful self-defence. The Crown says this defendant is guilty of murder.' She gives the jurors a hard stare and says, 'Feel free to make a note of that if you want to.' Some do.

'Of course,' she says, 'if a defendant raises this defence, it is for the prosecution to disprove it. And of course, any defendant who may have acted in lawful self-defence is not guilty. But how . . .' she strikes the lectern with the flat of her hand, sending a scatter of papers in the direction of Mr Merchant, 'how could anyone think it reasonable to hit a man again and again about head and face with a poker? How could anyone reasonably inflict this level of injury on an unarmed man?'

This is the moment for her to add the bit she has left out – that a defendant's state of mind may need to be judged in the light of her history, but no, Miss Roberts only says, 'If Mrs Marsh had to hit her husband at all – and the Crown does not accept she did – once she had him down, why didn't she leave the flat!' The barrister isn't asking a question. She is making a declaration of war. And, battle joined, she sinks into her seat, flushed with the belief of a job well done.

Mr Merchant stares at her. He is flushed too. I'm a little pink myself. Advertently or otherwise, Miss Roberts has told the jury only part of the law of self-defence. Though it was all written properly on her piece of paper, she has now omitted what might favour Mercy Marsh.

Mr Merchant is on his feet. 'My Lady . . .'

And in those two words I hear 'can defending counsel no longer rely on the fairness of his prosecutor?'; I hear 'what has happened to fair play?'; I hear 'help me'. And I will. Miss Roberts, looking pretty pleased with herself, seems oblivious to the fact that she has played a dirty trick on her opponent. Or to the fact that it's no part of prosecuting counsel's job to play tricks, dirty or otherwise.

So what is prosecuting counsel's job? It is to present the case. It is not to secure a conviction at all costs. Certainly not at the cost of convicting someone who should be acquitted. The trial is there to serve society and it cannot do that if it is less than scrupulously fair. A prosecutor has many things to do before and during the trial but in opening her case, Miss Roberts's job is to foreshadow coolly and carefully the available evidence; to explain why, logically, the jury should accept her arguments, and to set out the matters in issue between prosecution and defence. It may seem odd for the prosecution to be expected to set out the defence case. But that is what is needed if counsel is to present the Crown's case in a fair and balanced way.* Miss Roberts has done wrong. She has – cleverly it must be admitted – used rhetoric and stage gestures to whip up her audience against Mercy Marsh. And worse, she has misled the jury about the law.

Indignation comes from Colin Merchant in silken waves. He is a man who believes in the fairness of the system, and he is furious at what he sees as his prosecutor's unfairness. He is a man of great experience, with tricks aplenty of his own. For every one that Miss Roberts can pull out he will have two up his sleeve, but the last thing I want is for the trial to descend into that. Anyway, my duty is to ensure the trial is fair to both sides and no ambitious young prosecutor will stop me doing that. The first task is to prevent an undignified slugging match taking place in front of the jurors, who are now agog.

'It's all right, Mr Merchant,' I say, 'we can easily sort this out. The defence cannot fully open its case at this stage, but it can – indeed should – ensure the issues are properly set before the jury at the outset. If you feel that has not been done, I would invite you to address the jury . . .'

Miss Roberts frowns.

'. . . and to do it now.'

Miss Roberts gets to her feet.

'You will of course be brief, Mr Merchant.'

'But . . .' says Miss Roberts.

But me no buts, my dear, for Mr Merchant, every inch a Queen's Counsel, is turning to the jury and pulling his silk gown about him. He is drawing a breath. He is on home territory.

---

* Appendix L.

'Ladies and gentlemen,' he says. And this in itself is the mark of his experience, because with these words – rather than the more traditional 'members of the jury' – he is appealing not to the collective but to the individual heart and mind of each of the twelve. 'You have just heard a very full address by Miss Roberts on behalf of the Crown. She has said every bad thing she can about the conduct of Mercy Marsh. It is not for me to say she's wrong, but it is for me to say she may be wrong. Whether or not she can make you sure that Mercy Marsh is a murderer, we shall see. But if she wants to, she must do it on the evidence, not on her personal whim.'

This is tough stuff. It is coming close to public and professional criticism from a senior member of the Bar towards a more junior one. He speaks slowly, earnestly, distancing himself from Miss Roberts's hyperbole. And when she frowns and shakes her head, he does not allow the jury's attention to wander to her even for a second.

'I won't detain you for long,' he says, 'certainly not as long as the prosecutor did.' He pauses for the jurors to smile, to raise eyebrows at each other, and Miss Roberts looks down. Mr Merchant continues. 'It's not my business to tell you what to do. In due course you will make up your own minds and our society trusts you to do that without interference from anyone else. All I do now is beg you not to jump to conclusions. You have each taken an oath to bring in a verdict according to the evidence – and at the moment you haven't heard a single word of it. All you have heard is what Miss Roberts hopes it will be. She may be telling you to convict but she has no more idea of what really happened in the Marshes' flat that fateful night than I have. Neither of us was there. She is telling you to convict because she is employed by the Crown to put forward the prosecution case . . . as I am employed on behalf of the defendant. So all I ask you to do is to take time to pause; to ask yourselves what happened to make a woman like Mercy Marsh do what she did. To ask yourself what her state of mind was when she did it, because it is here that the key to the case may lie. If, for example, you were considering self-defence – and in opening her case Miss Roberts omitted to mention this vital point – in deciding if Mercy Marsh's actions were reasonable, you must ask yourselves if they were reasonable according to what she genuinely believed. It doesn't matter whether that belief was correct. A mistaken belief is still a belief. And here is an obvious thing, you might think . . . what she genuinely believed depends on what had happened between this couple before that night. About that, Miss Roberts has told you nothing. I say no more than that we should all wait and see what the evidence is before jumping to conclusions.'

He has spoken briefly but he has driven home the point. The jurors look at each other. They look at him. Two of them pick up their pencils. One makes a note. The other crosses through the note he had made at Miss Roberts's behest.

The jurors aren't the only ones intrigued. I am too. Because Colin Merchant said, 'If, for example, you were considering self-defence', which sounds as if he expects the jury to be considering something else too. I know him to be a careful man. He chooses his words for a reason. But self-defence is the only defence being raised, isn't it? Of course, on a charge of murder there are many possible defences, including diminished responsibility, loss of control, insanity, automatism. They are all complex. All require a lot of input from the judge. None have so far got a mention and all defences that might arise should be foreshadowed on the Digital Case System. Merchant is experienced enough to know that springing a defence on the prosecution late in the day can derail a trial. I've got enough problems with prosecution counsel, without the defence bending the rules too.

Anyway, if he believes he has another viable defence, why not say so? As soon as I ask the question, I know the likely answer. Everyone who has been in his position will know it. He believes there is a defence but his client doesn't want to run it. It happens sometimes. But on a charge as serious as murder, why would any defendant not take any and every chance to be acquitted?

Is it that, unlike self-defence, the defences of 'diminished responsibility' and 'loss of control' don't lead to outright acquittal? They only reduce murder to manslaughter. But it would be a cynical defendant who would abandon the chance of even this against the chance of getting off altogether; and Mercy Marsh doesn't strike me as a cynic. Besides, the likelihood of her acquittal on the basis of self-defence is thin-to-vanishing. What can she say that would justify smashing in her husband's skull till part of his brain disappeared into his spinal column?

She must have been advised of this by her legal team. And she doesn't look the sort to argue with an experienced silk. She doesn't look the sort to argue at all. But then, she doesn't look the sort to bang her husband over the head with a poker. She can't be more than five foot two, and I doubt she weighs seven stone. Where did she find the strength? What drove her? If asked, Miss Roberts would no doubt say those questions are irrelevant; that if she bashed in her husband's skull, what could she have intended but to cause him at least serious injury? And if you intend this and cause death, it's murder. Miss Roberts doesn't care what led up to the killing. But perhaps the jury will. And perhaps this is what Colin Merchant is banking on.

After the prosecution opening, Mr Merchant asks for time with his client – and seeing a glimmer of what he is dealing with, I am sympathetic. But there is the list officer and the seven-defendant case and . . . I look at the woman in the dock. I can see she is trembling. I give Mr Merchant the time he has asked for.

CHAPTER THREE

WHEN WE REASSEMBLE ON Thursday morning, the defendant is very pale. Her eyes are red, perhaps with exhaustion, perhaps with weeping. But the prosecutor does not look at the forlorn figure in the dock. She gets to her feet and calls her first witness. She has planned it all carefully, beginning with Rodney Marsh's last night alive. Evidence will come from Mr and Mrs Overton, neighbours who, as he died, sat in their flat, watching television, no more than two metres away on the other side of a party wall.

Esme crosses the court. Behind her an elderly man shuffles and grumbles. He is wearing thick glasses and a cardigan. He is so perfectly the picture of 'difficult old gentleman' that I find myself checking to see if he is wearing carpet slippers. Sadly he is not. He does, however, have hearing aids. Miss Roberts hasn't yet spotted this but Mr Merchant has and is looking down to conceal a small and private smile.

Mr Overton settles himself into the witness-box and now it is Esme's job to swear him in. She asks if he has a religion.

He cups a hand to the hearing aid behind his right ear. 'What?' he says.

Mr Merchant's smile broadens.

'Religion,' repeats Esme, louder this time.

He cups the other hand. 'As long as I'm away by lunchtime,' he says.

'Religion,' she bellows.

'No need to shout,' he says.

Time for me to intervene. 'Esme, let the witness affirm.'

Ever since Charles Laughton cross-examined Una O'Connor in *Witness for the Prosecution*, the idea of deaf witnesses swearing to what they have heard has been part of courtroom legend. It's a trope. It's a cliché. And now it is happening in front of me. It takes Miss Roberts exactly three questions to realize the extent of her difficulty. By raising her voice till she is red in the face, she extracts from Mr Overton that he has a hearing problem, has had it for years, that his hearing aids are working as well as they ever do, and that he does not intend to stay beyond lunchtime no matter what.

'My Lady,' she says, 'might the jury retire while I address you on a matter of law?'

'Of law?'

'Well,' she concedes, 'not exactly of law.'

'Not of law.'

'More of . . .'

'Of the form of the hearing,' prompts Mr Merchant, and someone on the jury guffaws.

'Well,' I say, consolingly, 'whatever it is, Miss Roberts wants to make an application about it so . . .'

So, off go the long-suffering jurors.

'Now, Miss Roberts? Do you want the witness to remain in court or do you wish to address me in his absence?'

'I don't suppose it will make much difference,' she says ruefully, 'but he had better leave.' And when he has been led out, 'My Lady, the witness is clearly having difficulty hearing and I apply for him to be able to use the induction loop which I understand is available to court users in this building.'

I nod. 'Mr Merchant, what do you say about this application? A witness who can't hear the question is unlikely to be able to help the jury with an answer.'

'My Lady, normally I could have no possible objection, but in this case there are unusual considerations. Mr Overton is being called to give an account of what he heard from the neighbouring flat. Miss Roberts expects him to say he heard an argument, that my client sounded aggressive in tone and language, and that this was what immediately preceded her act of aggression which in turn led to the death of Mr Marsh. It is, of course, my case that something very different happened, and that Mr Marsh was the aggressor. In my respectful submission the inability of the witness to hear clear questions in a quiet courtroom is proof in itself of the unlikelihood of his having heard anything at all from my client's flat. The jurors are entitled to have this demonstrated to them.'

'I agree that the witness's hearing difficulty may be of real significance to the jury – but it has already I think been amply demonstrated and they are unlikely to forget it. If they are in danger of doing so, I'm sure we can rely on you, Mr Merchant, to remind them. And of course I will do so in my summing up at the end of the case. I can see no purpose in common sense, in humanity or in law in making this gentlemen endure being shouted at.'

So when the jury comes back, Mr Overton is provided with the hearing loop and Miss Roberts tries again. But everyone has bad days, and this is one of Miss Roberts's. Her witness has lost patience with the whole process and is now sitting in the witness-box, hunched like a bad-tempered crow.

Yes, he snaps, he can hear better now, always could if only people would speak up. And yes, he is ready to resume his evidence but he has to be away by lunchtime and if there is to be any more wasting of his time he will leave immediately.

'No, you won't, Mr Overton,' I say. 'I'm very sorry we have had a problem but . . .'

'It isn't me who has a problem,' he says, hearing me perfectly now and fixing a grim look on Miss Roberts. 'It's her.'

'Well, whoever has the problem, the evidence is yours, and it is of great importance to this jury and you must give it. If we get on with it, I'm sure you will be able to leave the building very soon.'

So Miss Roberts starts again. 'Mr Overton, on the evening in question, did something happen that caused you to call the police?'

'No,' he says, hunching deeper in his seat.

'No?'

'No. I didn't call the police. My wife did. You'll have to ask her.'

'Let me rephrase my question. Did something happen which caused your wife to call the police?'

'Presumably,' he says.

'What caused her to do that?'

'You'll have to ask her.'

Miss Roberts digests this then says, 'Well, did you hear anything that might explain why your wife called the police?'

'Not really.'

'But surely . . . you heard some voices from next door.'

'You may have noticed I'm rather deaf.'

'And you,' murmurs Mr Merchant to Miss Roberts, 'are rather leading.'

The jurors enjoy this one. The guffawing man guffaws again. The woman beside him giggles. Miss Roberts shakes her head and turns to the CPS lawyer. He shakes his head and turns to the officer. All three of them shrug. Miss Roberts accepts defeat.

'My Lady,' she says, 'in the light of this witness's obvious difficulty, and the fact that there is another witness – his wife – who I am assured has no problem with her hearing . . . I will concede that the jury should not rely upon Mr Overton's evidence and I will ask him no further questions. I'll call his wife instead.'

Mr Overton has caught this all right. He smiles a wicked smile. 'No, you won't,' he says. 'My wife's gone to Hull.'

Miss Roberts isn't the only one who thinks she must have misheard, but it turns out Mrs Overton has indeed gone to Hull. She has a daughter and grandchild there and both have come down with flu. Mrs Overton has gone to minister to them. 'There's no knowing when she'll be back,' says Mr Overton with grim satisfaction. 'There's no knowing with the flu.'

CHAPTER FOUR

AND SO MR MERCHANT'S start to the trial goes better than he might have hoped. He will get through the day with no evidence from either of the neighbours. Still, the prosecution case is strong, and bit by bit Miss Roberts lays it out. There is the evidence of the young police officer, his palpable shock, even at this distance, as he relates what he saw. There is the forensic scientific evidence and that of the pathologist. There are the photographs of the flat, neat, ordinary, except that none of us can look at the area in front of the gas fire with an ordinary eye. In the course of the afternoon and the following morning details are added. The picture builds up. Mr Merchant does what he can but things are beginning to look bad for Mercy Marsh. Whatever her husband was doing by way of threat, why – at least after the first blows sent him to the ground and he had his hands up to protect himself – did she continue to beat him? Why didn't she just walk out? Run out? Go to the Overtons for help or call the police?

By Friday afternoon Miss Roberts has an officer in the witness-box telling the jury about the defendant's police interview, how Mercy had said 'it was me' and then refused to say anything else, though he had asked her many more questions.

'What questions?' asks Miss Roberts. As if she doesn't know. As if she and Mr Merchant haven't been through every word of those interviews, and more than once.

'Well,' says the officer, 'lots of things. She admitted killing him in what was clearly a very violent attack so we wanted to know why she did it. We asked about her previous relationship with the deceased. We asked whether there was any provocation or any need to defend herself against him. We asked if he was threatening her in any way and if he was, why she didn't stop once he was on the ground.'

'You specifically asked why in those circumstances she continued to strike him?'

'Yes.'

'And she gave no answer to any of these questions?'

'None.'

'So she was given an opportunity to explain why she did what she did, but she chose to say nothing.'

'Yes.'

Miss Roberts looks pointedly at the jury. Any account which Mercy gives now will be subject to the question 'why didn't you say so before?', which Miss Roberts will answer before Mercy herself can, by accusing her of having invented a defence to meet the prosecution case.

When the officer leaves the witness-box it is just after 3 p.m. Plenty of time for some more evidence before we rise for the day. But Miss Roberts asks if the jury might briefly leave us – and when they have, she says, 'My Lady, the Crown is hopeful of getting Mrs Overton to give evidence.'

Mrs Overton! I had almost forgotten about Mrs Overton.

'My Lady, Mrs Overton is still in Hull—'

'Nice place, Hull,' murmurs Mr Merchant.

'. . . She is still looking after her family, who are stricken down with a particularly—'

'Miss Roberts, I am not a jury. Just tell me what you want.'

'I want,' says Miss Roberts with dignity, 'to utilize section 51 of the Criminal Justice Act 2003.'

Mr Merchant and I look at each other, registering the blankness in each other's eyes. Honesty is sometimes the best policy. 'You had better give us a clue, Miss Roberts.'

'It is the section by which the court may require or permit a person to take part in eligible criminal proceedings through a live audio or video link. By virtue of subsection 3(d), an eligible proceeding includes any trial in a Crown Court.'

'Oh, that section 51,' says Mr Merchant.

'I'm betting,' I add, 'there's a subsection that—'

'Subsection 5,' says Miss Roberts. 'It requires you to consider all the circumstances of the case, particularly the availability of the witness and their views. Mrs Overton has strong views about leaving her family when they are suffering. Subsection 4 provides that the court may not give such a direction unless a) satisfied it is in the interests of justice to do so and b) the parties to the proceedings have been given the opportunity to make representations.

'I,' she continues, 'make a representation that it is clearly in the interests of justice for the jury to hear Mrs Overton in order to get the fullest possible evidence of events.'

Meanwhile I've found section 51 in Archbold and read it. I ask Mr Merchant if he has any representations to make. He searches for a reason to object but can't find one.

I keep reading. There's pages of the stuff. I can see that Miss Roberts has a point but that she hasn't drawn to my attention all the provisions of sub-subsection 5 – and I am beginning to learn how Miss Roberts operates.

'What about section 5, subsection 6, sub-subsection (d)?' I ask, in what I hope is a tone of innocence. 'The one that says I should consider the suitability of the facilities at the place where the witness would take part in the proceedings.'

'Ah,' says Miss Roberts.

'I was wondering when we could get to sub-subsection (d),' says Mr Merchant.

Now I have (d) in my grasp, I am not going to let it go. 'Miss Roberts, usually a witness will go to the local Magistrates' Court. Sometimes a police station. Occasionally local authority offices. Such places can be expected to provide suitable facilities.'

Miss Roberts frowns. 'I was rather hoping Mrs Overton might do it over her mobile phone from her daughter's living room.' Perhaps she follows the elevation of my eyebrows because she adds, 'She has a smartphone and I have ascertained that there is a video facility on it. I'm sure we can instruct her how to use it.'

I get my eyebrows under control. 'I really don't think so, Miss Roberts. I bear in mind that 6(f)(ii) requires me to consider "whether the direction might tend to inhibit any party to the proceedings from effectively testing the witness's evidence".'

Mr Merchant's expression suggests 6(f)(ii) is one of those things he best likes to reflect upon on a quiet winter's evening.

'In my judgement,' I continue, 'there should be a court official with Mrs Overton to ensure no one interferes with or coaches her, and that she is not in any way prompted during the giving of her evidence, especially during cross-examination.'

'Who could possibly coach her in Hull?' says Miss Roberts.

Who indeed?

But Mr Merchant is on his feet now. 'My Lady, if there is no court official present, how can we be sure she isn't using her phone to receive texts or other messages reminding her of things or instructing her? Or merely distracting her? Mr Overton might be asking what he is to have for lunch. And when she will be home to put it on the table. The rules are there to safeguard the system.'

Mr Merchant is right. There is a system to be followed. Though the rules are not immutable, Mrs Overton's evidence may be critical and this is a murder trial. I must be fair to both sides. I must also be as fair as I can to the list officer – but after all, we are making good time and we have another whole week in which to finish this case. So . . .

'Miss Roberts, it is important not only that justice is done but that it is seen to be done. If this lady is sitting in her daughter's living room in Hull, neither I nor you nor Mr Merchant can see what is happening around her. That is not satisfactory. Accordingly my ruling is this: I will adjourn the case until Monday morning so that Mrs Overton may give her evidence to the jury by a remote link, but she may only do so using a proper video system from a place where I am satisfied the process is appropriately overseen. I am afraid she must go to a local court building or other suitable facility.'

'But—'

'That is my ruling, Miss Roberts.'

She mutters something which, happily, I do not catch. In a sudden spirit of generosity, I add, 'In order to give you as much time as possible to arrange matters, on Monday instead of sitting at 10.15, we will sit at 10.30.'

At 10.30 on Monday morning Miss Roberts is back and in high dudgeon. 'It cannot be done,' she says.

'There is no court in Hull which can oversee the process?'

'The court isn't the problem.'

'What is the problem?'

Mrs Overton is not prepared to leave her daughter's home unless she can be absolutely assured she will be back by lunchtime. Lunchtime in the Hull household is, apparently, an event of . . . well, she would have to finish her evidence by 11.15 to accommodate this need. And it is already 10.30 and she is still at her daughter's . . .' Miss Roberts trails off miserably. Even she can see this, in the context of a murder trial, is ludicrous.

'Oh dear,' I say. 'Well, what do you want me to do about it?'

'Change your ruling,' says Miss Roberts. 'Let her give her evidence from her daughter's living room.'

I want to say, 'Dear woman, if it was unfair to allow it last Friday, it's unfair to allow it today. It can't become fair because you have a difficult witness.' But I satisfy myself with, 'The Overtons are not the easiest of witnesses.' And then, 'Might the Overtons' lunch be taken a little later, do you suppose?'

'Lunch in the Overton household,' says Miss Roberts with what dignity she can muster, 'is always taken at midday. Might we try again tomorrow? If I can arrange for her to give her evidence from the Hull court at 9.30 . . .?'

Can I justify adjourning the case till tomorrow? I think of the delay. I think of the list officer and the Seven Defendants and the Vulnerable Witnesses and the Press Interest. And could I prevail upon my own jury and defendant to be ready to sit by 9.30? Jurors have their own lives to lead. They have children to see off to school. Some have considerable distances to travel to court. And the cost to the public purse of wasting a court day is very substantial. On the other hand . . .

But Mr Merchant is on his feet. 'My Lady, Mrs Marsh is brought from a woman's prison to the west of London and her prison van has not yet arrived on any morning of this trial before 9.45. She must be able to hear Mrs Overton's evidence. I must be able to take instructions from her as the evidence unfolds.'

Well, that's that. If Mrs Overton's evidence is important enough to cause all this trouble, it's certainly important enough for the defendant to hear. In any trial, not least one as serious as this, the interests of both sides must be protected. I make a tentative suggestion that, if the jurors can all be here by then, we aim to sit at 9.45 next morning. 'You'll just have to ask your questions quickly,' I say.

Miss Roberts nods but Mr Merchant shakes his head.

'My client,' he says, 'is expecting the Crown to close its case this morning, and she is ready to begin her own evidence immediately after that. She has prepared herself. The waiting is a huge strain on her. It is cruel to make her wait another day.'

'Cruel?' Perhaps it is. It's a cruel world. It will certainly be cruel to the Seven Defendants and the Vulnerable Witnesses if next week's trial cannot be got on. You can't simply push it back by a few days, because expert witnesses become unavailable, barristers are booked to be in other courts, the problems are endless. But Mr Merchant is turning to look at his client – we all do. And I see now that she really does look stressed. Her pallor is chalky. There are dark circles under her eyes. When she pushes back a strand of thin grey hair, her hand is shaking. And after all, my job is to make sure my jury gets the necessary evidence . . . Suddenly I see a way around all this. I take a breath, check I can do what I have in mind, then say, 'I have a potential solution but . . .'

Four eyes narrow and fix on me.

'. . . I won't adopt it unless you both agree. Miss Roberts, you wish to call Mrs Overton to deal with what she heard on the night of the killing?'

'I do.'

'Mr Merchant, I imagine that before you get to the night of the killing, you will wish your client to tell the jury some of her personal background, perhaps about herself and the deceased and their relationship?'

'Yes.'

'Very well. The course I am about to suggest is highly unusual, but I see no reason why your client cannot begin her evidence today. She can deal with background matters. Then we can interpose Mrs Overton – if she chooses to join us – first thing tomorrow morning. If she is in place at the video link in Hull at 9.45 she will be finished surely by 11.15 and home in time to put lunch on the table. If we were to adopt that course, I think, Mr Merchant, there can be no prejudice to your client?'

He hesitates. No doubt he is trying to decide if he can use Mrs Overton for his own ends. She might give evidence damaging to Mrs Marsh about the night in question, but she might also give evidence helpful to the defendant about the nature of the relationship between the deceased and his wife. After all, that party wall had always been thin enough to hear through. Mr Merchant has a difficult judgement call to make. He pauses. 'Very well,' he says at last.

And so it is agreed. The jurors are brought in. I explain that, subject to one piece of evidence, the Crown will now close its case, and the defence will begin. And that tomorrow they may hear one last witness from the prosecution. I say, 'It is unusual to take witnesses out of order like this. Normally the Crown's case closes before the defence opens. However, the Crown's last witness is not available today, and we are all anxious not to waste time. In fact, I would like to sit tomorrow at 9.45, if you can all be here by then?'

Jurors look at each other but no one objects.

'Very well. Then the course I have described will allow us to get on with the case this afternoon. Both sides are content to proceed in this way. So we shall begin to hear the defence case now, and Miss Roberts will interpose her final witness tomorrow morning.' I don't add 'if the witness turns up in front of a suitable video link', though it's what I'm thinking.

CHAPTER FIVE

AND SO MR MERCHANT begins. 'I call Mrs Marsh to the witness-box.' We all turn, expecting to see her stand and come forward but she does not move. He tries again. 'Mrs Marsh?' Still she remains in her seat, apparently frozen.

'Mrs Marsh,' I say, 'this is the time when you may, if you choose, go into the witness-box. If you do, you will enter it just as any other witness would – the jury will be directed to listen to your evidence and weigh it up as they would that of any other witness.'

There is a long moment in which I wonder if she will ignore me too, but finally she stands. Each action seems to be in slow motion. Mr Merchant nods firmly at her. Encouraged – or defeated – she makes her way to the side of the dock, where a kindly officer opens the little door and helps her down the two steps. Esme is waiting and leads her across the courtroom.

'Would you like to be sworn on a Holy Book or to affirm?' asks Esme.

Mrs Marsh leans towards Esme and whispers.

'My Lady,' says Esme, 'the witness says she was brought up Catholic but hasn't been to church for a long time.'

The little woman in the witness-box is looking at me with something like panic on her face. There are hectic marks on her cheeks, bright against the pallor. I see her chest heaving. 'I want to do what's right,' she says.

'Really, Mrs Marsh, there's nothing for you to worry about.' Privately I doubt that is true. It seems likely she has a great deal to worry about. But I don't often get a witness who wants to make sure she is doing right before taking the oath, and I need to reassure her. 'The important thing is that you are making a serious promise to tell the truth, the whole truth and nothing but the truth, and you should make that promise in a way that binds your conscience.'

She nods. 'I'll swear on the Holy Bible, then.'

She takes the book from Esme and clutches it with a shaking hand, as if she fears she'll drop it. When she reads the words of the oath from the card in front of her, her voice comes in small breaths. I ask if she would like to sit and she sinks gratefully onto the little fold-down wooden seat. She takes a tissue from her sleeve but she does not weep. She is way beyond tears. She looks at the jury, at me and finally at Mr Merchant. It doesn't seem to occur to her that the person she needs to study – the one who is determined to undo her – is Miss Roberts.

'Let's begin,' says Mr Merchant, 'with your childhood.'

Miss Roberts gives an impatient toss of her head as if to say, 'What does the jury care about a killer's childhood?'

Mrs Marsh nods obediently but her neck is bent as if there is a yoke about it. I wonder if she is ill, but Mr Merchant – who knows her so much better than I – hasn't raised any problem, so I let it go. For surely he knows what he is about? He does. Slowly he draws from her the story of her life.

Mercy Blackthorn was born in a village in the north of England and grew up quietly with elderly parents and without siblings. How different her life might have been if Rodney Marsh had never gone on a cycling trip, or if he had followed the A-road that bypassed the village instead of the little B-road that went through it. How different if he hadn't stopped for his lunch in the local pub, or if she, a twenty-year-old, hadn't got a Sunday job clearing the tables there. Of course, if it hadn't been Mercy, it might have been some other girl smitten with his confident smile, his London ways.

'He made me see things differently,' she says to Mr Merchant's question.

'What things?'

A little pucker appears between her eyes as she tries to formulate her thoughts into words. 'He seemed to know everything.'

'To be omnipotent?'

'Only God is omnipotent,' she says with unexpected sternness. 'What I mean is he was older, more experienced. He knew more about things.'

'So you got to know each other?'

'He stayed for two days. And then he came back. And . . .'

'And eventually he brought you to London?'

She nods.

'To his home.'

'It was to be our home.'

'Very well,' says Mr Merchant, 'let's look at that home. Would you take up exhibit 3, the bundle of photographs.'

She seems to be having difficulty focusing but Mr Merchant is a steady pair of hands and finally she finds the page to which he is directing her and, together with the rest of us, studies the images of the flat where for so many years she lived with the man she killed.

'It's very clean and tidy,' says Mr Merchant.

'Cleanliness is important.'

'Next to Godliness.'

'Well, yes.'

He nods. He pauses. He stares at the photograph. 'But . . . what's this? On the skirting board . . .' He lifts the picture and once he points it out, we all see it. A dark mark, a disfiguration, some scuffing. Counsel take their instructions from their clients but I'm sure he hasn't got this from Mercy Marsh because the expression on her face, as she stares at the image, is one of real distress.

'Can you tell us what those marks are?' he asks gently.

It seems she can't. Or won't. The silence stretches taut and she is shaking visibly now. Finally Mr Merchant says, 'It looks as if something has hit the wood. Hit it hard, and more than once.'

She nods.

'But what could have done this?' He tone is musing now. 'The dents could be made by the head of a hammer, but aren't those claw marks too . . . ? Oh,' he speaks as if the light is dawning but I know the light dawned some time ago, perhaps in the long hours when he has sat over the papers, studying them, trying to work out how to help a client who won't help herself. 'A claw hammer, perhaps?'

'Perhaps,' she says.

Miss Roberts is on her feet. 'He's leading the witness,' she declares angrily. 'My Learned Friend is leading his client.'

He certainly is. He's practically dragging her. And – whatever the rules, I have no intention of stopping him. I satisfy myself with, 'Take a little care, Mr Merchant.'

He nods briefly but does not break eye-contact with the woman in the witness-box. 'What about the door?' he says. 'The door to the lounge.'

'What about it?'

'It's damaged.'

Miss Roberts is about to object that now he is giving evidence, but he stares at her and for a reason I don't immediately understand, she subsides.

Mrs Marsh turns the pages of photographs, one after the other. 'I don't see it,' she says a little desperately.

'No.' Colin Merchant imbues the syllable with a meaning it will scarcely bear. 'None of us can see it, but it's there all the same. The prosecution have put together this album of photos, choosing relevant ones from all those taken by their forensic photographer. Among the ones they didn't think were relevant was this one.' He holds up a sheet of paper and the jurors crane to see. 'I have copies,' he says. 'For everyone.'

Of course he has. The copies are handed around.

'I'd like to exhibit the image, My Lady.'

Esme is onto it. 'The album is exhibit 3, My Lady.'

'Then we'll make the new exhibit 3A.' I speak brightly, as if I'm pinning a child's drawing to the wall. But this photograph, I sense, will become important. And it could so easily have been missed by less conscientious counsel than this one.

Colin Merchant may have trawled through many hundreds of pages. It can be a thankless and little-remunerated task. It requires attention to detail. But sometimes – just sometimes – it pays off. And when it does the result can change the course of a trial. What is it he thinks he has found? Is it one of these rare discoveries?

'You can't see it when the lounge door is open,' he says, 'but when it's shut . . . there.' He takes a separate photograph from under his notebook and with a red pen circles something on it. He holds it up and turns it this way and that so we can all see where he indicates. 'There. It looks like a neat round punch mark in the painted wooden surface.'

So this is why Miss Roberts didn't object – she must have known her selection of photographs for the jury's bundle is far from impartial. Now however she is on her feet. She is practically howling. 'He's giving evidence. He's leading. He's breaking the rules.'

Is it only me who hears him whisper, 'Just like you?'

The picture with its scarlet circle is given an exhibit number – 3B – and passed around the jury then placed in front of the witness. 'My Lady,' says Mr Merchant, 'I will return to what caused this mark on the door later. But for the moment I would like Mrs Marsh to help us with another mark.'

I nod. 'But take care, Mr Merchant.'

'Let's look just above the gas fire at the mantelshelf. What is that shelf made of, Mrs Marsh?'

She shakes her head. 'Some sort of stone, I suppose.'

'And what is that in the shelf? You can see it best in exhibit 3, page 36.'

Obediently we all turn to the page. Now it has been drawn to our attention the chip is clear. It's larger than a chip. Quite a gouge really.

'Mrs Marsh,' he says, 'can you tell us what caused that?'

Mrs Marsh takes a sip of water. The glass trembles. The water slops. Is she frightened? Is she ill? But Mr Merchant ignores it all and presses on.

'There is damage,' he says, 'to the skirting board and to the mantel shelf and to the door. But perhaps we should concentrate for a moment not on what caused all this damage, but on who.' He pauses. Looks her straight in the eye. 'Was it you, Mrs Marsh?'

Her look of pure astonishment is clear to us all.

'No,' he says, 'we didn't think it was.'

This is going too far. This is pure and unacceptable comment, and Miss Roberts is back on her feet. She is learning that you don't play tricks on an experienced silk and get away with it. It's a tough lesson. But this time Mr Merchant knows he has overstepped the mark. He apologizes to me and to Miss Roberts. For good measure he apologizes to the jurors, though they are clearly enjoying it.

'So if it wasn't you,' he says, 'who was it?'

There is silence while she wrestles with a train of thought. Through what dark tunnels that train goes isn't clear, but it leads to this. 'I can be very irritating.'

Mr Merchant is too clever to try to work out how she has arrived at this answer. Instead he picks it up and runs with it. 'Very irritating to whom, Mrs Marsh?'

'Well . . . well, I suppose to Rodney.'

'You irritated him?'

'I think I must have.'

'Often?'

'Well, I suppose so.'

'Why do you suppose that?'

And all Mrs Marsh can do is look helplessly at the photographs, at the damage to skirting board and mantelshelf and door...

'What caused the damage, Mrs Marsh?' And when she doesn't answer, 'It may be hard, Mrs Marsh, but you have taken an oath on the Holy Bible to tell not only the truth but the whole truth. Can you do that?'

She looks like a cornered animal. 'A hammer,' she says at last.

To a judge – to any lawyer – even, I suppose, to poor Miss Roberts, it is a joy to see the job done so expertly. Well, perhaps not to Miss Roberts. But she will learn a lot from this. And one day she will show us all what she has learned.

'Now,' says Mr Merchant to his client, 'the deceased...'

'Rodney,' says Mrs Marsh softly.

'Rodney... Was Rodney a DIY enthusiast?'

'Not really.'

'Was he often...' – the perfectly timed pause – 'hammering things?'

She is silent for a long while. Finally she says, 'I'm not sure I understand.'

He knows that he must above all be patient. 'Look at the photographs,' he says, 'and show us what Rodney used the hammer for – apart, that is, from hitting the door and the mantelshelf and the skirting board.'

Mrs Marsh looks doubtfully at the album. Turns a page. Turns two. Shakes her head.

'Did he hammer nails?'

'No,' she says so quietly we barely hear.

'Well, if not nails, what else did he hit?'

He is willing her to say it. To say, 'Me.' To say, 'He hit me.' To say, 'If not on that day then on others.' To say, 'He put the fear of God into me. The fear of the devil. The fear of him. So that when on that day he came at me, I . . .' but no. She isn't going to say it. And since she is his witness, he can't suggest it to her, can't 'lead' her to the answer.* Perhaps she doesn't say it because it isn't true, though Mr Merchant wants so much that it is. Because, after all, what does he really know about the Marshes? What do any of us know about the lives of others?

Mr Merchant stares for a moment at his client, at the lowered head, the hands twisting about each other. 'My Lady,' he says, 'would that be a convenient moment to stop for today?'

In a courtroom, time needs to be spent in the search for the truth, but every hour that passes involves the spending of a lot of public money. I have a duty to protect both. 'There's a little of the afternoon left. Can you use it?'

Colin Merchant shakes his head. 'I don't want to take Mrs Marsh further in her account until we have heard all the prosecution's evidence. I understand My Learned Friend may have another witness to call tomorrow.'

Fair enough. The defence is entitled to know what the prosecution case is before they try to answer it.

And so we rise for the day.

---

* In examination-in-chief, the advocate asks questions of his own witness, allowing them to set out their account. The advocate may not 'lead' his witness, i.e. may not ask questions that suggest the answer he wants. In cross-examination, the advocate asks questions to break down the account of a witness for the other side, and can 'lead' and suggest to his heart's content.

CHAPTER SIX

This gives me an hour in my room before teatime – an hour to reflect upon the afternoon's evidence and the line taken by the defence silk. He has led the jury and his client into that neat little flat and to the damaged door, the damaged skirting board and the damaged mantelshelf – three specific signs capable of suggesting violence. 'Capable of suggesting violence' is a lawyerly way to put it. For what else could they suggest? But suggesting isn't proving. A suggestion isn't evidence. Only Mercy Marsh can give the evidence that her husband was a violent man. And she hasn't. This may, of course, be because he wasn't and she is a strictly honest woman. But then what is she doing advancing 'self-defence'? And if there was a history of domestic violence that made her fear she would be attacked, why, oh why, won't she say so? What am I missing?

I settle down in front of the computer and type into the search engine 'battered women'. I'm expecting to see stories of what women have experienced, advice on where to get help and how to find support groups. But the first thing that pops up is 'battered woman syndrome'. It's the second thing, too. And the third. In the International Classification of Diseases, 'battered person syndrome' appears as a subcategory of post-traumatic stress disorder.

That women are battered comes as no surprise, but that such cruel treatment in a domestic context can lead to a 'syndrome' – a recognized mental condition – is a more recent development. I wasn't expecting it to occupy such a prominent position in the zeitgeist of the internet. The condition, now defined as 'a pattern of signs and symptoms displayed by a woman who has suffered

persistent intimate partner violence', was proposed as early as 1979, building on earlier research by Martin Seligman going back to 1967.*
The words 'intimate partner violence' dance on the screen. They suggest black eyes, twisted arms, sexual assault. They suggest every sort of harm that can be visited behind closed doors by an abusive personality against someone close to them. Physical and sexual violence is, of course, the common currency of the Old Bailey courtroom and happens in pubs or down dark alleys or in doctors' surgeries as well as behind the closed doors of a home. But the idea that acts of violence in the home not only cause physical hurt, but can lead to a diagnosable state of mental illness, is startling. The point isn't so much that the violence causes bodily injury as that it causes injury deep in the psyche too.

What exactly is this 'battered woman syndrome'? I thought I knew, but as I read on, I find it is a subtler and more insidious beast than I had imagined. At its heart is the continuous exertion of power by one partner over another, creating a sense of oppression and inadequacy in the weaker party. The aggressive partner uses repeated cycles of violence and reconciliation. He[†] places great stress on how hard he is trying to make the relationship happy, so that with each fresh episode of abuse, the victim . . . what? . . . thinks her partner is omnipresent and omniscient, and that the fault is all hers? That is what I am reading on the internet. I think of Mrs Marsh's words, 'I must be very annoying' and 'he seemed to know everything', and I feel the hairs on the back of my neck stiffen.

But no, even if she was a battered wife, and even if she had

---

* The matter was first extensively researched by Lenore Walker in 1979 as she examined the situation of women who had killed their abusive husbands. She drew upon work done by Seligman in 1967 and his theory of learned helplessness in which he explored why women stay in relationships with men who abuse them.

† Though abusers are not exclusively men.

developed the syndrome about which I am reading, why would she kill her husband instead of . . . well, just leaving? She is helpless to walk out of the dock, but what was to stop her walking out of the front door in the long years before that killing? I keep reading and find a suggested answer which completes the circle, going back to Seligman's work in the 1960s. He argued that the victim, beset by self-blame and unable to resolve matters, develops feelings of helplessness which, he wrote, 'lead to depression and passivity, making it difficult to marshal the resources and support system to leave'. He called it 'learned helplessness'.

And has Colin Merchant read up on all this before me? Have his eyes focused on these words? Has he reflected and come to conclusions which I cannot see? I make myself examine the evidence so far presented and catch myself shaking my head.

I think about this until teatime, then I take the problem downstairs to the judges' tea table. It is G's birthday and to celebrate the occasion she has brought in a chocolate cake. She has joined us recently at the Old Bailey, and it's a delight to have her. There is an air of celebration. H loosens the strain on his waistcoat and prepares his napkin for duty.

'The eating of chocolate cake,' he says, 'is incompatible with higher thought.' He may have a point. In fact the eating of chocolate cake seems to be incompatible with any thought beyond, in H's case, calculating his chances of a second slice. When all that remains are crumbs and contented sighs, 'Here's my problem,' I say, and lay it before the gathering.

On the other side of the table S leans forward. Cake does not interfere with the ascetic of S's thought processes. 'It isn't your problem,' he says. 'You're the judge. You're not her counsel and you're certainly not a psychiatrist. It's not for you to go looking for defences.'

'But,' says kindly G, 'if the poor woman has been abused over years . . .'

S pushes his spectacles back up his nose and frowns. 'Strictly speaking, being a battered partner isn't a defence, though it can give rise to . . .' his long fingers stroke the air, '. . . to situations where certain defences do apply. So, if your Mrs Marsh was attacked, "self-defence" might arise. If she snapped following repeated attacks in the past, "loss of control" might apply. If she had developed battered woman syndrome, "diminished responsibility" is a possibility. And if you keep poking around,' he fixes me with a cool eye, 'you may have to sum up the lot of them.'

There is an audible gulp which, I realize, has come from me. G gives me a sympathetic nod.

Back in my room I consult the textbooks, Archbold and Blackstone, the A and B of criminal court practice. I'm hoping S is wrong but I know he isn't. If there were to be evidence that Mercy Marsh was a woman battered by the man she killed, I may have to direct the jury on self-defence and on loss of control and on diminished responsibility. I will be setting them the equivalent of a university law exam. I will have to give them the information to deal with it, and to convey that information in a way that each of them – no matter their intellectual capacity or educational background – can follow. But I am getting ahead of myself, because at the moment there is no evidence she was battered. The evidence only shows . . . what? That there are three areas of damage to her home. That's it. You could be suspicious. You could speculate. But you could not conclude a fact from this . . . could you? I am allowed to leave an issue for the jury's consideration, only if there is evidence upon which they could come to a factual decision. I look at the situation from the high, clear ground which S occupies. Currently there is no evidence that Rodney Marsh physically abused his wife, and it doesn't seem his widow is about to provide any. If there is no evidence, it is not my business to speculate that there may be. My business is to ensure there is a fair trial. The ethos of fairness has created a system where Mercy Marsh has legal aid for a first-class barrister. There will be more legal aid if that barrister has good reason to instruct a psychiatrist. If he can't do that because his client won't give him instructions that justify it, well . . . it's not, as S says, my problem.

Tuesday morning brings a happier-looking Miss Roberts. I ask if she has her missing witness.

'I do, My Lady.'

'Really? On a video link from Hull?'

'No, My Lady. Her family have recovered and she has travelled back to London overnight. She is here and ready to give evidence.'

Well, well. 'You want to interpose her at this stage?'

'I do.'

'Mr Merchant?'

Colin Merchant has already agreed and to object now would require a very good reason which, it seems, he hasn't got. The jury files in. When they discover who the prosecution witness is, their eyes brighten. They enjoyed Mr Overton and have hopes of his wife. So do I. But Mrs Overton, comfortably plump under her heavy coat, gives every appearance of being a sensible body. She follows Esme to the witness-box. As she climbs into it, she pulls her coat around her and takes us all in with a sweeping gaze. To Mrs Marsh she gives a small, tight nod before Miss Roberts reclaims her attention. Her voice, when she takes the oath, has a Yorkshire burr.

I ask if she would like to sit.

'No, thank you,' she says. 'I'll stand on my own feet.' She turns to Miss Roberts, who takes her through the basic facts – her name, that her flat abuts the Marshes', that she has known them for many years.

'Now,' says Miss Roberts, 'the night of the killing—'

'No, dear,' says Mrs Overton. 'That isn't where you want to start.'

'Yes, it is.'

'No, it isn't. You want to know how they lived, the two of them.'

'No,' says Miss Roberts, 'I want you to tell us about the night Rodney Marsh died.'

Mrs Overton is silent but her expression says she suspects Miss Roberts is a foolish lass.

'Mrs Overton, that night was it you who called the police?'

'Yes.'

'Why did you do that?'

'Because of what was happening in the Marshes' flat.'

'And what was happening in the Marshes' flat?'

'Nothing,' says Mrs Overton.

The jury leans forward. Miss Roberts leans back. Surely even Mr Merchant must feel a twinge of sympathy for her. We all have our nightmares, and the Overtons are hers.

'But you asked the police to attend.'

'I told them to get themselves there as quick as they could.'

Wary now, Miss Roberts asks, 'If nothing was happening, why did you want them to come quickly?'

'Because I feared something bad had already happened.'

'To Rodney Marsh?'

Mrs Overton is now quite satisfied Miss Roberts is a foolish lass. 'Of course not,' she says. 'I phoned them because I was afraid something bad had happened to Mercy.'

Miss Roberts blinks hard. 'But if nothing was happening . . .'

'It was because nothing was happening that I was worried.'

'I don't understand,' says the unhappy Miss Roberts.

'That,' says Mrs Overton, 'is because you won't let me explain about the Marshes.'

Mrs Overton is after all providing considerable entertainment-value for the jury. But there is evidence to be drawn from this lady and Miss Roberts seems unable to draw it.

'Mrs Overton,' I say, 'would you like to explain?'

She nods. 'It's hard to understand if you didn't know him. To me and my husband he was always pleasant. Neighbourly. Can I carry your bin in for you, Mr Overton? Can I get you anything while I'm at the shops, Mrs Overton? But inside that flat he was a . . .'

The jury cranes its collective neck, anticipating her choice of word. Mr Merchant is holding his breath.

'. . . a tyrant,' she says.

And in the dock Mrs Marsh buries her face in her hands.

'It wasn't every night, but it was often enough. He would shout. Call her names. Complain and criticize. I couldn't hear everything, of course, but I heard enough. And once he started, he would go on for hours. Hours. I don't know how she put up with it. I wouldn't have. I would have left any man that treated me like that. I asked her why she didn't go. She said, "But I love him." That was always her answer. "But I love him."' Mrs Overton turns to me. 'Women can be fools sometimes,' she says. And I can only nod.

I understand. Miss Roberts, however, it seems does not. She looks as if she has been hit by a lorry and is trying to work out where hurts most.

'Anyway,' says Mrs Overton, 'the shouting started again that night. It was the usual thing. I was expecting it to go on for a good while so I went to turn up the sound on the TV, but I didn't get across the room before . . .' She stops. I like to think it was a deliberate pause for the drama of the thing.

'Before what?' says Miss Roberts.

'Before it all went suddenly quiet.' She is silent herself for a moment, remembering. 'It was as if they – or, as it turned out, he – had been struck dead.' Another pause. And then, freed from the shock of her recollection and brisk now, 'I went to the door and looked out. I saw their front door was open. It must have been her, I suppose. She could have run away, but she didn't.'

So that was why the door had swung open when the young

officer knocked. Mercy Marsh had looked out but gone back and not even shut the door behind her.

'Of course, I didn't know that then. I was frightened he had finally killed her so I called the police.'

Miss Roberts absorbs this, decides that she hurts all over, and sits down. Mr Merchant stands.

'To be clear,' he says, 'the shouting you heard that night was the sort you had heard innumerable times before?'

'Innumerable,' says Mrs Overton, relishing each syllable.

'It was the voice of the husband?'

'It was.'

'In the past it had gone for hours at a time?'

'Yes.'

'But this time all was sudden silence?'

A nice Shakespearian turn of phrase, Mr Merchant. But no time to enjoy it because he is asking the next, the critical question. This is not his witness but that of the prosecution, and he is free to lead her where he will. 'And did it ever go beyond shouting, Mrs Overton? Did he ever strike her?'

She purses her lips. 'She never complained of it. She never complained of anything. But in the days after the shouting she would often wear a heavy cardigan or a high-neck sweater.'

'So you thought . . .?'

Miss Roberts is too miserable to intervene so I do. 'No, Mr Merchant. You may not invite the witness to speculate. But you may ask her if she knows why Mrs Marsh wore such clothing.'

He asks the permitted question.

She replies, 'I know that I thought it was because he had bruised her.'

Well, no one can say I didn't try.

'I suppose,' Mrs Overton muses, 'she finally snapped.'

We are now all supposing the same thing, but this is a question of law for me and of fact for the jury. It is not one for Mrs Overton. Gently I remind her not to speculate but only to tell us what she saw and heard.

'Hmmm,' she says, 'but I still don't understand why she put up with it for so long.'

And why do they, these women? If the evidence of Mrs Overton is true – and even Miss Roberts would find difficulty gainsaying it – why do women like Mercy Marsh put up with these things?

But I must park this thought at the back of my mind because Mr Merchant has no further cross-examination and Miss Roberts has no re-examination, so I release Mrs Overton from the witness-box, and she walks out of the courtroom leaving the rest of us in silence, to digest what we have heard.

Coffee aids digestion. Off goes the jury for another break while I grasp at the shore on which we have washed up.

'Well,' I say, 'where do we go from here?'

Where indeed? For here is something new. Here is evidence, if the jurors believe it . . . from which they can infer domestic abuse. The very thing that Mrs Marsh has failed to say, but which Mr Merchant has been quietly driving at, is suddenly out in the open. He should be cock-a-hoop, but he isn't.

He says, 'My Lady, I am in a difficult position. In the light of this evidence, unforeshadowed by Miss Roberts—'

'How could I foreshadow it when I didn't know about it?' she hisses.

'As I say, in the light of this new material, I need to take instructions from my client. But since she has begun to give evidence, I am not permitted to do so.' He's right. There is a rule against it. 'This,' he says, giving Miss Roberts a hard look, 'is what comes of the Crown being unable to call its witness at the proper time.'

I reach for oil to pour on the murky waters. 'Is it such a problem, Mr Merchant? After all, I have the power to override the rule if I need to in the interests of justice. I can give you leave to speak to your client if you think it necessary.'

'I do,' he says.

I ask Miss Roberts if she objects, but she seems drained of the power to do so. And it is more than this. She is looking worried. I could almost persuade myself she is looking older, as if a weight has dropped on her. She turns to the CPS lawyer and the police officer behind her and there is a deal of whispering. I give them the time they seem to need. Finally there is a reluctant nod from the lawyer and Miss Roberts stands.

'My Lady,' she speaks slowly and as if she is walking in a narrow gulley and must concentrate on loose stones and other hazards, 'I have no objection to My Learned Friend speaking to his client, provided he gives an undertaking to restrict himself to the new evidence.' Surely this can't have been what all that whispering was about?

Mr Merchant gives the undertaking. Counsel's word is his bond. That's how the system works.

'And I must tell Your Ladyship about another matter,' says Miss Roberts. 'In the light of this new evidence . . .'

Ah, here it comes.

'In the light of the new evidence, I may have further material to disclose to the defence. I must ask for time to review the position.'

Disclosure. In my courtroom, above my head hangs one of the swords of the City of London. It might as well be that of Damocles. Failures of disclosure are the bane of judges and can be the death of trials. Disclosure is such a simple word but, in law, so complicated. Here's what it's about. It is the responsibility of the prosecution to ensure that any material in its possession, upon which it does not rely but which might assist the defence, is disclosed to them. It is in this material that Colin Merchant will have found the photograph of the damaged door. Anything which does not help either side is filed away as 'undisclosed'. Miss Roberts has held back something because it did not help her and she did not see that it could help the defence. Now she thinks it might. She is behaving – at last – as prosecuting counsel should. That, too, is how the system works.

I am hard up against time constraints in this trial, but whatever the costs, disclosure must be sorted out. It's no good pressing on only to risk getting things wrong. A misstep might end up in the Court of Appeal with an order for a retrial. Worse, it might lead to an injustice that cannot be put right by a retrial. However inconvenient, Miss Roberts must have the time she needs. Both I and the list office will have to live with a further delay. I send a message to the jury – with my apologies, ladies and gentlemen, you have the rest of the day off. Come back tomorrow, please. Usual time. Hope for the Seven Defendants, the Vulnerable Witnesses and the Press Interest is receding.

CHAPTER SEVEN

AND SO I'M BACK at my desk in my room when Esme brings me a chocolate-covered marshmallow and says, 'I think Mrs Overton is telling the truth.'

As it happens, so do I.

She is silent for a while. 'Still,' she says at last, 'I don't understand why she didn't just leave him. I would have. So would you.'

But Mercy Marsh didn't leave, and though I could explain Seligman to Esme, I certainly am not allowed to explain him to the jury. There are, of course, plenty of psychiatrists who could. They could examine Mrs Marsh and give an opinion as to whether she was suffering from the syndrome. And if she was, this would open up a range of defences to her. All this could happen. But it won't unless her lawyers instruct a psychiatrist, and they can't unless she instructs them that she is indeed the victim of domestic violence. I rarely see a defendant standing smack in the way of their own best defence, but I seem to be looking at one now. And the mystery is why.

I must, however, be mindful of S's warning. He said this was not my business. But isn't my business to see justice done? I think of Seligman and the suggestion that victims can be overwhelmed by self-blame and then depression; and that this in turn can lead to passivity and an inability to find a way out of their problems, even by leaving. But if Mrs Overton is right, Mercy Marsh said she stayed because she loved her husband, and I saw nothing in Seligman about this. Perhaps I wasn't looking in the right place. I open my computer to recheck but I have another thought. I go to the place where I have found illumination in the past – to the online archives of the Old Bailey, which cover trials from 1674 to 1913.

I enter a search for 'killing – all subcategories'. Under 'key words' I type in 'wife husband'. I hesitate. Then I add the word 'love'. On the screen there appears a long list of cases, a long list of heartaches. The marshmallow grows sticky in my hand. I change the word 'love' to 'poker' and find a surprising number of these too. I try combinations of key words working through from 1913 backwards and it isn't long before I find Emma Byron, known as Kitty.

In 1902 poor Kitty was being tried for the murder of Arthur Reginald Baker, with whom she lived as his wife though there was a Mrs Arthur Baker elsewhere, and lucky for her she was elsewhere, because Arthur Baker seems to have been a man of the Marsh kidney.

The account begins with the evidence of Arthur and Kitty's landlady, who stood, as Mrs Overton had, in the Old Bailey witness-box and told the court how Arthur was drunk nearly every day, how the couple were always causing disturbances. She explained how one day when he was kicking up a row, she went into their room and saw Kitty's hat torn in pieces on the floor and everything in disarray, and how she gave the couple notice. Later Kitty came to apologize for the noise and said, 'Well, next week you will hear something very dreadful.' When the landlady asked what, Kitty told her there was to be a divorce between Arthur and his wife, adding, 'Well, Madam, don't you tell him if I tell you, because he bangs me so.' The landlady had said, 'As you are not his wife, why do you support all the ill-treatment he gives you?' Kitty replied, 'I love him so,' and when asked, '... what do you live with a brute like him for?' had replied, 'Because I love him, and I have lost my character, and I cannot get any work.' The landlady had asked her, 'Why are you always screaming like that?' and Kitty said, 'Well, how can I help it when he comes and strangles me, and puts his hand on me like that; how can I help it?' The landlady finished her evidence by saying Arthur was always knocking

Kitty down, that as soon as he came home, the quarrelling began, and then you heard a bang; that when he was sober he was a perfect gentleman, but he was very seldom sober.*

I read and reread the words 'I love him so . . . I love him'. This from a woman who – because of her man – has lost everything but him. There is something frighteningly reminiscent in all this of what has been playing out in my courtroom.

And are Kitty and Mercy Marsh alone? Surely not. There is nothing new in the world. So I press more keys and up from the past rise Sarahs and Marys, pokers and knives, more violent men who beat their partners and women driven to kill them. That is not to say some of these women weren't senselessly violent too, but it soon becomes clear that Mercy and Kitty stand in a long line of victims of domestic abuse who wouldn't, couldn't, walk away from their abusers and ended things by ending them. I think I will skip the judges' tea today. Let someone else have the chocolate thingummies. I have more than enough to chew over.

And so we come to Wednesday and we still have to deal with the fallout from the problems of disclosure, the rest of Mercy Marsh's evidence, counsels' speeches and my summing up. It's possible to do it all by the following Monday, but it's tight. Should I warn the list officer? Not yet. Sufficient unto the hour is the evil thereof. The first thing is to find out how great that evil is. So I leave the jury in their room and go to see how things are progressing in court. Esme gives the customary three raps and opens the door for me. She intones the familiar words that summon all manner of persons having business there to draw near and attend, and I see that the business occupying the two barristers is troubling them. Mr Merchant looks as if he hasn't slept. Come to that, so does Miss Roberts. She is first on her feet.

---

* For Kitty's fate, see later in this story.

'My Lady, following the evidence of Mrs Overton yesterday, I have been reviewing the question of disclosure. I have handed to Mr Merchant a further document. May I pass up a copy to Your Ladyship?'

She may. She does. I read. It is a single sheet of A4 paper badly photocopied but clear enough. Part of a file of GP notes recording three attendances by Mrs Mercy Marsh to the surgery. The reason for each is innocuous enough. First she had a persistent sore throat. There was, apparently, a highly infectious streptococcal infection doing the rounds. Nothing strange here. Except that the doctor – perhaps through years of experience and acquired wisdom – makes a small note at the end of his examination. His patient is tender around areas of the neck he wouldn't expect, and there are small dark smudges, no bigger than the tip of a man's finger, for which she can give no account. On the two further visits, months apart and for equally innocent complaints, he takes the trouble to examine her thoroughly. Once, he finds a bruise on her left upper arm – an easy thing to happen to anyone – except that she has a matching one on her right arm. Another time he sees a long scrape on her shin – not normally suspicious, but this doctor has noted it. Does he suspect she has been struck with something? Or kicked?

Mr Merchant should be pleased, for he has Mrs Overton's evidence under his belt, and here at last is something for him to investigate. A doctor to whom he can speak. A cloth that can be lifted to uncover what lies beneath the relationship between the Marshes. Surely now Mercy Marsh will let him pursue what has become an obvious line of defence? And how much time will that take?

Cautiously I ask, 'You want an adjournment, Mr Merchant? You want to see this GP and take a statement from him?'

But Colin Merchant closes his eyes briefly and says, 'Those are not my instructions, My Lady. It is not my client's case that her husband was a . . .' He stops.

'Yes, Mr Merchant?' By which I mean you'd better say it, you'd better get it out in the open so we can all see the mess we are in.

'My client does not wish to speak ill of the man she has killed. She is overcome with . . .' he seeks the right word – the one that will unlock things, '. . . grief,' he says. 'She is overcome with grief and no one will allow her to grieve.'

And here's a thing I hadn't thought of before. We expect a battered woman to hate her abuser. We expect her to take the chance for escape, or at least to be grateful for help and release when the chance is offered. It simply hasn't occurred to me that a battered woman – certainly one who has developed battered woman syndrome (frequently known by its abbreviation, BWS) – may genuinely believe she loves her abuser, and perhaps she genuinely does. For who can define love? And can you think of a greater torment than to have killed the thing you love, and to be allowed no punishment? Perhaps that's it. Perhaps in her heart, even if not in her conscious mind, Mercy Marsh wants to be punished, wants the court to give her penance so that she may be absolved. But why then wouldn't she have pleaded guilty to murder? And suddenly I see the answer to that too. She cannot plead guilty to murder because she cannot bring herself to acknowledge she ever *wanted* to hurt her husband.

These thoughts wash through the synapses of my brain like waves. I see it, but I don't understand it. I'm no psychiatrist. I'm a lawyer. That's all we are, we judges. And as a lawyer, the situation is clear. It's life that isn't clear. And death.

So Mr Merchant, who should be able to rollick through the trial, swinging psychiatrists on his gown-tails and kicking Miss Roberts up and down counsel's row, can't. He can't because his client, who looks as if a breath of wind could knock her over, is standing firm upon the simple proposition that the man she killed was worthy of her love. She will not sacrifice his memory upon the altar of her innocence. She will not speak ill of him. She will not let Mr Merchant do so. And if Mr Merchant can't help her, neither can I.

I suppose I should be grateful there is not to be a further delay, but all I can do is say, 'The jurors are waiting. Are we ready to continue with the trial?'

And Mr Merchant only nods.

CHAPTER EIGHT

So Mrs Marsh returns to the witness-box, today leaning on Esme's arm. She seems barely able to walk.

'Mr Merchant, is your client quite well?'

'Well enough to complete her evidence, My Lady.' And turning to Mercy Marsh, he sets about his business. 'Yesterday,' he says, 'we heard Mrs Overton say that she frequently heard the deceased shouting at you. Is she right?'

'I wouldn't call it shouting,' she says.

'Mrs Overton thought you might have been bruised. Did you have any dark marks on your body?'

'Perhaps,' says Mercy Marsh, 'I had dust about me. I like to keep the place clean.'

'Dust?'

'Perhaps,' she says.

Mr Merchant sighs. 'All right, Mrs Marsh, let's turn to the evening of your husband's death. Tell us, please, in your own words, what happened.'

She hesitates. The Bible on which she took her oath the day before lies on the clerk's desk. She stares at it then looks away. 'I'm really not sure,' she says.

'Try and think. It's not in dispute that you picked up a poker and struck your husband repeatedly. The jury wants to know why.'

For a long while she is silent. Finally she says, 'I felt I had to.'

'You felt you had to?'

'That's what I thought then. Now I think I was wrong.'

'Still,' Mr Merchant grasps at this straw, 'the jury is concerned with your thoughts at the time, even if those thoughts were based on a misunderstanding.'

Another silence then, 'I thought perhaps he was going to kill me. Not that he would have. But in my stupidity . . . I can be stupid, you know . . . in that moment . . .'

'And what made you think that?'

Colin Merchant is willing her now to say 'because he has almost done it before'; to say 'he has put his hands around my neck, pressed till I blacked out'; to tell the jury what it is men like him do to women like her. But a barrister, asking questions of his own witness, cannot lead her to the answer he seeks. Only a cross-examiner can do that. And Miss Roberts can hardly be expected to suggest that Rodney Marsh got what was coming to him because he had, through long years of abuse, driven her to it. Let's face it, the rules were not made for defendants like Mercy Marsh.

So Mr Merchant asks all he is permitted of his client. He makes no more progress, sits down and Miss Roberts gets to her feet.

Two women – one prematurely old with no appetite left for life, the other young and hungry. Mercy Marsh is ready to be eaten up, and if anyone can do it, it's Katrina Roberts. She has her name to make. Future briefs pile up like clouds in the air, and like clouds they can float away. To bring them within her grasp she has only to impress the CPS lawyer who sits behind her, watching. She has only to say to this hopeless, helpless witness, 'You claim you mistakenly struck your husband repeatedly on the head with a poker? You did it until he fell to the ground and then you carried on doing it? That was quite some mistake, wasn't it, Mrs Marsh?'

She has only to say this, or something like it. And yet she doesn't. I look more closely, and now I see she doesn't look hungry so much as tired. She exchanges with the lawyer a look that I can't understand. Has some row taken place between them? She turns to start her cross-examination and I wait for the fireworks but when she speaks, it is quietly.

'Mrs Marsh,' she says, 'I want to get to the truth.'

And I do too.

'You have taken an oath to tell the truth, the whole truth and nothing but the truth. Do you understand those words?'

Mercy nods. From the expression on her face, you might think she was being led to the gallows.

'You swore on the Holy Bible. Do you respect that Bible?'

'Yes.'

'Then I would like you to have it with you as you answer my questions.'

Esme sets the book in front of the witness and Mercy lays a hand on it.

'Now,' says Miss Roberts, a flash of yesterday about her, 'let's stop worrying about what happened between your husband and yourself in the past, and concentrate on what happened that final evening. Take up exhibit 3, if you please.'

Mercy relinquishes the Bible and picks up the exhibit. Under Miss Robert's direction, we turn to a page showing in the corner of the living room a tiny dining table and two chairs. Here it comes after all, I think. She cannot resist breaking this witness, and why should she. It's what she is trained to do. A talent she has honed over years for this very moment. It is hardly her fault if Mercy Marsh has reduced herself – or been reduced – to a state where she is her own worst enemy.

So this is Miss Roberts's moment. But she doesn't take it. Not yet. Her voice remains neutral. 'You see on the table the remains of a meal. You had eaten supper?'

A whispered, 'Yes.'

'Except that one of you hadn't eaten – or not much. One plate is almost full. That plate was yours, wasn't it?'

Mercy nods miserably and, anticipating the next question, says, 'I wasn't hungry.'

'I don't accept that,' says Miss Roberts. 'If you weren't hungry, why did you put the food on your plate? No, Mrs Marsh, you both sat down to eat. Rodney finished his meal but you barely ate. Tell us why. The truth, if you please.'

The jury leans forward. So do I. So does Mr Merchant. It must be occurring to him – as it is to me – that Miss Roberts, who has so far fought her corner with venom, now isn't. Now it's almost as if . . . can it be? . . . she is, very skilfully, both pursuing her own case and giving the defendant a chance to state hers. She is driving Mercy Marsh into the place where the wretched woman refused to go for her own counsel. The extent of this daring can be measured by the darkness in the face of the CPS lawyer.

The witness removes her hand from the Bible, sees Miss Roberts eyeing this, and replaces it. 'Rodney said I'd burned the food,' she says at last. 'He was angry. It's an old oven. It's easy to burn things.'

'You didn't eat your supper because it was burned? Or because your husband was angry with you?'

Mercy thinks how to answer. Finally she says, 'I can't eat when I'm upset.'

'And after he finished his meal? What then? Was he still angry?'

'It was very stupid of me to burn his food.'

'So he was still angry?'

Mercy sighs and nods. Perhaps unconsciously, Miss Roberts does the same. There is none of yesterday's panache. 'What happened next?' she says coldly.

Mercy retreats into, 'I can't remember.'

Miss Roberts is having none of it. 'Of course you can remember. At least you could remember when Mr Merchant asked you. You said – if you spoke the truth – that you thought your husband was going to kill you.'

Mercy puts a hand to her head. 'Did I say that?'

I nod.

'Well, if I said it, it's true. I've taken an oath. But if I did think it, I made a mistake.'

'We'll come to that in a moment,' says Miss Roberts. 'First I want to know why you thought it.' The voice is like steel now. Ruthless. No, not ruthless. Not if that means pitiless. And it is a fair issue to explore, for if Mercy Marsh had no good reason to believe her husband was going to kill her, or none she is willing to give, the case against her is strong. But if there is a reason, she is now being given the chance to tell us. Until now, fairness has not been the hallmark of Miss Roberts's prosecuting style, but here is a new Miss Roberts. She seems to have grown up overnight. Perhaps she spent those dark hours thinking about her failure to open the case properly, her failure to disclose what now clearly needed to be disclosed. Perhaps she has spoken to senior members of her Chambers about the responsibilities of her job. Perhaps it has occurred to her there is more to this job than winning.

For prosecuting counsel, how far to push can be a tricky business. On the one hand, all barristers depend for their living on impressing those who can brief them. For many, one of the most important sources of work is the CPS. On the other hand, the Bar works on the reputation of its practitioners. Good reputation depends on behaving honourably. Barristers who throw away their good name deserve the impoverishment of profession and purse that follows. And Miss Roberts is too good – or will be one day – to waste herself.

Good prosecutors pursue all available avenues to support their case, while maintaining strict fairness. And here is the new and fair Miss Roberts. I can't know if she came to this in the lonely hours of the night, or if she just woke up wanting to do what is right. But I do know – I can see it in the darkening glower of the CPS lawyer and the bemused face of the officer – that she is putting herself at risk in order to give Mercy Marsh another chance to say what she has previously refused to.

'So,' she says again, 'bearing in mind the oath you've taken, what exactly did Rodney do before you killed him?'

Silence.

'Mrs Marsh, I will keep asking until you answer, because that is why we are all here.'

Another silence. Then, with a deep sigh, Mercy Marsh lays her hand on the Bible and accepts she can't fight this any more. Her voice is faint as she says, 'He came towards me. He had that look he has when . . .' She puts a hand to her neck. Is this an unconscious action as she remembers the past? If not, if it's an act, it's a very good one. 'It's not his fault,' she says. 'He couldn't help himself when I made him angry.'

And out it all comes. How Rodney was so kind, except when he lost his temper. So thoughtful, except when she made him cross. So gentle, except when he wasn't. He was always so sorry afterwards. He would hold her hand and stroke the bruises and promise never to do it again. 'He couldn't help himself,' she says. 'Not when I pushed him to it.'

Miss Roberts lets her talk, then asks, 'How long did this go on for?' I can't read the tone. She is giving away nothing. She's just asking.

Mrs Marsh considers. 'It began about six months after I came to London.'

'Twenty years?'

Twenty years. Two decades of living in fear that today would be the day she was killed.

'So why,' asks Miss Roberts in a tone of practised and polite bewilderment, 'didn't you leave him?'

And Mercy Marsh looks her full in the face, apparently puzzled that – after all the difficult questions – she is being asked such an easy one. 'Because I loved him,' she says. 'I still do.'

Those words again. Because I love him. It's what Kitty and so many have said over the years. Miss Roberts does not attempt to belittle the woman in the witness-box, nor to scorn her. She only nods.

Mr Merchant stares at his prosecutor with a look of respect. If she has offended the CPS and lost her prosecution practice, she has at least gained the regard of a senior member of her profession. But a glance at the CPS lawyer shows that even his face has softened. So perhaps Miss Roberts will be all right. After all, no one in the courtroom can doubt that Mercy Marsh is a witness doing her best to tell us the truth . . . or at least, her truth. We rarely hear simple truth spoken in the witness-box, but we know it when we do.

Miss Roberts, however, hasn't forgotten she is there to prosecute a murder. She just sets about her job in a different way. She needs to prove Mercy Marsh was not acting in self-defence.

When I sum up self-defence to the jury, I will set it out like this:

If you conclude
(i) the defendant believed or may have believed, genuinely even if mistakenly, that it was necessary to use force to defend herself from an actual or imminent attack (subjective question) AND
(ii) the amount of force used was reasonable in the circumstances as the defendant genuinely believed them to be (objective question),

she is not guilty.

Miss Roberts turns her attention to the second limb, that of reasonableness. 'Let us suppose for a moment,' she says, 'that you genuinely if mistakenly believed you had to defend yourself . . . surely you are not saying it was reasonable to strike your husband's head again and again with a poker?'

Mrs Marsh thinks. Reflects. Says, 'I really don't know.'

Miss Roberts, like the rest of us, is unused to this degree of honesty. It stops her in her tracks. But when she finds her next question, it is perfectly judged. 'I mean,' she says, 'if you are telling the truth, there was nothing special about that evening. He had behaved in this way a hundred times. You had never needed to beat him to death before. What made it reasonable to do so on this occasion?'

And Mr Merchant bows his head, knowing, as he has always known, that his client has no answer to this. Mercy Marsh cannot explain what happened to her that day. She does not know. And this is where 'self-defence' fails. Miss Roberts has done a good job. The CPS should be pleased with her. She has efficiently and fairly scuppered self-defence. But she isn't finished yet. Perhaps she wants to ensure Mr Merchant can't pull a rabbit out of the defence hat – and she knows there are two possible rabbits that could reduce murder to manslaughter. One is if the defendant's responsibility was diminished by reason of mental illness. The other is if she lost her self-control because of how the deceased behaved. Neither has been raised in this case, and she wants to make sure they can't be.

'I don't suppose,' she says casually, 'that you have any sort of mental illness?'

Like a lamb to the slaughter Mercy says, 'No.'

'And you are not saying that your husband did something that made you lose your self-control?'

'Of course not.'

When all the questions are done, the defendant returns to the dock. She seems quite exhausted. The dock officer hands her some water. She thanks him and sips. She has given all she has to give. The jury too looks drained. Even I could do with a cup of tea. The light and heat concentrated on a witness can sometimes be too much to bear.

CHAPTER NINE

THE EVIDENCE IS FINISHED and I send everyone away because I now have a lot of thinking to do. Tomorrow counsel will make their final speeches. To do so, they must be clear what defences I will let the jury consider. I will work it out overnight and tell the barristers my conclusions in the morning. If they want to argue with those conclusions they will have a chance to do so. I will then sum up the case on Friday. It looks like I will meet the list officer's deadline after all. But first I must sort out in my own mind the question of what defences in law arise on the facts of this difficult case.

Once in my room, I phone S. 'Have you got a few minutes?'

'Have you got any Earl Grey?'

Soon he is in my armchair – the one he deems most conducive to analytical thought – stirring his tea while I pace about in front of him.

'I have a three-pipe problem to offer you.'

His eyes sparkle. 'Set it out,' he says.

I have barely begun when there is a knock on the door and G appears. 'Come in,' says S. 'A team effort is required here.' Five minutes later H arrives in search of something – he forgets what – helps himself to tea, goes to the drawer where I keep my biscuits and thumps himself down in the remaining armchair.

'It's like this,' I say, and stop because actually I'm not sure what it is like. Not like anything I have come across before.

'Facts,' says S, taking a blue pen from his breast pocket. 'Give us facts.'

So I do while he makes neat notes.

When I have finished, he puts away the blue pen and takes out a red one. 'The law's straightforward. You have to direct the jury on any defence disclosed by the evidence. Let's look at each possible defence in turn. Merchant is running self-defence, so let's start with that. There is, I suppose, no doubt that it was she who caused the death?'

'None, but there's enough evidence for a jury to conclude she might have been attacked and needed to defend herself.'

'To defend herself, yes. But as to the reasonableness of the force used...'

'Part of his brain ended up down his spine.'

There's a silence.

'Well,' says H at last, 'the jury will have to consider it, but she'll be one lucky lady if they buy it.'

S nods, puts a red exclamation mark on page 1 of his notes and turns to page 2. 'For any murder, the prosecution has to prove she intended to kill or at least cause grievous bodily harm ... Is it possible she did not have this intent?'

'Brain,' I remind him. 'Spine.'

We shake our heads. A red exclamation mark appears on page 2. Page 3 is 'manslaughter by reason of diminished responsibility'. S sets out the law for us. There's an ocean of material to wade through but we don't need to go beyond the shallows. The Bench Book says the defendant has to prove an abnormality of mental functioning, and that expert evidence will be crucial to establish this.*

'I take it there is no expert evidence?'

'None.'

'So you can't even ask the jury to consider this.' He draws a red line through page 3 and turns over to 'manslaughter by loss of

---

* Appendix M.

control'. I tell them how Miss Roberts got the defendant to say the deceased did nothing to provoke her to lose her self-control.

'Neat,' says S. 'Door closed. Lock snapped shut.' The red line again. No issue to go to the jury here.

I spend the evening reflecting, but I know I cannot justify leaving to the jury anything but self-defence and lack of intent . . . both of which have S's red exclamation marks hanging over them. Still, my job is only to give the directions impartially and clearly. It's not difficult, just sad, because somehow we are not getting to the truth.

Next morning, in the dock, Mercy Marsh looks unstrung. She seems to have given up all hope. Counsel on the other hand are looking unaccountably chipper. They sit close together, poring over a shared document.

'Mr Merchant, Miss Roberts.' They stand politely. 'To make your closing speeches, you will need to know upon what defences I intend to direct the jury, so—'

'My Lady,' says Mr Merchant, 'before we get to that point, I need to tell the court something.'

Oh, for Heaven's sake, what now. We've had errant witnesses. We've had disclosure. What else have they got to throw at me? I'm about to find out.

'I must tell Your Ladyship that I am very concerned about my client's health. Particularly her mental health, which seems to have deteriorated sharply in the last few days. I am beginning to wonder if she is properly understanding her situation and my advice.'

'You needn't sound quite so pleased about it, Mr Merchant.'

'I beg Your Ladyship's pardon. I didn't mean to sound pleased.'

'And isn't it rather late in the day to raise such issues? I understood your client did not wish a psychiatrist to be involved in her defence.'

'She does not, My Lady. Not at all.' He exchanges a look with Miss

Roberts, who pushes the papers they had been studying towards him. 'But this isn't about a psychiatrist being involved in her defence. It's a different matter. Does Your Ladyship have in front of her the Bench Books?'

There are a myriad of the things. They tell judges how to deal with evidence, trial management, law, sentencing, youths, those who have particular mental or physical problems, those from diverse backgrounds . . .

'All of them, Mr Merchant?'

'I had in mind the Equal Treatment Bench Book, My Lady.'

Esme, who is clearly in on the secret, produces the court's copy with a flourish.

'Paragraph 106,' says Mr Merchant.

Esme already has it open. I read aloud. 'Mental Disability. Ways to find out whether the defendant has a mental health condition. Paragraph 106: Judges need to be aware if mental health is an issue, both so that all reasonable adjustments can be made, and in order to make the most appropriate disposal decision. Either because of the stigma attached or because of lack of self-awareness, many defendants will not have informed the criminal justice system that they have a mental disability.'

'Paragraph 108,' says Miss Roberts, 'states that various behaviours may alert a judge to the possibility that an individual has a mental disability. If concerned, a judge can obtain further information in a number of ways. And then,' she looks down modestly, 'Your Ladyship may be particularly interested in the last item in the list, which says medical reports can be requested by the judge at any point during court proceedings . . .'

Well, clever old counsel.

'Let me be clear,' I say to Mr Merchant. 'You want me, of my own volition, to order a psychiatric report?'

'Yes.'

'Because . . .'

'. . . because you have seen the defendant's condition deteriorate in the course of the trial and you are concerned about this.'

Well, that's true. 'And the purpose of the report is to . . .?'

He looks me straight in the eye. 'To ensure you can identify any problems and achieve a fair trial. If I have sight of such a report, it might enable me to do the same.'

I think about it. Such reports help the judge know what directions to give to achieve fairness, the number of breaks a defendant might need, and in extreme cases whether she is fit to be tried at all. But this trial is almost over. What directions could I give now?

Counsel vie to get in first. Miss Roberts graciously cedes the ground. Mr Merchant says that if it emerges his client is ill and allowances should have been made for her condition, I would have to decide whether the trial has been fair. And if it hasn't, I would have to consider what to say to the jury. And if any unfairness couldn't be cured I might even have to discharge them and order a fresh trial.

'The Crown,' says Miss Roberts with a touch of her old sternness, 'doesn't want a conviction which unravels in the Court of Appeal because we were unaware of something as significant as underlying mental illness.'

Well, none of us want that, do we. The purpose for which I could order a psychiatric report is very different from the purpose for which Mr Merchant wants one – but at least it would lift the veil and perhaps show if there was truly a risk of injustice here.

'It might take a while to identify a psychiatrist . . .'

'I have already identified one,' says Mr Merchant.

From the dock there is wail of despair as Mercy Marsh realizes where this is going.

'Mrs Marsh,' I say as gently as I can, 'this isn't about Mr Merchant instructing a psychiatrist for your defence. It is about me instructing one to ensure this trial is fair. That's my job and I hope you won't try to stop me doing it?'

She blinks hard. Pulls at strands of her hair, the skin on her neck. She really isn't well.

'How long will this expert take to make a report? I will take it orally if that is quicker than putting it in writing.'

'Today is Thursday. We'll have it by next Tuesday.'

Next Tuesday! 'And which of us,' I say, 'is going to explain this to the list officer?'

CHAPTER TEN

As it happens, none of us has to. After all we have been through, the problems of the list officer are about to evaporate. Whatever god oversees the lists is working in his mysterious way. In a prison somewhere within the M25 a defendant due to stand trial the following week sees the light – or perhaps the dark – and decides to plead guilty. His four-week slot becomes free and the Seven Defendants, Vulnerable Witnesses and Press Interest will slip neatly into it.

As for my case, well, for once the system which so often clunks and grinds, shifts into gear. Mr Merchant's psychiatrist is given precious weekend appointments to see his client. Mercy Marsh, perhaps moved by my plea, is cooperative. Cogs mesh. Wheels turn. And by Tuesday morning, counsel and I have copies of her report. I can scarcely believe it until I see Dr Alyson, after which I believe it completely.

She is in her early sixties, iron-grey hair marshalled into a bun, a little mascara for appearance's sake and a business suit. This is someone who knows her stuff. And her stuff – oh, sensible Mr Merchant – is battered woman syndrome. She climbs briskly into the witness-box and watches me as I scan her document.

'I understood you wanted my report as quickly as possible,' she says, 'so I have used bullet points.'

Bullet points are all I need. I thank her for working over the weekend. I thank the prison for accommodating her. I thank Mr Merchant for sorting things out, and since it seems churlish not to, I thank Miss Roberts as well. Having worked myself into a general state of gratitude, Mercy Marsh spoils it by giving an audible groan and slumping forward in the dock. I suppose I have got used to her increasing pallor and the way she closes her eyes from time to time. I shouldn't have because now . . . now what have I missed? Whatever it is, Dr Alyson isn't waiting for me to gather my thoughts. She is already striding from the witness-box towards the dock.

I know when I'm not wanted. So while Mercy is being attended to, I go back to my room to read Dr Alyson's report. Her qualifications and experience are impressive. So is her thoroughness. In the three and three-quarter hours which she spent with the defendant, she got deeper than we did in the courtroom. She has drawn from Mercy details of childhood and concluded she was a nervous little girl, very willing to love and be loved by her elderly parents. As to her meeting and marrying Rodney Marsh, Dr Alyson says Mercy saw it as passing from the protection of parents to husband. She soon found it wasn't. In the early months of marriage, Mercy attended her GP's surgery with routine problems which, within a year, were far from routine. She didn't complain of injuries but the GP saw and noted them. She complained of 'nerves', sleeplessness, feeling low, but would not accept she might have mild depression. When he observed that her pupils were dilated and asked if she had taken drugs, she seemed astonished. When he pointed out the catalogue of small injuries, she said she was accident-prone. He noted an elevated heart rate and blood pressure but she insisted this was only nervousness at visiting the surgery. She said she was fine. Fine was a word she used a lot.

Dr Alyson's report now moves on to her own observations of the defendant. What the GP described as 'nervousness', she calls 'hypervigilance' and 'an abnormal startle response'. What the GP noted as 'feeling low', she calls 'distress'. She notes what I have seen in court – the constant pulling at her hair or twisting of hands. Of the marriage, twenty years of it, Mercy did not tell Dr Alyson that she was beaten. Instead she said she slept poorly, that she had bad dreams, and finally she admitted these dreams came when she was awake as well as asleep. They were dreams of being hurt. By her husband? Well, she supposed, some were. Why would she dream such things? Well, sometimes when she had been stupid or careless and upset, Rodney might have been driven to strike her.

Dr Alyson says such waking and sleeping 'dreams' are typical of flashbacks – the reliving of a traumatic event, which is typical of post-traumatic stress disorder. Other classic symptoms of PTSD, she says, include distress, anxiety, hypervigilance, an enhanced startle response, irritability. Overly engaged stress hormones can manifest in dilated pupils, increased heart rate, elevated blood pressure, sleeplessness, exhaustion, an inability to focus. She hardly needs to point out that these signs were all evident to the GP.

Dr Alyson's task wasn't to provide a defence but to help me understand if I was giving the defendant a fair trial. She has a neat way of combining the two. If the defendant is suffering from PTSD, I have taken no steps to ensure she has been able to follow the trial, given her no extra breaks, made no allowances for her. It is a sobering report. Of course, it is not the judge's responsibility to override counsel in his dealings with his client. And it is not counsel's responsibility to override his client. But surely it is the responsibility of all of us to ensure that the trial in which we are engaged does not – through the oversight of any one of us – lead to a miscarriage of justice.

When I return to court, Dr Alyson is already in the witness-box.

'I don't think Mrs Marsh is well enough to come into the dock,' she says, 'but I am ready to explain any part of my report Your Ladyship doesn't understand.' I don't tell her I fear I understand it only too well. 'Mercy Marsh,' she continues, 'has all the symptoms of PTSD. If her marriage involved a longstanding and abusive relationship, that is a likely cause of PTSD. Victims unable to stop the abuse can develop a psychological paralysis. Their self-esteem is destroyed. You don't want to hear about how this might raise the defence of diminished responsibility. You only want me to tell you if you have conducted this trial fairly. If she is suffering from PTSD, you probably have not.'

'I see. And in your opinion, *is* she suffering from PTSD?'

She looks me in the eye and says, 'Yes.'

Doctors rarely indulge in such clear views. Mostly it's 'the pattern of behaviour is capable ...' or 'diagnoses are difficult ...' But Dr Alyson calmly takes us through the observations that underlie her conclusions.

'Had I been asked at the beginning of this trial,' she says, 'I would have strongly recommended Mrs Marsh be monitored for signs of flashbacks that removed her mentally from her immediate environment, of distress that made it difficult for her to concentrate, of exhaustion from sleeplessness and of fight-or-flight responses affecting her perceptions. I would have recommended regular breaks to minimize the effect of such events. Otherwise I must assume that at least in parts of this trial – and I cannot tell you when or at what length – she will not have been effectively participating.'

I think back over the trial; of the times I have pressed on because ... well, because I was being pressed by the thought of the next trial. But what is the point of any trial if it fails to provide justice? Esme refills my water glass. 'Remember,' she whispers, 'her own counsel was encouraging you to go on.' It's true but, dear Esme, it's no excuse. Mr Merchant is no more a psychiatrist than I am. And I'm the one in charge.

'My Lady,' says Miss Roberts, cutting through my self-castigation, 'may I take the liberty of analysing the position?'

It's the first time Miss Roberts has sought leave before taking a liberty. And she has an interest in getting this right – at least, she has an interest in not being taken apart by the Court of Appeal. So I give her free rein.

'The Crown sees the problem like this. *If* Dr Alyson is right, the defendant may be suffering from PTSD. *If* so, two things follow.

First, we may not have taken appropriate steps to ensure she could participate effectively. Second, PTSD at the time of the killing might have provided her with a potential defence of "diminished responsibility".

I agree with your analysis, my dear, but where does that leave us? Since no one else seems inclined to answer this, I have a bash at it myself. 'I suppose the only question is whether we can put these things right in the course of this trial, or whether I must discharge the jury and we must start again.'

'I think,' says Miss Roberts, 'Your Ladyship may be conflating two issues – the disadvantage and the diminished responsibility.'

I take her reproval for intellectual frailty on the chin. Colin Merchant comes to my rescue.

'I rather fear the two issues are irrevocably intertwined,' he says. 'A defendant suffering from the syndrome may be incapable of giving the instructions upon which, in her own interests, I should have acted.'

He is right. The answer to both questions rests on whether Mercy has a mental illness. Dr Alyson says she has. But would a psychiatrist instructed by the Crown agree?

'I can instruct a psychiatrist this afternoon,' Miss Roberts says.

I look at the dock, where a small figure sits white and shaking. I look at the jury-box, now empty of jurors, and wonder if I can really keep them waiting while the doctors do their work. I look at the door that leads down to the cells where the guilty begin to serve a sentence that can be measured in decades.

Counsel are following my gaze, and apparently my thoughts.

'My Lady,' says Miss Roberts, 'the Crown has a proposal to make. It is one we have reached after discussion with Mr Merchant.'

'All thoughts are welcome,' I say.

'This one certainly will be,' she says. 'Your Ladyship will appreciate the evidential landscape has shifted considerably since the beginning of the trial. Though Mr Merchant will need a full psychiatric report from Dr Alyson on the issue, we for the Crown can see that she is likely to conclude there is a possible case for "diminished responsibility" here. If she does, we would instruct a report from a psychiatrist of our own. If – but only if – both psychiatrists are satisfied that at the time of the killing the defendant was suffering from PTSD as a result of what is called "battered woman syndrome", the Crown would drop the charge of murder and accept a plea of guilty to manslaughter by reason of diminished responsibility.'

I turn to Colin Merchant. 'And would the defendant plead guilty to such a charge?'

'My Lady, what Miss Roberts and I propose is that just such a second count be added to the indictment. I can say that Mercy Marsh would plead guilty to it.'

I try to grasp the information. 'So if both psychiatrists agree she was suffering from mental illness at the time of the killing, she will plead guilty to Count Two manslaughter, and the Crown will drop the charge of murder?'

'Yes,' say the barristers in unison.

'I suppose we can be confident Dr Alyson will find that Mrs Marsh had PTSD, but if the Crown's psychiatrist does not, the trial of murder will go ahead.'

'Yes,' they say.

'But,' adds Mr Merchant, 'we both agree it couldn't be done with this jury. It is far too late in the trial to put a new issue like that before them.'

They are right. This jury, which has listened so carefully to the evidence for over a week now, will not get to bring in a verdict. But the likelihood is that no jury will – certainly not if both psychiatrists find Mercy Marsh was suffering from PTSD. And surely they will – for surely this woman meets all the criteria about which I have been reading.

CHAPTER ELEVEN

It takes three weeks to get the two full psychiatric reports. By then my jury has long gone, but it doesn't matter because both psychiatrists agree that Mercy Marsh was and still is suffering from post-traumatic stress disorder. A second count of manslaughter has been added to the indictment. Mercy Marsh has pleaded guilty to it. When we reassemble, Miss Roberts tells the court that after careful consideration the Crown has decided to accept the plea and not to proceed with the charge of murder. Behind her the man from the CPS is nodding as if this proposal had all been his idea in the beginning. Which just goes to show how good an advocate Miss Roberts is.

Every year many, many women suffer violence in their own homes, the very place where they should feel and be safe. It happens to men too, of course, and their suffering is as important, but this story is about the women who form by far the greater number of victims. Almost always the problem is there to be seen, but people turn away or don't recognize what they are seeing. They close their eyes to the bruises. They close their ears to the screams. Too often what happens behind closed doors stays there.

The violence these women endure at the hands of abusive partners may be physical or sexual, mental or emotional, and very often involves all these things. The number who die is tragically large. Some – probably several hundred each year – commit suicide. Almost the same number are murdered. Some are too ashamed to tell anyone what is happening, often blaming themselves rather than their torturer; but many make repeated calls for help, to friends, police or social services, before they either are killed by or kill an abusive partner.

That women have used violence against those who inflicted violence on them is a simple fact of history. That they are entitled to the same defences as anyone else is obvious. For them, as for the assailant in the street, the pub, the workplace, there is a huge difference between an *act* of serious violence and an *offence* of serious violence. If a woman runs her partner through with a meat skewer, that is an act of violence; but for it to be a criminal offence, she must have intended to do it, and for it to be a serious criminal offence such as wounding with intent to cause grievous bodily harm, she must also have intended the harm she caused. Women under physical attack in their own homes have as much right to defend themselves as anyone else, anywhere else. This isn't special pleading for women who injure and kill their partners – these are fundamental principles of our law.

So far, so clear. What has not always been clear is the effect on a victim of daily domestic abuse, of living daily in fear. Historically it has sometimes created sympathy in sentencing – though not always. Poor Kitty, who despite the fact that the jury on convicting gave the strongest possible recommendation to mercy, was still sentenced to hang. But our society has finally managed to get itself beyond mere sympathy, beyond even empathy. We have recognized not only the plight of women trapped in domestic violence, but have also begun to understand the way it can alter their perceptions and their very thought processes. It has taken modern psychiatry to grasp that constant exposure to violence in the place where a woman should be safest and at the hands of the person who should care most for her, can lead to an altered form of thinking. It has taken modern psychiatrists to consider the possibility that this can amount to a form of PTSD. These cases are now well recognized in the courts.*

Perhaps we just need to be grateful for the fact that, in understanding the ongoing fear and violence some women face on a daily basis, we have come a long way. That shouldn't stop us from recognizing there may be a long way to go yet.

---

* Appendix N.

4: No Evil Angel . . .

THE BOY CAN'T BE *more than eight or nine years old. He is dark-skinned and has the thinness that comes from never being still. His bright eyes are, at the moment, half hidden under brows drawn together in concentration. His attention is on the canvas bag slung across one shoulder. He walks in the shadows, crossing the estate by way of the circuitous path he knows the drug dealers use. It brings him out by the park and he disappears through the iron gate and into the bushes. He is less careful now and you can follow him by the disruption of the leaves and branches. He skirts the children's playground and the gritty sandpit. He passes the tennis court with its cracks and weeds. He is heading for the place where the hedge meets the thickest of the bushes. When he gets there he crouches down. His white T-shirt catches the early sun. His dark curls are hidden in the twining of the leaves. You can't see his face at all, but you can tell his hands are busy with something. If your eyes are keen you can pick out the canvas bag he has cast aside. If your ears are sharp you will catch a series of sharp metallic sounds followed by a click. If you are sensible, this is the moment you will move away, because the boy is about to stand, to turn, to emerge from the bush and lift what he has been carrying until it is level with his face. He will struggle a little with the weight but he knows how it must be done because he has seen his father do it. He knows he must line it up with his eye and squint through the sight in order to focus. He knows he must squeeze the trigger. And then he knows no more.*

Back in the flat where the boy lives, his grandmother arrives home. She has been at work, an early shift, 5–8 a.m. The job – cleaning offices – used to be easy enough, but these days she has trouble with her legs. She used to be home before Ty went to school. Now she isn't surprised to find he has already left. She turns towards the kitchen, thinking she will make a cup of tea. It is then that she sees the door to the hall cupboard is open and that the stool from Ty's bedroom is there. She can see how he has placed it, so he can stand on it and reach up. She goes to it and lays a hand where his feet have been. Eventually she lets her eyes follow where her thoughts have gone, to the top shelf. With great difficulty she hoists herself up onto the stool and pushes aside a half-used pot of paint. She sees behind it the oily blanket and, where the bag had been, an empty space. She doesn't want tea any more. She doesn't want anything but to have her grandson safe beside her again.

CHAPTER ONE

THIS MONDAY MORNING BRINGS me a new trial about which, as yet, I know nothing beyond its name – The Crown v. Adams and Adams. I have come into the Old Bailey early to access the documentation on the Digital Case System, but I can't. Apparently the system is having difficulty digesting this late transfer from another court. So am I. These transfers happen from time to time. A trial overruns in one place while in another something 'goes short'.* We help each other out. This one arrived amid a flurry of emails at the end of the previous week. All I know about it is there are two defendants who both seem to be called Michael Adams. The charges are not as serious as most we see at the Old Bailey. It's nothing more than possession of a prohibited weapon, a sawn-off shotgun. So far, so not-very-interesting.

My usher today is Jim, and he doesn't think it's interesting either. Like most of us, he resents mopping up another court's overspill. He is a dour and canny Scotsman who walks under a cloud of dispirit. He has been around a long time. You can't pull a fast one on Jim, though he has been known to do just that to pretty well everyone else. He is an arch and skilful manipulator. Among the things he likes to manipulate is the courtroom in which he is working. Jim is a heavy smoker and it is convenient for him to be on the ground floor, where he can pop out to the car park to do damage to his lungs. I worry about Jim's lungs. So when he says, 'My Lady, we're sitting in

---

* Trials 'go short' for a variety of reasons. For example, a defendant may plead guilty, or the Crown may find it doesn't have the evidence to proceed.

Court 13 today' and I say, 'On the ground floor?' and he says, 'That's where it is generally to be found, My Lady', I am wary.

Court 13 is never good news. Quite apart from the atavistic fears that make some defendants, witnesses and jurors jumpy, my room is on the third floor, where Courts 9–12 are found (don't ask – or if you must, see the footnote).* Sitting in Court 13 means that many times a day I must go up and down the judges' stairs or use the judges' lift. I am not a fan of either. The judges' stairs have a rubber floor and a curious smell. The judges' lift demands that you present it with a special pass before it will cooperate, and even then it likes to make unscheduled detours via the basement car park. Not, you understand, that I am overly influenced by this. I am mainly concerned about Jim's lungs.

Jim, who is sensitive to these things, picks up the note of suspicion in my voice and proffers, by way of explanation, 'It's the legs, My Lady.'

This is something else about Jim. He carries on a constant internal dialogue which – when it becomes audible to the rest of us – requires we figure out the bits we haven't heard. The legs, for example. I have no idea whose legs they are or what train of thought has brought Jim to them. Before I can enquire, Jim – perhaps feeling something more is needed – offers, 'She's on the blink.' It emerges, after some probing, that it is a defendant who has dodgy legs and cannot climb the stairs to the third floor where is my courtroom; and it is the lift which should therefore carry the legs up to me which is on the blink. The lift . . . no doubt because it is cousin to the judges' lift . . . is often temperamental. Lots of things at the Old Bailey are. I would be myself if there were any

---

* The old part of the building houses Courts 1–4 on its first floor. Courts 5–8 flow from them into the new building, which is directly adjacent to the old and joined internally. Courts 9–12 are above them on the third floor of the new building, so Courts 13–16 have been slipped in on its ground floor. Courts 17 and 18 are on the ground floor of the old building.

mileage in it. But there isn't. I have a defendant with dodgy legs so we must sit in a court on a lower floor, and there's an end of it.

All the way down the stairs, I rage against my fate. These legs have no business here. This isn't a Bailey case. Surely someone could find a court other than mine for them. Surely I needn't be bothered with this bit of unlawful shotgunnery. Surely . . . My inward grumblings bring me to the door of the court and Jim is throwing it open. I must enter and face the Michaels.

But when I do, they aren't. They aren't Michaels at all. Well, one of them might be. He is a tall, broad Black man in his forties, wearing a white shirt and smart jacket – no doubt brought in by his legal team. But the second defendant is quite different. She is a tiny woman with grizzled hair. Her face is wrinkled with age and consternation. She gazes around as if she cannot understand what is happening or why everyone is standing. When the dock officer nudges her, she lays a hand on her co-defendant's arm and leans on him to get to her feet. Here, then, are the Dodgy Legs.

She does not look like a gun-runner. Except that maybe she does, because I've come across them before – these women who allow themselves to be led into crime by their men. As soon as I see them together in the dock, I know. At least I think I know. I think this man is a son or possibly a grandson – someone, at least, whom she loves and who has used her and betrayed her and whom she will still defend before she defends herself. I have seen it most often with young women who are convicted of housing a weapon for their boyfriends; convicted while they keep silent about the real wrongdoer. This old lady is a new and painful twist on the old story.

She is not Michael, it turns out, but Michaela. No doubt she was named for her father and her son for his grandfather. Perhaps a trail of Michael Adamses goes back across generations and geography; loyalty to each other bred in the bone and registered at the time of birth. Perhaps.

I look about my courtroom. The public gallery is open and in it are the usual tourists, together with a few young men who nod towards the dock and have presumably come to support the defendants. When they catch me looking at them, they sink back under their hoodies, but they sit quietly enough and cause no trouble.

I turn my attention to counsel. Three of them – one to prosecute and one for each defendant. At the Old Bailey, where cases are usually among the most serious in the criminal calendar, we judges are spoiled because we see the most experienced and best counsel. We know them. We trust them to know their job. But this case has come with unknown counsel who practise on the outer limits of London.

The prosecutor is called John Collingwood. Jim sums him up in a damning whisper – Too Polite, Too Thorough, Too Slow. And Jim knows these things. I look at the man. Of middle-height and with a comfortable spread of stomach, he must be in his fifties – old enough to have been appointed a QC, but he hasn't been. Perhaps he has never applied for the promotion. 'Silk', after all, is reserved for 'high flyers'. Still, this case doesn't need one of those. It needs a decent, fair prosecutor prepared to put in the work. The two counsel defending are very different. Both are women and worryingly young. New Generation. That doesn't mean they aren't good at what they do – far from it. Everyone has to gain their experience somewhere. They make an interesting pair. I look at their names on the list Jim has given me. Jasmina Shah represents Michael Adams. She is tall, fine-boned and immaculately dressed. I wouldn't normally notice counsel's neckwear, but her collarette* is so white and fits with such precision around her slender neck, I cannot but stare. And it is in such contrast to that of Fiona Fontaine, who is for Michaela

---

* Male barristers wear white wing collars with tabs or bands tied around them. Women usually wear a linen 'bib' which encircles the neck and to which the bands are attached.

Adams. Miss Fontaine's linen is held together with a safety pin and her generous proportions spill out of various gaps in the rest of her clothing. The women do not look at each other. Am I sensing a cut-throat here? A 'cut-throat defence' is where the defence of one defendant is directly damaging to that of another. And when it happens, the usual winner is the Crown. I study the barristers. The body language is not encouraging. But when I ask if we are ready for a jury panel and John Collingwood says, in his gentle, courteous voice, 'We are, My Lady', the women turn on him simultaneously, like young lionesses eyeing prey. Perhaps they will work together after all.

'Jim,' I say, 'a jury panel, if you please.'

'Fine by me, My Lady,' says Jim, 'if you can get the jury bailiff to give you one. But I can't.'

'Is there a problem?'

'Not so much a problem. More, a queue. There are three other trials starting this morning and we have to wait for them to have first pick of the new jurors.'

I understand. The other cases will be 'proper' Old Bailey cases, most likely murders with multiple defendants and due to last for three or four weeks, perhaps more. It can be difficult to find jurors to sit on long cases. Particularly now the school holidays are about to begin. The jury bailiff will have to send to each of these courtrooms panels of up to fifty people, from which the other judges will listen to pleas to be excused. They will allow some of these pleas, where there are pressing personal or professional commitments, family problems, ill health . . . even holidays booked and paid for. My case will last a bare two weeks and I must take what's left of the panels.

'The jury bailiff says she won't have anything for you before 2 p.m.,' says Jim, trying not to look smug. And I can hardly blame him for relishing a morning free to visit the car park whenever he wishes.

John Collingwood gets to his feet. 'Perhaps Your Ladyship has not yet had an opportunity to become familiar with the facts of this case. This enforced delay will allow you the opportunity to . . .' He hands up a file of papers, which Jim places in front of me. 'There are . . . complexities . . .' says Mr Collingwood.

'Complexities?'

'Also, in opening my case to the jury I would wish to refer to certain matters to which Miss Shah objects.'

'It's Ms Shah,' says Ms Shah. 'Not Miss.'

Mr Collingwood blinks, apologizes, turns back to me and says, 'It would be helpful if Your Ladyship would rise and read my opening note and then . . .' he hesitates and settles for safety with, 'and then *we* can make our submissions about the disputed material.'

'Is it only Ms Shah who is raising a point of law?'

'I understand,' says Mr Collingwood, 'that Ms Fontaine has no submission at this stage.'

'It's *Miss* Fontaine,' says Miss Fontaine.

So I'm to be sent up the rubber stairs to my room, where I am to study this case with 'complexities', demoted by the jury bailiff to the afternoon list. As I get up to leave court I remember The Legs. 'Miss Fontaine,' I say, 'I understand your client has a problem with her legs. If during any part of the trial she finds it difficult to stand when I enter or leave court, she need not do so. I will know that no discourtesy is meant.'

CHAPTER TWO

THE THING ABOUT CRIMINAL cases – the thing that makes them more gripping than cases about drainage pipes or dry shipping – is that they tell stories. They are about people. And their problems. Defendants or victims or witnesses or their families, none of them come to the Old Bailey for fun. Except maybe the tourists. And they soon learn better. Those using the courts are often at the worst point of their lives. And who can define that? Certainly it will include those charged and facing imprisonment. And certainly it will include those who have been hurt or whose loved ones have been killed. But the complexities of which Mr Collingwood spoke will throw a new and painful twist on this suffering. For, as I read, I discover the tragedy of this case – as awful as most tried at the Old Bailey. If the Crown's allegations are true, as well as being defendants in danger of substantial prison sentences, these defendants must be enduring agonies of pain at what has happened to a child they love, not least because it is their fault.

I read, impatiently at first, then with more attention, and finally with a grim soberness. I read of the little boy betrayed by those who, despite what must be their natural love for him, put him in harm's way. I think of him, scarred and blinded. And I wonder who will care for him if the two in the dock – the two whose fault this is – are locked away in prison.

At 11.30 I am ready to go back into court to hear counsels' submissions. Ms Shah gets to her feet.

'My Lady, I seek to exclude from the evidence and therefore the

Crown's opening, any reference to the injuries to the child Tyler Adams. Those injuries have no probative value to the issues before the jury which are simply "did either or both of these defendants ever have that gun and ammunition in their possession?" The child's injuries have no probative value on this point but they are capable of prejudicing the jury against the defendants.'

I take a moment to absorb this. Ms Shah's submissions are as precise as her linen. Point one, evidence is only admissible if it has relevance to the issues in the case. Point two, the allegations are that each defendant at some time had possession of the firearm and ammunition – possession in the legal sense, i.e. had control over it. Point three, Michael Adams is said to have stored the canvas bag with its contents in his mother's flat some time before the day of the incident in which Tyler was injured. Ergo, the facts of that injury can have no value at all in proving his guilt or innocence. They will, however, certainly affect the jury's view because it will touch their hearts when only their minds should be touched.

'Accordingly,' she concludes, 'no reference to Tyler should be made at any stage in the trial.'

'When you speak of minds and hearts, Ms Shah, I suppose you are talking about that part of the mind which acts logically and that part which responds with emotion.'

'Well, obviously I don't mean the actual organ of the heart.'

'Hmmm. I'm not as sure as you are that different aspects of the mind can be so easily divided up. But I see the logic of your argument.'

And I do. What happened to Tyler Adams, and the damage that a sawn-off shotgun – or any firearm – can do, lies at the root of our legislation prohibiting its possession, but how does it prove whether his father was the one who brought the gun and ammunition into the flat in the beginning or whether, while it was there, his grandmother knew, and had control over it? The pinkness of Mr Collingwood's neck suggests he too is seeing the point. He half rises, ready to reply, but first I must see whether Miss Fontaine has anything to add. In view of the earlier indication, I am expecting the answer 'no', or at most, 'I support Ms Shah's submission'. But when I cock an enquiring head in her direction, she heaves herself to her feet.

'Actually, My Lady, I do have something to say.' Inspiration has arrived late with Miss Fontaine but it is here now. 'In my submission,' she says, 'the "disputed material" is relevant to my client's case, which is that she did not know the canvas bag was in her hall cupboard, but she well knew Tyler was ... is ... a curious and bright child, and that, loving him as she does, she would never knowingly have exposed him to danger. I wish to persuade the jury that the obvious risk the gun and ammunition posed to her beloved grandchild shows her ignorance of the presence of those items in her home and therefore her innocence of the charges against her.'

Very neat, Miss Fontaine. Too neat for Ms Shah, who is left furious and floundering. Too neat for the man in the dock, who growls low in his throat and stares at his mother in a way I don't care for. Miss Fontaine doesn't care for it either. She quickly adds, 'It is Mrs Adams's case that though she doesn't know how the gun and ammunition got into her cupboard, she does not, cannot, believe her son put them there.'

I consider asking if she thinks it was the gun fairy who did it, but she is already hurrying on.

'Be that as it may, I submit that the material is relevant to my case. If Your Ladyship were to exclude the material at the behest of Ms Shah, I would seek to put it back in on behalf of the second defendant.'

Miss Fontaine speaks so vehemently that strands of hair creep from under her wig and her collarette parts company with her shirt. When Ms Shah hisses, 'You never said that before,' Miss Fontaine replies, with endearing honesty, 'I didn't think of it before.'

Miss Shah has been caught out, but she is a quick thinker. Also a realist. And the reality she sees – no doubt neatly numbered in her clear mind – will be something like this:

1. Even if I persuade the judge to stop the Crown telling the jury about Tyler, she won't stop Miss Fontaine doing so if it is relevant and probative to Mrs Adams's case.
2. The judge is very likely to decide it is relevant and probative to Mrs Adams's case because – well, it is.
3. This would make any triumph I have over Collingwood pointless. I should never argue pointlessly – it achieves nothing except to irritate the judge.
4. Is there an alternative argument I can use . . .? Yes, there is.

'My Lady,' she says, 'had Miss Fontaine explained her position to me earlier—'

'I couldn't explain it if I hadn't thought of it,' says Miss Fontaine reasonably.

'. . . had she thought of it earlier, I should not have troubled Your Ladyship with my submission . . .'

I nod.

'. . . but if my submission would otherwise have found favour with Your Ladyship, I would analyse the matter in this way.' And in two neat points (oh, she is a master of the neat point) she lays before me another argument. 'First: it is the duty of the court to achieve a fair trial for both defendants. Second: if a fair trial for my client requires the material to be excluded and a fair trial for Miss Fontaine's client requires the material to be admitted, the solution is to try the two defendants separately.'

Mr Collingwood, who until now has allowed the ladies to scrap unhindered, sits up.

'Oh, I say . . .' He seizes his Archbold and shakes it as if to make it give up the law he needs.

'Try chapter 1, paragraph 279,' says Ms Shah briskly. 'The passage is headed "Separate Trials of Counts Lawfully Joined and of Defendants Lawfully Charged".'

It's not the snappiest of titles but it is apposite. We read through "Power to Order Severance and Application of Principle". We skip "Similar Sexual Offences", ditto "Bad Character of One Defendant" and finally land on "Severance as Between Defendants". The discussion covers six paragraphs – over two pages of tiny print rigid with statute and case law. I stare at the detail. 'Would counsel like a little time to look at all this law?'

'Yes,' says Mr Collingwood.

'No,' says Ms Shah.

'Very well,' say I. 'Mr Collingwood can have time with the law and Ms Shah can have a cup of tea.'

We sit again at midday and, it being Ms Shah's submission, she begins.

'My Lady, I accept that only in exceptional cases should separate trials be ordered for defendants jointly charged with the same offence. That principle is well established. Indeed it is so old that it may be due for review.'

The case law to which she is referring goes back to 1977, which I suppose to Ms Shah seems like ancient history. Not so much to those of us who were there. It was a big year for 'severance'. Three times the Court of Appeal took the opportunity to visit the subject.[*] The law has been settled ever since. I have got used to it.

'Ms Shah, I hope you're not going to ask me to overturn the Court of Appeal's judgements?'

She laughs a little too gaily. She would love me to do just that. Sometimes we'd all like give the court above a gentle kick. But lower

---

[*] Moghal (1977) 65 Cr.App.R. 56 CA; Lake (1977) 64 Cr.App.R. 172 at 175; Josephs and Christie (1977) 65 Cr.App.R. 253 at 255 CA.

courts are bound by precedents set down by higher ones. 'No, My Lady,' she says. 'In fact, I rely upon the Court of Appeal because though it set down the rule, it recognized there might be exceptions . . .' she pauses, 'Your Ladyship will recall the case of Josephs and Christie (1977) 65 Cr.App.R. 253 at 255 CA.'

Her Ladyship doesn't entirely recall but isn't about to say so. 'And you say your client is the exception that proves the rule?'

'I do, My Lady. I respectfully submit that the nature of the injuries to this little boy are such that any jury hearing of them will be hopelessly prejudiced against the defendant.'

'Miss Fontaine doesn't see it that way.'

Ms Shah gives Miss Fontaine a long and contemplative look. 'I cannot account for Miss Fontaine's analysis of her client's best interest. I can only account for my own.'

'I understand your submission. Let's see if Miss Fontaine has anything to say.'

Miss Fontaine rises to her feet, pushes her errant hair back under her wig and her neckwear into something approximating its intended shape. 'A joint trial,' she says, 'puts my client under considerable pressure. She would be much more comfortable if she were tried separately.'

I decode this as meaning that if her son gave her the gun, or she knew he put it there, or even that she knew no one else could have done so, she is in a difficult position. He is, after all, her son. And by his looks, not a man to be tangled with. I sympathize but the law doesn't.

'The law,' I say, 'intends one jury to try all linked matters unless that cannot be done without such prejudice as makes the joint trial unfair. Even if I accept your client is in a difficult position, can you really argue it creates the sort of prejudice that should lead to severance?'

'No,' says Miss Fontaine sadly, 'I suppose not. But . . .' more brightly, 'if Ms Shah is right, your ruling would produce that additional happy outcome.'

I turn to the prosecutor. 'And what do you say, Mr Collingwood?'

Mr Collingwood has by now come to grips with Archbold. 'The Court of Appeal has said there are powerful public reasons why joint offences should be tried jointly.' He lays a hand on chapter 1, paragraph 279 as if drawing strength from it. 'A joint trial saves money and time and witnesses having to give the same distressing evidence twice. Most important, it enables the same jury to hear all the relevant evidence. The Court of Appeal has recognized the risk that if they hear only part of the whole – the part which each defendant might wish them to hear – they may be misled.'

'But what,' I say, 'if a joint trial involves admitting evidence in relation to one defendant where it is inadmissible in relation to another?' It is a coy question since we can all see the answer set out on the page.

'Shall I read out what Archbold says?'

'Please do, Mr Collingwood.'

So he does.

'It is accepted practice that a joint offence can properly be tried jointly even though this will involve inadmissible evidence being given before the jury and the possible prejudice which may result from that . . . in such a case the trial judge should warn the jury that evidence is not admissible as against a particular defendant.'

'Down to me, then?'

'As you say, My Lady, down to you.'

'Very well. I will rise to consider the matter.'

CHAPTER THREE

NOT THAT THIS DECISION needs much consideration. The law is clear and logical. These defendants must be tried jointly, and if evidence is inadmissible against one of them, I must make that plain to the jury. Besides, the point relied on by Miss Fontaine – that no one who loved the child would have exposed him to such a risk – might be thought to benefit Ms Shah's client too. I must, of course, make sure the words of my ruling accurately apply the law to the facts, because if there is a conviction, counsel will pore over my words to see if they can be appealed. If they can, the ruling will be pored over again by three judges in the Court of Appeal (Criminal Division) – known to its friends as the Crim Div. I understand how the Crim Div works, having sat there myself. It is an exhilarating experience, but all brain, no jury. And I know that the hapless Crown Court judges whom the Crim Div say have erred are often those who failed to ensure their rulings showed their logic. Of course, sometimes there is no logic. Or the logic is seriously skewed. But it's the job of a judge to ensure everyone can understand what they have done and why. No problem, just rigorous work, to which I now settle down.

So the actual decision isn't troubling me. But something else is. Miss Fontaine has hinted that her client is being pressured by her son – no, that's putting it too high. She has suggested her client feels pressured by being in the dock with him. They are not the same thing. The first involves active wrongdoing by Michael Adams. The second might be only a mother's natural wish to protect her son. But when I think of the bulk of the man and the fragility of the woman, I am not comfortable. At present, however, there is no complaint against him, and so no judicial decision to be made. The best I can do is keep an eye on things.

Lunch is served in the judges' dining room, and I am pleased to find myself sitting next to S. He has been at the Old Bailey longer than any of us, and is used to casting his cool, analytical mind over our stickier cases – of which I am beginning to think my current trial might, despite initial appearances, be one. Protocol requires I don't talk about work over lunch, which is reserved for entertaining the Sheriff's guests, but my unease about the Adamses has taken me past protocol. S is prodding his fish with a dubious fork. I think I might just run Michaela Adams past him, but the guest on his other side is ahead of me. This man is an archaeologist and it seems he and S have a common interest, for they are suddenly and deeply engrossed in the barrows of Bree-land. This takes them through the main course. I think my chance will come with the pudding but no, by then they are on to the thugs from the south. Finally, 'I had no idea you were so interested in archaeology,' I say crossly. Both S and his neighbour suspend spoons and words. They stare. I know I have said something stupid, and anyway, the moment has passed. It is five minutes to two and chairs are pushed back and the judges must return to work.

As I head towards the stairs, S appears. He is carrying a large book, which he presses into my hands. 'Tolkien,' he says. 'The Barrows of Bree-land. For every action, consider too a compromise.'

Back in court I give my ruling but S's words echo in my mind. So I add the following: 'I will, of course, warn the jury against prejudice. I will tell them they must not be influenced against either defendant by the horror of the events that occurred. But I ask all three of you not to make my task or the jury's harder by . . .' I search for the telling phrase, '. . . by upping the ante. Mr Collingwood, you have no interest in creating prejudice, so please take care to adduce the simple facts as neutrally as possible. Miss Fontaine, you have no interest in fostering discord in the dock, so please find some compromise.'

Ms Shah, appeased, nods. So do the other two.

And now Jim is ushering the newly formed jury panel, twenty-seven of them, into court and chivvying them into something like a line along the far wall. They are a sulky-looking lot. Perhaps they are jaded by trailing round three other courtrooms with three other judges to whom they have already explained that they simply can't take weeks off work, can't find childcare, can't miss the family holiday . . . can't do the jury service for which they have been summonsed. I never understand the reluctance to sit on a jury. Once jurors get into it – certainly at the Old Bailey – they are almost always fascinated and deeply engaged. That comes later, though. First I have to find twelve I can swear in.

Jim climbs up to my Bench and thumps down in front of me a sheet of paper. 'Note,' he says. 'Third on the left. Troublemaker.' I look at the handwriting. It is indeed that of a troublemaker. Fussy. Tight. I scan the content. Mr Gerald Fordham, it seems, is taking his grandson fishing on Friday. In fact, he plans to take his grandson fishing every Friday during the school holidays and is not prepared to disappoint the nine-year-old. So, regretfully, he is unable to serve on a jury. Signed Gerald M. Fordham, Esq.

Well, none of us want to disappoint a child, Mr Fordham, but jury service is one of the very few civic duties (together with paying taxes) that we ask of those in our society, and your grandson would no doubt be proud that you are doing it. If we want to live in a world where the law is enforced, surely the sacrifice of Friday fishing isn't too much to ask. I have a sudden image of Ty Adams. After all, Mr Fordham, you're a lucky man to have a grandson to take anywhere.

I look at the wavering line against the wall. Let's see if we can put some backbone into them. 'Ladies and gentlemen,' I say, 'before we begin the process of calling the names of those who will form the jury, I am going to ask the prosecutor to tell you, in a nutshell, what the case is about. If you find you have any personal connection with the events described, or with anyone involved, please let me know. This is very important, because those who undertake the responsibility of doing justice must be able to approach the task impartially and without any sort of bias.'

John Collingwood gets hastily to his feet. He reads out the names of the defendants and witnesses – the dramatis personae. Then, in a few short sentences, he tells the waiting panel about the little boy whose father and grandmother are in the dock; about the dark cupboard in the flat on the seventh floor of the tower block that stands among half a dozen other blocks on the estate in north-west London; about the oiled cloth and the sawn-off shotgun and the ammunition. And as he does so, the echo of the explosion seems to resonate around us and twenty-seven shocked faces turn to look at those in the dock who – to give them their due – lower their heads. But it is not the defendants I am watching. It is Gerald Fordham. I see he feels it. A little boy ... someone's grandson. Well, let's see if his name is called. And if it is, let's see what happens. I give the jury panel some further instructions. The case is only expected to last two weeks, but if they have any problems, they should approach the Bench and explain them to me.

The clerk rises, takes the pack of name cards and shuffles them with a practised flourish. He pulls one off the top of the pile. Nola Nnadi. A fine-looking Black woman walks forward. She is perhaps in her mid-thirties, well dressed, and when she approaches the Bench to speak to me, articulate. She explains that she works for the government and has arranged cover at work for up to three weeks (sensible woman!) but there is one day when she will need to attend a meeting at 4 p.m. The commitment is an international one and she wonders if we might rise a little early that day. Of course we can.

She takes her seat in the jury-box. If only all jurors were like this. But they are not. The second name called proves it. In answer to the clerk, a man in his thirties, very thin and nervous-looking, scuttles across the courtroom. I think he is going to approach me but he hesitates, seems to think better of it and takes the place next to Ms Nnadi. There is something about The Scuttler that makes me uneasy, but he has raised no difficulty and it's not my job to create one.

At the third and fourth names, two men walk to the jury-box and look around with interest as if they are taking their seats in a theatre. Which in a way they are. More follow without complaint and I am beginning to relax, when number eight causes me to forget about number two. Number eight is in his late twenties. He looks like he might not have washed this morning, and certainly hasn't shaved or combed his hair. He is wearing grubby jeans and a T-shirt with a slogan on it which I try to ignore. If he raises a problem I might find myself inclined to excuse him, but when he approaches me it is only to ask what times he would be expected at court. I tell him we sit from 10.15 to 4.15 each day. He frowns but goes to the jury-box, where he slumps into his appointed seat. He closes his eyes. I, briefly, do the same. They say you can't judge a book by its cover, but who *they* are and whether they know what they are talking about is another matter. No time to worry about number eight now. Nor number two. On we go. Number eleven is a pleasant woman who comes forward to tell me she has a family holiday booked and paid for but she has a clear two weeks before she goes away, and is very happy to serve if I tell her the case will be over by then. A holiday booked and paid for is one of the exceptions that requires me to excuse a juror from jury service, so I look at counsel. They whisper to each other, then Mr Collingwood says they are confident two weeks will provide ample time for the completion of this case.

'Very well,' I say to number eleven. 'You have my assurance. You will be free to go on your family holiday.' And she nods and smiles and takes her place. That leaves only number twelve. The clerk draws the top card from the pack and calls out – wouldn't you know it – Gerald Fordham. I brace myself. It's been a tough morning but I can take it. I don't have to though, because Mr Fordham averts his eyes and walks meekly over to take the last seat in the jury-box. So. An injured grandchild has captured his attention and his care.

One by one the twelve jurors are called on to take the oath or affirmation, promising to bring in true verdicts according to the evidence. And so the stage is set. The players are in their places. The play's the thing. But the ending is not yet written, and who will turn out to be hero and who villain not yet determined. John Collingwood rises to his feet.

Mr Collingwood's opening is a quiet, careful, thoughtful thing and the jurors are all attention. Even juror number eight manages to keep his eyes open, and number two stops shivering and looks about him. The detail will come with the evidence upon which the verdicts will be based. All the prosecutor needs to do at this stage is to set out his stall so we can see what he has to offer.

'Members of the jury,' says Mr Collingwood . . . and this in itself is a milestone, for it recognizes that these twelve people are one unit, joined in their promise to do justice. They are a jury, and that is a thing with a long and honourable history,[*] designed to serve society as the engine of fact-finding in a criminal trial. 'Members of the jury,' he says, 'this is a short and relatively simple case, but a very serious one.'

This morning I might have disagreed with him, but not now.

'You have two defendants in your charge,' he says, 'a mother and son. Each is alleged in Count One to have had in their possession a

---

[*] See *Unlawful Killings*, p.15.

prohibited weapon, namely a sawn-off shotgun. Each is alleged in Count Two to have had in their possession twenty rounds of ammunition.' He looks along the two rows, the twelve faces concentrating on him. Apparently satisfied each is listening, he continues, 'Although they are indicted with the same charges, the Crown says the son's wrongdoing is far greater than that of the mother. It is he, says the Crown, who sourced the gun and ammunition, and he who took these things to his mother's flat and left them under her care. Her wrongdoing is limited to knowingly allowing these things to remain in her home. It may not sound much, but the law regards the provision of a safe house to store dangerous weapons as a serious offence. That is because without such safe houses to keep the weapons out of the hands of police, they couldn't be used or hired out for the commission of dreadful crimes of violence. And, make no mistake, members of the jury, a gun together with its ammunition has no purpose other than the commission of dreadful crime – the infliction of terror and injury and death. And in this case those consequences were truly dreadful.'

He pauses again, pours a glass of water, sips, makes the jury wait. Is he doing exactly what I asked him not to? Is he playing on the jury's emotions? He catches sight of my face and shakes his head. It is an almost imperceptible movement. Can I trust him? We'll see.

'Let me make it clear,' he says, 'the Crown accepts that what happened was neither intended nor foreseen by either defendant – but it could not have happened if they hadn't kept and safeguarded that unlawful weapon. The victim of their wrongdoing was a little boy whom, the Crown again readily accepts, they both loved. Michael Adams's son, Michaela Adams's grandson. Eight-year-old Tyler lived with his grandmother in a flat which, over the next weeks, we will all get to know well. How Tyler . . . everyone calls him Ty . . . came to leave the flat that morning with the gun and ammunition in a canvas bag we shall never know. But the Crown submits that when you have heard all the evidence, you will be sure that is where he got it. He was a bright little boy, curious, as children are. And his curiosity brought him to a dark place. What followed,' Mr Collingwood catches my eye and keeps his voice steady, his words uninflected, 'has left him scarred and blind.'

I picture him, this little boy, opening a cupboard door, reaching up to a shelf, those curious fingers moving things aside until finally they close on the canvas bag. Had he seen it hidden, or did pure mischance lead him to it? Did it open at his touch? Was it heavy when he lifted it? Did his heart quicken with excitement? And when he got to the park? Was the gun already loaded, or did he do that himself? If so, how did he know what to do? Did he aim the gun at something or just point it in the air? And then ... and then the explosion that had shattered the quiet of the morning, and shattered him. When you tear apart skin and flesh, nerves and organs, you can't always put them back together again. Ty will live but he will never be the child he was; never be the person he might have been.

John Collingwood tells the story without drama, but however you look at it, this play is a tragedy. When he has finished, the afternoon is drained and so are the jurors.

'Tomorrow,' I say, 'we will sit at 10.15, and the Crown will call its first witness.'

CHAPTER FOUR

Next morning, at ten past ten, Jim knocks on my door. I am in the act of settling my wig on my head but one look at his face stops me.

'Juror number eight,' he says. Three weighted words.

Juror number eight. No surprise there. 'Does he have a problem?'

'I don't know,' says Jim, 'but we have. He's not here.'

I look at the clock. Not yet quarter past the hour. Jim follows my hopeful glance and shakes his head. 'I told them to be here by ten o'clock. The other eleven are.'

'Maybe he's having travel difficulties.'

'Maybe,' says Jim. 'Maybe not.'

'Let's check where he lives and see if his tube line is disrupted.'

'I have. It isn't,' says Jim.

No arguing with that. And nothing to be done but wait. That's how it is. Once a trial starts, the judge is in the hands of others. Not just one other but dozens of them. Before an Old Bailey judge can start the court day, prison vans must deliver the prisoners, witnesses and counsel must arrive, and so must all twelve jurors. In a trial with, say, seven defendants, that requires up to thirty people to get themselves to my courtroom before I can begin work. Here are some of the usual things that go wrong:

- public transport has broken down/gone on strike/flooded or frozen or been covered with the wrong sort of leaves
- a juror's childcare arrangements have come unstuck because the child has come out in spots/the carer

has come out in spots/the carer's child has come out in spots
- the juror has come out in spots – or any of the gamut of health issues available to the enthusiast
- the juror has a job interview to attend/a funeral to attend/a dental appointment
- heavy traffic is delaying the prison vans. Note: heavy traffic comes as a perpetual surprise in the optimistic world of the prison van.

Here are some of the less usual things:

- the first prison van is stuck in one end of the Blackwall Tunnel because protesters have glued themselves to the other end
- the second prison van, alerted by the dilemma of the first, has taken a different route and got lost in the Limehouse Link
- on leaving prison, one of the defendants was found to have a toothbrush impressively reconstructed to do fatal injury. Note: it was found because, less impressively, he tried to conceal it up his anus
- there are no prison vans, or if there are, no drivers because of staff shortages due to summer colds/winter colds/low morale/a global pandemic
- a juror's water pipe has come adrift and until she can remember where the stopcock is, she cannot remove her hand from where it is holding things together.

But usual or less usual, they all have the same effect. So . . .

'So,' says Jim, 'if he's not here in fifteen minutes, I'll get the jury bailiff to phone him.'

Jim is as good as his word, but if Eric – for so number eight is named – has a phone, he doesn't answer it. He does, however, turn up. At 11.30. Jim reports his arrival. 'Overslept,' he says. The scent of Jim's disgust mixed with his tobacco is heady. And to give Eric his due, when I finally get into court, he is so shamefaced that I downgrade my words from 'bollocking' to 'firm line'. I remind the whole jury of the serious job they are here to do, the cost to the public purse of time wasted, and the fact that every minute we don't sit has to be added on to the end of the trial. 'So please,' I say, 'make sure you set your alarm clocks.' I do not address Eric specifically but the other eleven turn to look at him anyway. I can't help feeling sorry for him. He appears as unkempt as the day before, and even heavier-eyed. But it is, after all, very early days. So I add, 'We'll say no more about it,' – Gerald Fordham looks as if he has a deal more to say about it – 'but in future I expect everyone to be here on time. Now, let's get on with the evidence, shall we?'

'Yes,' says the lady with the family holiday booked and paid for.

'Yes,' says Michael Adams from the dock. And when everyone looks at him he adds, 'Well, my mum needs a verdict here.'

For the record, Michael Adams's mother looks as exhausted as Eric. I should have explained that, unlike most of my defendants, Michaela Adams has not been remanded in custody to await her trial. Somewhere along the long road that has brought her here, she has been granted bail. A kindly magistrate or judge has looked into that haggard face, taken note of the dodgy legs and decided that she is not likely to: (a) abscond; (b) interfere with witnesses; or (c) commit any further crime (if she has committed one at all). These being the three general criteria for withholding the right to bail, she has been granted it.

Mrs Adams would no doubt have found the regime in prison very hard, but I am wondering now how difficult it is for her to get herself and her dodgy legs to court each morning. There's not a lot to be said for being remanded in custody, but it does relieve a defendant of the need to organize her own transport. I have a brief image of her struggling on tubes and buses, and make a mental note to ask if arrangements can be made to help her. Technically this is not part of my responsibility. But if it interferes with her ability to participate in the trial – well, that *is* my responsibility. Sorting out the problems of defendants, jurors and witnesses falls within Judge Territory. And in the territory of every trial, there's always someone who needs a little help. I look around the courtroom, taking in Mrs Adams, her son, and the jurors in seats two and eight and twelve. Which one, I wonder, is going to cause me most grief before I'm done with this case? But I never will be done unless we make a start, so I invite Mr Collingwood to call his first witness.

Miss May – Miss Victoria May – is young, perhaps no more than twenty, and she has been waiting to give her evidence since ten o'clock this morning. The Old Bailey's witness support suite is as good as you will find anywhere and better than most. It comprises a number of rooms staffed by kindly volunteers. It offers space and privacy, tea and sympathy, distraction and a shoulder to cry on. But for a nervous witness, the waiting can still be painful.

When she is finally brought into court, the strain is showing. I try not to look at Eric as she takes the oath in a quavering voice, tries to control her shaking hands. Mr Collingwood takes her through her story. The poor girl had been walking the family dog. They always went to the park because . . . well, she doesn't know why really, they just always did. She had let the dog off the lead. He was well trained and obedient but the explosion had terrified him and he had bolted. She had been calling and searching for perhaps five minutes when she came across the child.

So far she has managed to give her account without weeping, but the memory of the little boy, the blood, the smell of oil and explosive, undoes her.

'Miss May,' I say gently, 'we can pause if you need to, but it won't go away. We will have to come back to it. Would you like a short break, or shall we try to get through it now?'

She takes a sip of water, blows her nose and takes a moment to order her thoughts. Then she straightens her back and says, 'I'd rather get it over with.'

She is thinking of Ty. I guess we all are. This is what Ms Shah was trying to avoid. But how can this story be told without bringing him into it? In the dock, the Adamses have their eyes down and I can make nothing of them. Even so, they each give a very different impression. It's odd how some defendants seem to fill the courtroom simply by their presence, while others barely register in the space they occupy. Michaela Adams is of the latter sort. She seems to be wishing very hard to vanish. How must she feel, hearing Miss May describing Ty in a pool of his own blood? Come to that, how does his father feel?

When Mr Collingwood has finished with Miss May, it is the turn of defence counsel to cross-examine.

'Ms Shah?'

'No questions, My Lady.'

'Miss Fontaine?'

'Nothing, My Lady.'

I stare at the pair of them. If neither defendant is challenging Miss May's evidence, and neither wants any further information from her, why has she been brought to court? There is a sensible rule that if no counsel needs to question a witness, rather than make her come to court, her statement can be read to the jury and its content becomes her evidence. Of course, there are times counsel ask for a witness then find that what she says under oath does not require challenge or elucidation. But whatever has happened in this case, surely Miss May could have been spared the ordeal of reliving what she saw? Should I make a fuss about it? Demand to know who asked for her attendance and why? Or should I trust counsel to have acted properly? I am tempted but . . . but . . . what is to be gained? It is done now, and can't be undone. It has made me jumpy, though. Watchful. In opening, the description of what happened in the park went further than I might have wished. Then a young and distressed witness has been brought to court unnecessarily. What next?

'Next, My Lady,' says Mr Collingwood, 'I propose to deal with the evidence of the paramedics who took Tyler to hospital and the doctors who treated him there, but all counsel have decided it can be done briefly and by agreed facts.'

Well, that's better. Agreed facts are a sensible way of putting unchallenged information before a jury with the minimum of fuss. They are what they say. Counsel can take any material in their possession – statements, hospital records, recordings of 999 calls . . . anything; and by agreement draft simple propositions of fact which all agree are true and accurate. These agreed facts or admissions are just as much evidence as any other in the case – and they have the advantage that the jury knows all parties agree they are correct. I explain all this to the jury, and Mr Collingwood hands out written copies for them. There is one for me too. I read:

Admissions pursuant to Section 10 of the Criminal Justice Act 1967

The following facts are agreed on behalf of the prosecution and defence:

1. A 999 call was made by Miss Victoria May at 07.29.
2. The first paramedic arrived at the scene at 07.43.
3. An ambulance arrived at 07.47.
4. Tyler was given medical treatment at the scene and when he was deemed stable, was taken to hospital, where he arrived at 08.31.
5. The patient was handed over to medical staff at 08.40.

6. Doctors treated Tyler and he was admitted to the children's ward, where he remained for three weeks and four days.
7. During that time he was operated on three times, twice at the hospital and once at a specialist eye hospital.
8. He has received skin grafts for injuries to his face, arms and chest. The wounds are well healed and the grafts successful, but visible scarring remains. The injuries to his eyes have healed but the damage to his sight is thought to be irreparable. He has no sight in his right eye, and only limited residual sight in his left eye.

Mr Collingwood reads all this out in a steady voice. A silence follows. How much more of this does the jury really need to hear? To my unspoken question, Mr Collingwood says, 'There is a last area of evidence relating to the incident in the park and I would like to deal with it now so that tomorrow we can return to court and concentrate on events in the flat.'

And so there is one more piece of evidence in this long day, and it will come from the ballistics expert. He walks to the witness-box, a neat man of quiet authority who takes the oath without referring to the printed card. How many times has he done this? For how many guns and how many mangled bodies? Enough to make me confident he knows his job.

'The weapon,' he tells us, 'is a single-barrelled sawn-off shotgun. Shotguns are designed with a long barrel which generally has no inner wall "rifling".* They are therefore often known as "smoothbore". This one shoots straight-walled cartridges containing "shot" which is made up of numerous small spherical projectiles. It has a semi-automatic repeating action which cycles each time the

---

* Rifling is a series of helical grooves on the internal surface of a firearm's barrel which impart spin to the projectile, improving stability and accuracy.

shotgun is fired, ejecting the spent shell and reloading a fresh one into the chamber.'

Mr Fordham puts his hand in the air. 'I need another notebook,' he says. When Jim has given him what he needs, together with a pencil sharpener, Mr Collingwood takes us back to the evidence.

'You said the shotgun is "sawn-off"?'

The witness nods. 'Yes. Its barrel has been reduced in length.'

'Does that mean it won't work?'

'Not at all. But it does mean it's less accurate.'

'Why would anyone do that to the gun?'

'Perhaps because it makes it easier to hide, and easier to carry without being seen.'

'I see,' says Collingwood. 'And what in law is the status of such a weapon?'

'In this case, what remains of the barrel is so short it is a prohibited firearm. You cannot lawfully possess it.'

Mr Fordham's newly sharpened pencil scratches noisily.

'Now,' says Collingwood, 'the cartridges. I understand twenty of them were found.'

The witness consults his notes. 'That's right. Two had been loaded into the gun, fourteen were found in the canvas bag and another four on a shelf in the hall cupboard of the flat where one of the defendants lived.'

'Were they all the same?'

'No. There was a mixture of 12- and 20-gauge cartridges.'

'Oh dear,' says Mr Fordham as the tip of his pencil snaps.

'The gauge of a firearm,' says the witness, 'refers to the diameter of the barrel, which in turn dictates the size of cartridge which should be used. The diameter of the projectile is called its calibre. The two need to match. In this case the shotgun required 12-gauge shells.'

'Could the 20-gauge shells be used in it?'

'Not without potentially disastrous consequences.' The expert pushes aside his file of notes and looks directly at the jury. 'Although this firearm is designed for 12-gauge shells, it is possible to inadvertently load 20-gauge shells into it. If you do, and if the gun is fired, the shell won't emerge as it should. But it can slide past the chamber and get stuck in the barrel.'

'Is that what happened in this case?'

'I believe so. Two cartridges were loaded, the first a 20-gauge shell, the second a 12-gauge. When the gun was fired, the first shell became lodged right down in the barrel. Either the second had been automatically loaded into the chamber, or possibly the child did it himself, not realizing what had happened to the first. In any event, the 12-gauge cartridge was fired and impacted on the one that was lodged. He was unlucky. It could have just led to the barrel splitting open like a peeled banana, but in this case it led to a significant explosion. In short, it blew up in the boy's face.'

Mr Collingwood sits down and Ms Shah stands up. 'Does it require any great physical strength to load the gun?'

'Not if you know how to do it.'

'So it could have been done by the grandmother or even by the child himself . . .?'

'Or by anyone else who knew how.'

Ms Shah sits. Miss Fontaine stands.

'Anyone including his father . . .?'

'Anyone who knew how.'

Miss Fontaine sits. The two women glare at each other. It's more than enough for today.

CHAPTER FIVE

NEXT MORNING, AT TEN past ten Jim knocks on my door. I am in the act of settling my wig on my head but one look at his face stops me.

'You know that film *Groundhog Day*?' he says.

This time Eric turns up at 11.15.

I have him brought into court without the other eleven. 'Mr Bridges, this can't go on.'

'I don't know what to say . . . I'm really sorry.'

'I'm sure you are, but is this to happen every day?'

He shakes his head helplessly. 'I don't know.'

'What time did you go to bed?'

'Um . . . seven o'clock.'

'Seven in the morning!'

'Seven in the evening. I just didn't sleep right through. Not, that is, until I slept right through the alarm.'

I send Eric back to the indignation of his colleagues, and turn to face the barristers. 'It happens sometimes,' I say. 'Perhaps he has a sleep disorder. Has anyone noticed anything amiss about him?'

'Does Your Ladyship mean apart from his always being late?' says Mr Collingwood.

'He does seem to drift off during the day,' says Miss Fontaine.

'I would suggest a tentative diagnosis of narcolepsy,' says Ms Shah.

'I would suggest it's modern youth, no discipline,' mutters Jim.

That leaves only me, and I say, 'Here's the problem. If he continues to be late I will have to discharge him. We can't have a juror who is only here for part of the day and not entirely here then.'

'Is he in contempt of court?' asks Ms Shah.

'He would be if he were doing less than his best to get here on time. But contemnor or not, I would still have to discharge him, and I don't want to go down to eleven jurors at such an early stage of the trial. Not if I can help it.'

'The law allows it,' says Ms Shah. And it does. But even Ms Shah speaks with less than her usual certitude.

The law says that as long as I start the trial with twelve jurors, I can finish it with as few as nine. Judges have to discharge jurors for all sorts of reasons, including unexpected illness and bereavement. But the system is designed for twelve minds to work on the problems thrown up by a trial, and the fewer the minds, the less desirable it is. There are all sorts of knock-on effects. And if we lose a juror on the third day of trial, who knows where we will be in a week's time.

'I'll give him one more chance,' I say. 'And maybe an alarm clock with a loud ring.'

Today's agenda, now we are finally getting to it, involves officers who attended Michaela Adams's flat. Events in the park had attracted many people from the estate. From them police discovered the identity of the little boy and where he lived. Given the circumstances, police weren't prepared to go there without an armed unit, which included PC Patten. He has been a police officer for over nine years and a firearms officer for nearly four. He drove the armed response car, a Trojan, with a front-seat communications operator and a rear-seat navigator. In the vehicle's safe were three carbine rifles. Each officer wore an armoured vest covering them from shoulder to waist, and each had a holstered Glock handgun and a taser. It seems a lot of firepower to deal with one elderly lady whose legs will barely carry her. But, as PC Patten points out, they had no idea who was in the flat or what guns were there. On arrival, they slung the carbines across their bodies and made their way to the seventh floor, where they followed procedure, shouting that they were armed police and that the occupants should open the door then stand back with hands raised and visible. Their body-worn camera footage is played. We hear the words called out but the door remains closed. We watch the grainy images as two more officers appear with a ram with which they run at the door. It rocks on its hinges then bursts open. As the armed officers walk steadily forward, we see a small, dark hallway and in the shadows, a figure sitting on a stool by the open cupboard.

PC Patten gives us a commentary that explains the footage. One of the unarmed officers restrained Michaela Adams while others with firearms searched the flat. 'I went to the back bedroom,' says the PC, 'and established it was empty. I could see it was used by a young boy.'

'What made you think that?' asks Collingwood.

PC Patten pauses, thinks. 'The posters on the wall, I suppose,' he says. 'The toys. And when I went to the living room I saw framed photographs of a boy. It all matched with what we had been told of the child in the park. I went back to the woman in the hall. She said, "My grandson." I asked if she had any idea how he might have got access to a firearm.'

'And what did she say?'

'She said, "Is he OK?" I asked again if she knew how he could get a firearm. She didn't reply but she looked at the top shelf of the hall cupboard. I got an officer to take her to the sitting room while I searched the cupboard. On the top shelf I found a half-used pot of paint and behind it an oily cloth. I pulled the edge of the cloth aside and saw loose cartridges so I let go of the cloth and left it for forensic examination. I then went to Mrs Adams and arrested her on suspicion of unlawful possession of firearms[*] and I cautioned her.'

---

[*] For the purposes of this legislation, a firearm includes not only a gun but also ammunition.

'The words of the caution, officer?' says Mr Collingwood.

'I told her she was under arrest. I said . . .' he clears his throat and recites the words engrained in him by countless repetition, 'you do not have to say anything but it may harm your defence if you do not mention when questioned something which you later rely on in court. Anything you do say may be given in evidence.'

'And did she say anything?'

PC Patten shakes his head. 'She seemed not to understand so we thought it better not to ask anything further.'

Ms Shah begins her cross-examination by telling the officer she represents Michael Adams and asking him to confirm there was no sign of her client at the address. She quickly establishes there were only two bedrooms, one clearly occupied by the elderly woman, the other by the child.

'There was no other sleeping accommodation?'

'No.'

'None of my client's clothes?'

'No adult male clothing at all.'

'No extra toothbrush?'

'None that I noticed.'

Satisfied that she has distanced Michael Adams from the flat, she sits down and Miss Fontaine stands. There can be no distancing of her client from that cupboard. The best she can do is drum up a little sympathy for the woman in the dock.

'PC Patten, it was obvious that you were dealing with a frail old lady. Did you really have to restrain her?'

'There's a protocol, Ma'am,' he says. And then, with a wry smile, 'If she had a gun and shot one of us, it wouldn't do less damage because she was old.'

'Did she ask about her grandson?'

'On the way to the police station she kept saying, "Is he OK? Is Ty OK?"'

'And what did you tell her?'

'The truth. That I thought he was injured but didn't know how badly.'

'What did she say to that?'

'Nothing. But . . .' he pauses, looks over at the dock, 'in fairness to her I think she was in shock.'

Miss Fontaine, grateful for any mercy, sits down, but the small point in Mrs Adams's favour has an effect in the dock, where her son – perhaps he thinks if the jury blames his mother, they will acquit him – turns to glower at her. She in turn leans forward, hands to her head. I'm not sure what is going on, but I don't like the look of it.

'Jim, would you take the jury out for a moment?' And to the jury, 'Ladies and gentlemen, I won't delay you for long. I just want to raise a short matter with counsel.' When Jim has led the jury out, I turn to counsel.

'Miss Fontaine, your client looks unwell. Would you see if she is all right?'

The barrister scurries to the back of the court, speaks briefly to Michaela Adams and returns to her place. 'My Lady, Mrs Adams is feeling rather faint. I think that hearing the evidence of PC Patten has distressed her.'

I look at the clock. Quarter to one. Eric Bridges has already caused us to lose a chunk of the morning, but this is Mrs Adams's trial. She is entitled to hear the evidence in a state when she can concentrate on it. 'We'll rise now,' I say, 'and see how she is at two o'clock. When we reassemble, I would like a dock officer to sit between the two defendants.'

'Why?' demands Ms Shah.

'Because my judgement requires it,' I say.

CHAPTER SIX

Lunch seems to revive Mrs Adams. At least, when we return to court, she looks brighter. The afternoon's evidence is less stressful, though no less interesting. It involves the results of laboratory tests on items seized during the police investigation. First into the witness-box is the fingermark expert. He is a bullish-looking man who, when he speaks, has an endearingly soft voice.

'The skin on fingers, palms and feet,' he says, 'is made up of non-continuous friction ridges. They can suddenly end or branch into other ridges, creating patterns we call characteristics. These characteristics are individual to each person. Along the ridge edges are tiny pores which emit sweat. When you touch a surface, an impression in sweat is left. We are able to recover those impressions and compare them against the known fingermarks of a suspect. If we find sufficient matching characteristics, identity is established.'

Mr Fordham makes diligent notes while Mr Collingwood asks, 'Did you examine both the gun and recovered cartridges for fingermarks?'

'I did. And also the buckle and leather straps on the canvas bag.'

'Did you recover any marks?'

'Yes, on the buckle, strap and gun we recovered eleven clear prints. On three of the cartridges we recovered partial prints. I was provided with the fingermarks of both defendants and the child. All the marks I recovered matched those of the child.'

'There were none that matched either defendant?'

'There were none at all save for those of the child.'

'Do you have any expert opinion about that?'

The bull's head drops and the soft voice rises. 'I do,' he says. 'Once a fingermark is deposited on a surface it can last for ever unless it is removed either by being accidentally rubbed away or deliberately cleaned off. Prior to the events in the park, that weapon had certainly been handled – not least because it had been sawn-off. If indeed it had come from the hall cupboard, someone had put it there. Given all this, the absence of any other fingermarks suggests strongly that the weapon and cartridges had been wiped clean at some time before the child took them.'

'You think that likely?'

'I do.'

Mr Collingwood sits down and it is Ms Shah's turn. 'Even if you are right, you certainly can't say who cleaned the gun and ammunition.'

'I can't.'

'It could have been years before and in another part of the country.'

'I cannot tell you where, when or by whom it was done.'

Ms Shah sits. Miss Fontaine is about to stand but she hesitates. I know the signs. I've been in this position myself back when I was at the Bar. She has a question to ask but she knows it's dangerous, knows she might get the wrong answer. But Ms Shah has made a point and the two of them have locked horns in this trial, so Miss Fontaine takes a breath and plunges in.

'You say it is likely the gun has been cleaned. But you can't say it definitely was.'

'Nothing is ever certain. But if I said "likely" I was in error. I don't think it's likely.'

Miss Fontaine smiles.

'I think it's highly likely.'

Miss Fontaine stops smiling. She knows – we all know – she has scored an own goal. Ms Shah gives her a look of contempt. Mr Fordham writes at length then snaps shut his notebook.

The next witness is another forensic scientist – this one with an expertise in gunshot residue. Miss Swinson is a large and agricultural-looking lady. I see, as she marches across the courtroom, that her legs are encased in lisle stockings of the type that take me fondly back to my childhood. She affirms, settles herself into the witness-box, studies the jury as might a university teacher eyeing her latest crop of disappointing students, and sets about her task. 'A firearm,' she says, 'is a weapon with a barrel capable of launching one or more projectiles by the rapid expansion of high-pressure gas which in turn is caused by the deflagration of a chemical propellant.'

Mr Fordham nods. This is meat and drink to him. The grandson, once proficient in the art of the rod, will no doubt be moved on to other things. The rest of the jury, however, blinks hard. Mr Collingwood seeks to clarify.

'What do you mean by deflagration?'

It is an innocent question but it causes Miss Swinson to stare as if at an idiot. 'I am speaking,' she says sternly, 'of exothermic combustion.'

Now it is Mr Collingwood's turn to blink hard.

'The physics are fascinating, Miss Swinson,' I say. 'The chemistry also. But do they matter?'

'Matter! Do they matter!'

In the face of her indignation, I retreat. 'Well, naturally they matter in general. What I mean is do they matter to the issue this jury has to decide? Do they matter to the question of who put the weapon in the cupboard and who knew it was there?'

Her indignation wavers as she concedes that on these limited issues, the pure science has no relevance. Over to you, Mr Collingwood.

'What is relevant,' he says, 'is the matter of gunshot residue. Could you . . .'

Miss Swinson certainly can. 'Gunshot residue is a cloud of fine debris expelled from the firearm when it is discharged. It contains components from the ignition of the primer. These may be burned, unburned and partially burned particles which are not visible to the naked eye, being between 1 and 10 microns in diameter.' Even Mr Fordham has difficulty with this one. Miss Swinson takes in the depth of our collective ignorance and says, 'A micron might be best understood as one thousandth of a pinhead. The particles I most commonly find are lead styphnate, barium nitrate and antimony sulphide. I also find copper, brass or nickel from the jacketing material. Other particles may include...'

The jury is lost. So am I – and I've heard it all before. 'Mr Collingwood, it would be helpful if you could control your witness.'

He mutters something. Possibly, 'If only.'

It can be hard for an expert to temper their knowledge and language to the level of the rest of us. But that is their job. 'Perhaps,' I say, 'it would help if Miss Swinson told us what she was tasked to do, and then we can draw out the evidence that answers that task.'

'I was asked,' she says stiffly, 'to examine samples taken from a cupboard shelf. They included swabs of the shelf itself, samples from a cloth and swabs from a paint pot. Also samples taken from inside a canvas bag, together with further cartridges found at the scene. I did not examine the gun itself nor the outside of the canvas bag, because the gun was fired in the park and gunshot residue emitted on that occasion would have skewed the results. My purpose was primarily to establish whether a gun had been stored in the cupboard prior to being taken to the park.'

Mr Collingwood takes up the reins. 'And how would the presence or absence of gunshot residue on the items from the cupboard that you examined help in determining that?'

'When a weapon is fired, a cloud of GSR is discharged. It will be deposited on persons or objects in close proximity.'

'Deposited?'

She gives him a long look, assesses his level of intelligence and settles for, 'What goes up must come down.'

'And what happens to the GSR once it has been deposited on a nearby person or thing?'

'That depends. In theory it will remain where it lands until it is shed, washed off or rubbed away by cleaning or by contact with something else. If the gun had been fired, I would expect it to be contaminated with gunshot residue. If it was then placed in a cupboard, it is likely that some of that residue would contaminate things with which it was in close proximity.'

Mr Collingwood is making progress. 'Very well,' he says, 'now we understand the theory, tell us what – if anything – you found on the items submitted to you by the police.'

She consults her notes. 'There was a great deal of residue on the samples taken from the cloth in the cupboard. This, together with the state of the fabric, suggests the gun had been wrapped in it when still heavily contaminated from a previous firing. There were some particles, but only a few, on the paint pot and on the swabs taken from the shelf. There were particles on each of the cartridges I examined, both those still in the cupboard and those in the bag in the park. There was significant residue in the canvas bag. Since the bag was recovered from the park and the gun was not put back in it after the child fired it, I conclude the contaminant got there at an earlier stage and after an earlier firing.'

'Is there a scenario that would fit these facts?'

'The findings are consistent with the gun being fired on an earlier occasion and, when still contaminated, being wrapped in the cloth together with the cartridges and placed in the canvas bag. They are consistent with the gun, at some stage, being unwrapped and removed so that residue fell onto the shelf and paint pot.'

'One last question. If the gun had been wiped clean – perhaps to remove fingermarks – what . . . ?'

Miss Swinson is way ahead of her counsel. 'If it was placed in the cupboard in a contaminated state then later removed and wiped clean, it would suggest the wiper knew about fingermarks but not about gunshot residue. If he had known, he would have wiped the cupboard and its contents too.'

'He or she,' says Ms Shah from her seat, and I cannot bring myself to reprimand her.

Mr Collingwood sits down. He is mopping his face with a handkerchief. I'm not surprised. Gunshot residue is hard work. It's ten minutes to four and we still have cross-examination to get through, but if the jury's collective face is anything to go by, they need a break. Ms Shah sees it too.

'My Lady, my cross-examination of this witness is important to my case,' she says. 'I can't be expected to deal with it at a time when the jury is too tired to concentrate. They must have a break before we go on. Perhaps we should adjourn till tomorrow?'

Miss Swinson looks aghast. 'But I have to be at another court tomorrow morning. Can't we finish now?'

I don't want to cause difficulties for another judge, another trial, another jury but I can't disagree with Ms Shah. She is entitled to the jury's full attention. So I ask counsel, 'If I give the jury a ten-minute break, and we then deal with cross-examination today, what time will we finish?'

They put their heads together. Ms Shah speaks for them. 'No later than 4.45,' she says.

It's only half an hour beyond our usual time. Not so bad. 'Shall we try to achieve that?'

Eleven jurors nod but not Eric Bridges. 'I can't,' he says. 'I just can't. I have to . . . I must . . .' He stops.

I wait for him to explain but he doesn't. His face is red. He seems on the verge of tears. I have no idea why but I am suddenly concerned about this juror who – like all of them – has his own life to lead beyond the door of the court. I make a decision.

'Mr Collingwood, would you kindly get details from Miss Swinson about her commitment tomorrow, then contact the prosecutor in that case and ask if it is possible for her to give her evidence later in the day. Perhaps another witness can be called before her.' I turn to the jury. 'We will sit at 10.15 tomorrow.' They push back their chairs and gather themselves to leave. As Jim moves to take them out, I murmur something to him.

CHAPTER SEVEN

'Mr Collingwood, Ms Shah, Miss Fontaine, I have asked Jim to bring number eight back into court.'

Three sets of eyebrows rise.

'The time has come to find out what is going on with him.'

'But . . .' says Ms Shah, then can't seem to think how to finish the sentence.

I do it for her. 'But I have a juror who can't sleep at night, can't wake up in the morning and can't stay awake when he gets here. He can't stay an extra thirty minutes when I need him to and he can't tell me why. Don't you think that warrants a few questions?'

They don't argue. I ask them to remain to hear what emerges, but I don't want to press Mr Bridges on personal matters in front of so many people, so everyone else must leave and the public gallery must be cleared. Mr Adams is taken down to the cells. Mrs Adams is sent to wait in the concourse beyond the door of the court. There is no one left in court but me, my clerk and counsel when Jim knocks and re-enters with juror number eight.

I turn to them. 'Mr Bridges, don't look so worried. You're not in any trouble. I just want to see what the problem is and if we can help.'

He twists his hands in an unconscious gesture of despair. Now he stands without the other eleven, I see he is younger than I had thought, perhaps only in his late twenties. The greyness about him looks less like grime, more like lack of good food and rest. It is as if he is tired through to the bone. 'I know I'm letting you all down,' he says, 'but I'm doing my best.'

And suddenly I believe him. 'Shall we take it step by step? Why don't you sit.'

He takes a seat in the jury-box.

'Now maybe you could start by telling me why you have been late every morning.'

His eyes are fixed on the desk in front of him. His lips are firmly closed. I think I'm not going to get an answer, then suddenly he looks up at me. I don't know what he sees but whatever it is, he finds himself able to say, 'Because I don't sleep at night.'

'Why not?'

A shake of the head. 'It's Amy,' he says. 'It's not her fault. She's only three months old. But when she cries it sets the boy off.'

'The boy?'

'My son. Alan. He's two. He's had enough to cope with. We all have. So I sit with Amy and if she cries I pick her up before she can wake her brother.'

'You sit up all night?'

'Until my mum comes, at seven in the morning.' His eyes are heavy with defeat. 'It's been hard since my wife died.'

The baby is only three months old. Did she die in childbirth? Was she already ill? Was there an accident? Whatever happened and whenever it was, the grief must be very raw. This is what happens when you send out juror summonses wholesale. You ask people to come and sort out the lives of others when they are struggling to deal with the living and the dying in their own. Many try to delay their service, but some slip through the net.

'You are coping alone with two young children?'

'My mum helps.'

'But why didn't you tell me in the beginning? I would have excused you.'

'I know,' he says. 'But I was frightened . . .'

'Of me?'

'No,' he says. 'Of course not. I'm frightened that if I can't do what I should... what is expected... they'll take the children away from me. I know jury service is important. You said so. And it's only two weeks. And my mum has arranged to come over every day. But she has to get back to my dad in the evenings.' He pauses. 'That's why I couldn't stay late. I'm sorry about that.'

So here it is. The stark reality of people's lives. And now I must think this through. My job is to ensure the trial is fair to all parties, and to see it to its conclusion. That means a jury must hear all the evidence and make findings of fact. This is best done when twelve jurors work on it together, their collective experience engaged in the job. On the other hand I can go on with fewer. I can certainly discharge this struggling father. And if I make him stay? Half the time he will arrive late or be too distracted or exhausted to concentrate properly.

'Mr Bridges, I wonder if you would be kind enough to wait outside the door for a moment while I discuss this with counsel.'

When he has left, we look at each other, counsel and I. We shake our heads. For the first time all four of us are in agreement. Common humanity dictates what I should do. 'It's hopeless. I must let him go.'

For the last time Jim brings juror number eight back into court. 'Mr Bridges, thank you very much for the efforts you have made to serve, but it is clear to us that at the moment you are not able to do so. You have commitments to others which must take priority. Please understand this is no reflection at all on your ability to cope with your young family. You certainly won't have difficulty with social services over this. It is purely a decision made by me. I am discharging you from this jury.'

He thanks me with tears of relief in his eyes. And he is gone.

So we have lost Eric Bridges, and through him a deal of time. I need to take stock of things. My initial calculation had been three days for the prosecution witnesses, but we are already on the fourth day and still not at the end of the Crown's case. We may then need another two and a half days for the defendants' evidence, and perhaps two more for speeches and summing up. On this basis I won't send the jury out to consider their verdicts until Thursday of the second week. I need their verdicts by close of play on the Friday because I have promised juror number eleven she can go on her holiday (booked and paid for) the following week. At the end of the day I need verdicts on two defendants whose cases involve separate considerations. This is looking very tight. Still, having parted company with Mr Bridges, it should be plain sailing now. Right?

Wrong!

Next morning brings my remaining eleven jurors and a note. From juror number two. In all the excitement over number eight I had quite forgotten number two. Jim lets the note flutter onto my desk like an injured bird. 'This jury,' he says with a grimace.

I read and my heart sinks. Juror number two – The Scuttler – is worried. He has noted three people in the back of the public gallery. I have too. They are the ones I saw at the beginning of the trial. They have come along each day. Juror number two doesn't like the look of them. Well, I'm not sure I do either but they are sitting quietly enough and they can't help their looks. The Scuttler, however, says he believes they must be friends or family of the defendants and therefore may well be violent. This frightens The Scuttler because he lives not far from the park in question. Well, honesty compels him to say he lives two miles away, but in the circumstances he is sure I understand his fears . . . he may be followed home or spotted when he gets there. He is afraid that if he finds the defendants guilty he will be in danger, because he knows the estate where Mrs Adams lives is full of aggressive people.

On the whole, jurors are sensible and rational but . . . And this is the sort of note which I have a duty to disclose to the barristers in the case. So Jim makes copies of the sad little scribble and goes off to find counsel.

If there is a weakness in the jury system, this is it. I have a juror who, having heard only part of the Crown's case and none of the defence's, has already concluded the defendants are violent and likely to have violent associates. And he thinks that such associates would be prepared to use violence on him and are capable of tracing him in order to do so. These things are enough to have defence counsel up in arms. But that isn't all. The Scuttler is frightened of repercussions if he brings in a guilty verdict, which will have Mr Collingwood objecting to him. And to cap it all, the wretched man has been studying the public gallery when he should have been concentrating on the evidence, which worries me. In fact, it all worries me.

Back in court they stare at me as if it's all my fault.

'No,' says Ms Shah.

I haven't asked her anything yet, but when I do the answer will still be no.

'We can't keep him,' she says. 'He clearly isn't impartial.'

'I agree,' says Miss Fontaine.

'I don't know why My Learned Friends are so concerned,' says Mr Collingwood. 'If he is too frightened to convict, it's the Crown who will suffer. He'll have to go.'

It's what they are all saying. But if I lose another juror I will be down to ten – and that before we reach the end of the prosecution case. And if we overrun, there is the risk of losing the lady-with-holiday. I might have to discharge the lot and start all over again at some future date. Even if I manage to retain the rest, a reduced jury makes it more difficult for them to reach verdicts. This is because a jury of twelve allows me to accept a verdict on which at least ten of them agree, with two outliers. My current jury of eleven still requires the agreement of at least ten. But if I lose juror number two and go down to ten, at least nine will have to agree. The lower the numbers and the fewer the permitted dissenters, the more difficult it is for them to reach a verdict. If they can't, the jury is 'hung' and must be discharged, with all the costs to the public and heartache to the participants of a retrial. On the other hand, to continue with a juror who is unable to be true to his oath is worse than useless – because what is the point of a trial which isn't scrupulously fair? He hasn't actually said he can't act in accordance with his jury oath, but . . .

'As good as,' says Ms Shah. And she may be right.

In such situations, there is a procedure. I must have The Scuttler into court and ask him some questions. So, as before, I have the court cleared save for counsel.

'*Groundhog Day*,' says Jim and stumps off to fetch juror number two.

The Scuttler comes in looking miserable and nervous. He pushes a flop of lank, dark hair out of his eyes, where it immediately falls back. I decide briskness is the way forward. 'Now,' I say, waving his note at him, 'what is the problem?'

The hand with which he points to the note is shaking.

'You are worried about people in the public gallery?'

He looks at the empty dock, then at defence counsel. When he speaks his voice is a whine. 'If the barristers are going to tell the defendants what I say, I'm not saying anything.'

Now I'm in a difficult position. I have no power to stop counsel telling their clients what is happening, and even if I could, I wouldn't. Defendants have a right to know what's going on in their trials.

'Let's just see if we can get to the bottom of what is troubling you. Are you willing to tell me if anyone has approached you?'

'No,' he says.

'No, they haven't approached you, or no, you won't tell me?'

He gives it some thought. 'No, they haven't, but I'm worried they will.'

'Has anyone tried to follow you?'

He gives the same answer.

'Would it help if I arranged for the jury to come and go each day by a private door on another side of the building?'

'There's three of them,' he says. 'They could be watching all sides of the building.' And, warming to his theme, 'They could be in telephone contact with each other. They could watch the entrances to tube stations.'

I suppose there is no end to the things 'they' could do, and there's no point in telling him his imagination is running away with him. He is where he is, and it's a dark place. It is possible for a judge who perceives a real threat to arrange for jurors to be brought to and from court by private vehicle, but here there is no measurable threat to justify such a step. Nothing has happened outside the morbid mind of a frightened man. That he is frightened, I have no doubt. The knuckles of his clasped hands are white under the taut skin. He is pale. He is shaking. There is a sheen of sweat across his forehead. I recall that first day and his demeanour then. He was frightened before the case even began.

'I could perhaps screen off the public gallery.'

'What use is that? They've already seen me.'

I try a few other tacks but nothing can ease his torment. So there is only one question left. And it is one I have to ask.

'You have taken an oath to bring in true verdicts in accordance with the evidence. Do you believe you can honestly and without prejudice keep that oath, or is your fear so great that it would affect your mind?'

He is silent for a moment, then he says, 'I'm very frightened.'

It's obvious I'm not going to get past this; obvious he is stuck and we are stuck with him. I turn to counsel. 'Does anyone have any other question they would like asked?'

'Yes,' says Ms Shah. 'Has he spoken to any of the other jurors about his apparent fears?'

'What does she mean "apparent fears"?' says The Scuttler.

But Ms Shah's question is a valid one, because if he has said to others what he has said to us, he may have contaminated their minds too. I reassure him and tell him to answer.

'No,' he says. 'I haven't spoken to the others. I keep myself to myself. I don't want to be any part of this. I just want to go home.'

I send him to wait outside the courtroom while I speak to counsel. All three are on their feet.

'All right,' I say, 'who wants to go first?'

'It doesn't matter who goes first,' says Ms Shah. 'We all think the same. He's got a fixed view that the defendants or at least one of them associates with people who – he has an equally fixed view – are violent. It's illogical. It's ridiculous.'

Illogical, probably. Ridiculous . . . hmmm . . . I sort of see how he has got himself to where he is. Most of us work on a mixture of observation and intuition. Pure logic isn't our natural mode.

'And anyway,' she says, 'he's made it clear he cannot adhere to his oath.'

It would be more correct to say he can't assure me that he *can* adhere to his oath. But essentially, she is right.

'So,' she says, 'it is my submission that he must be discharged from the jury.'

Miss Fontaine and Mr Collingwood nod vigorously.

And my job is to make a decision. To apply the rules. But always to bear in mind that the purpose of the trial is to get 'true verdicts in accordance with the evidence'. So when it comes down to it, whatever the problems of having only ten jurors, they are nothing to the problem of having one who can't act impartially. Either The Scuttler is able to judge this case dispassionately and fairly, or he isn't. And if he isn't, he must go. So it's thank you and goodbye to juror number two.

CHAPTER EIGHT

JIM IS INSTRUCTED TO get The Scuttler out of the building without contact with the remaining ten. I worry they will be upset by the diminution in their ranks but when they file back into court they seem to take it in their stride. They settle down without demur. And now we do make progress. Over the rest of the day and the next, small pieces of evidence slot into place, each adding to the bigger picture. They include the unchallengeable fact that the DNA of both defendants was recovered from swabs taken from the cupboard shelf. But after all, is it surprising if the DNA of someone who lives in or visits the premises is found there? This is the question asked by Ms Shah of the prosecution's DNA expert.

'Not very surprising,' he says.

Ms Shah smiles. Mr Collingwood frowns.

'But,' says the expert, 'it is noteworthy that more of Mr Adams's DNA was found in swabs from that shelf than anywhere else in the flat.'

Mr Collingwood smiles. Ms Shah frowns.

'And exactly how many other swabs from how many other areas in the flat were examined?' Her tone is imperious. Daring him. And in the face of it, he hesitates.

'I would have to check,' he says. 'But I can tell you that nine were taken from other areas of the *cupboard*, and only one of them contained his DNA. That one came from the upper inside of the cupboard door. It is all consistent with him going straight to that shelf.'

'And exactly what conclusion do you draw from that?' asks Ms

Shah, lifting her chin so that her very white collarette gleams dangerously.

'Well . . . er . . . that he accessed the upper shelf.'

'And if he did? There was a half-used pot of paint there, was there not? Do you have a problem with a son helping his mother with a little DIY?'

'My field is DNA,' says the expert cautiously, 'not DIY.'

And with this she must be satisfied.

By mid-afternoon on this first Friday we are through most of the prosecution case. So when one of the remaining jurors sends a note saying she has a headache and would I mind rising a little early, it's not a problem. Mr Collingwood says the last area of his case can be agreed between counsel and put in writing for the jury on Monday morning. Everyone needs a break. So off I go for the weekend, in a happier frame of mind knowing that we can deal with the defence cases and counsels' speeches between Monday morning and Wednesday lunchtime, that I can sum up on Wednesday afternoon, and that I can send the jury out by Thursday morning. Can I, after all, hope for verdicts by the end of the second week?

On Monday morning the jury is back and apparently as eager to get on with things as I am. Only numbers one and eleven seem a little distracted. The former perhaps thinking about her high-powered job, the latter about her holiday. Mr Fordham has asked for another notepad and his pen is poised for action. We're ready to go.

The Crown's case finishes swiftly and Ms Shah gets to her feet. 'I call my client,' she says, and Michael Adams heaves his bulk up and out of the dock and across the courtroom.

He is a curious presence in the witness-box, so broad that he seems to fill it. When I point to the folding seat behind him, he lowers himself onto it gingerly but even sitting, there is an air of muscle and menace about him. Still, he makes an effort to temper his voice to what Ms Shah has no doubt told him is an appropriate

NO EVIL ANGEL . . .

softness. No defence counsel wants the jury to feel intimidated by their client. In the dock his mother sits, head bowed while her son declares he barely visited her.

'I know nothing,' he says, 'about any gun.'

When he has said this in every way Ms Shah can devise, she sits and he must face cross-examination. Miss Fontaine goes first.*

'Never visited the flat?'

'Well, hardly ever.'

'Hardly ever visited your son?'

He hesitates, perhaps trying to decide if it is better to be a bad father or a gun-runner. Finally he settles for, 'I'm a busy man.'

Miss Fontaine appears to reflect. 'Well, you went there often enough to leave your DNA on the cupboard shelf.'

'That had nothing to do with any gun!'

'No? Well, what did it have to do with?'

He looks at his own counsel. 'Do you remember the paint pot?' he says, and of course we all do. 'I touched up the paintwork for my mum. I got the pot from the shelf and put it back there.'

Mr Fordham's eyebrows arch sharply but he dutifully notes the answer.

'I don't suppose you noticed a sawn-off shotgun and a bag of cartridges while you were up there?' says Miss Fontaine.

But sarcasm is wasted on Michael Adams.

Mr Collingwood fares no better. There is one only moment when the defendant seems to lose control and says hotly and unwisely that Ty had no business poking around in cupboards and that taking other people's property can be viewed as theft. But after the startled silence that follows his outburst, he pulls out a handkerchief – nice touch, Ms Shah – and mops at his eyes. 'Poor little boy,' he mutters.

---

* Where there are co-defendants, co-defending counsel cross-examines before the prosecution does.

And 'it's all so terrible'. And 'scarred and blind'. Miss Fontaine makes a face suggestive of vomiting but it is, after all, Michael Adams's son, and the jury looks impressed.

By 3 p.m. the first defendant has completed his evidence. He returns to the dock pretty much unscathed, but he must know his moment of greatest danger may be yet to come when ... if ... his mother gives evidence. What will she be persuaded to say about her own knowledge of the gun, and if it wasn't her, who did or had the opportunity to put it in her cupboard? Ms Shah says she has no other witnesses to call and closes her defence. Over to you, Miss Fontaine. There is a collective hush as we wait to see if she will call her client to give evidence. She rises to her feet, tugs at her vagrant collarette. Opens her mouth. Closes it. Turns, nods to the dock and says, 'Mrs Adams, please come forward to give your evidence.'

So we are to hear from the little woman who has barely raised her eyes throughout the trial. Except, it seems, we aren't – because Mrs Adams doesn't come forward. She doesn't even stand. She just sits, head bowed.

Miss Fontaine tries again. 'I call Mrs Michaela Adams.'

Nothing.

'Miss Fontaine,' I say, 'perhaps you would like to have a word with your client?'

Miss Fontaine hurries to the back of the court and whispers urgently. I cannot see Michaela Adams's reaction because she is overshadowed by the bulk of her son leaning over her in apparent solicitude.

'Miss Fontaine, would it be better if we rose for a short time and you spoke to your client privately?'

Twenty minutes later she sends a message asking if I will sit without the jury and without the co-defendant. I don't know what she wants to tell me, but her desire to speak in the absence of the first defendant suggests it isn't anything to his credit. She must know,

NO EVIL ANGEL . . .

however, I cannot shut out a defendant, particularly one who is about to be bad-mouthed by another. I indicate that I will sit without the jury and without either defendant, but all three counsel must be present and Ms Shah must be free to pass on anything said at this hearing, unless and until I rule otherwise.

I am expecting to hear about intimidation and fear – perhaps a renewed application, even at this stage, for a separate trial. But Miss Fontaine says only that her client seems unwell ... or, no, not unwell, but unable to focus and in distress, and might she have overnight to compose herself and to see if she is more able to cope in the morning.

What a case. We seem to spend more time out of court than in it. But some trials, some juries, some defendants are like this, and still the thing must be got through. There is an hour of court time left and I don't want to waste it, but what can I do? If I demand Miss Fontaine proceed now and she can't get her client into the witness-box, the elderly woman will have lost her chance to explain herself to the jury. Mr Collingwood and Ms Shah will have lost their chance to cross-examine her. And after all, it is understandable that someone in Mrs Adams's position is overwhelmed and needs a little time.

'Tomorrow morning,' I say. 'But you must proceed then, Miss Fontaine, with or without your witness.'

CHAPTER NINE

OVER TEA, G ASKS how the case is going. Ever since she heard about the little old lady with the legs, she has taken an interest. S and H are interested too. So I tell them about the time pressures and the need to finish within two weeks if I am not to lose juror number eleven. G asks if it matters very much if I lose number eleven to her holiday so I tell them about numbers eight and two. I tell them about the events of the day and Mrs Adams's refusal to move when called by her own counsel to go into the witness-box.

H says that if I'm under time pressure, I should be glad if Mrs Adams doesn't give evidence because that will save a good few hours, and I won't have to sum up what she says.

G gives him a hard look and passes him the biscuit barrel in the hope, I suspect, that if his mouth is full, he can't talk.

I shake my head. 'But her counsel was so sure she was going into the witness-box. What do you think is going on?'

S carefully removes the pink sugar from his iced gem and puts both pieces in neat alignment on the table before saying, 'It rather looks like coercive conduct by the son.'

'Never heard of coercive conduct between mother and son,' says H, absent-mindedly eating both pieces of S's deconstructed biscuit.

S watches the swell and gulp of H's throat and finds he has to go. So do I. I need to think about what S has said. I've seen bullying and intimidation between defendants in the dock often enough, but is this something more insidious? Something which might actually go to the root of the offence alleged against Mrs Adams? Is she a victim of controlling or coercive behaviour by her son? And if so, does it . . . should it . . . play any part in this trial?

Coercive control is a phrase increasingly used in the criminal courts. It usually refers to a pattern of behaviour – physical, psychological, emotional or even economic – designed to 'subordinate' another person. It may involve violence, intimidation, domination. It induces dependence. If Michael Adams had used coercive control against his mother, he might have committed a criminal offence contrary to the Serious Crime Act 2015 section 76.* But Michael Adams is not charged with this offence. And even if his mother felt pressured into wrongdoing by her son, under the Serious Crime Act it would provide her with no defence.†

Should I worry about this? Whether I should or not, I do. All evening. And next morning I find there is indeed something to worry about though, as it turns out, it isn't Mrs Adams. We are due to sit at 10.15 and I am not expecting to see Jim until shortly before then, but at 9.30 he knocks on my door. He raises one hand. In it is a note.

'Not another one!'

'I told you this was *Groundhog Day*,' he says.

'Number eleven and the holiday? Oh, why didn't I just excuse her in the beginning?'

'Not number eleven,' says Jim.

'Worse?'

'Much worse. It's number one.'

My lovely sensible number one. Number one, who has caused me no moment of difficulty apart from rising a little early one day . . .

---

* See Appendix O.
† Unless she reasonably believed death or serious injury would follow if she didn't comply, in which case the defence of duress might be available.

well, two days, once for her committee meeting and once for a headache. 'Whatever is the matter with number one?'

'You'd better read the note,' says Jim in a low voice.

So I do.

She must be in her mid-thirties. Certainly not more. She is beautiful and bright. And she is dying.

She has known for some time, she tells us, when I have cleared the court and it is – yet once more – just counsel and me. That is, she has known for some time that she has a brain tumour but it was only in the last few days she was told how hopeless it all was. The headache that made her ask to rise early on Friday had got worse and worse. In the end she had gone to hospital, where she spent the weekend while they did further tests. She thought I should know because . . . well, because . . . She stops.

What do you say? What does anyone say? Apart from how sorry I truly am. It must, of course, be the end of this trial, because I will now be down to nine and I still have juror number eleven to let go at the end of the week. But how can the inconvenience of any retrial be measured against this?

Nothing must be said to make this young woman feel that she is causing us any problems. I will simply discharge her and she isn't to worry about the trial at all. She is to put it right out of her mind and concentrate on . . . well, on what?

But when I say this, she frowns. 'No,' she says. 'I'm not asking to be discharged. I'm not going to keel over in your courtroom. Things won't happen that fast. The tumour is growing and the headaches will get worse, but I'm on different medication now and most of the time I will be OK. At least for a while.'

'But surely . . .' Surely she has things she needs to sort out, to do, because time is . . .

Perhaps she understands what it is I cannot say.

'Look,' she says, as if I am the one in need of comfort, 'I'm going

NO EVIL ANGEL . . .

to die and it will be quite soon, I suppose. There are few things which I can really achieve with the life that is left to me – but one of them is to complete this case. I want to see it through to the end. Please. It matters to me.'

I want to say 'of course', 'anything' – but I must be cautious because I have a job to do and it is to protect the integrity of the trial, so, 'Do you believe you will be able to . . . concentrate?'

'Unless a headache comes on, I am fine. If it does, I promise I will tell you.' She grins. 'Even if I didn't, you would see.'

Ms Shah is nodding. Miss Fontaine is nodding. Mr Collingwood has pulled his handkerchief from his pocket and nods behind it.

Still I hesitate. I don't want to promise what I cannot fulfil. Even were I to let this brave young woman remain and the trial continues, if we don't get verdicts by the end of the week, I may still have to discharge them all. I can't tell her this because nothing must ever be said to any juror that might make them rush things. But if on Friday I lose number eleven to her holiday . . . if I go down to nine . . . I think I will discharge the lot because I just don't believe we should resolve such a serious case in a way so far from ideal.

I don't know whether she reads my thoughts or misreads them, but she says, 'You really should let me, because one of the others has already cancelled a family holiday to see this through too.'

'A family holiday booked and paid for?'

'That's the one,' she says.

CHAPTER TEN

EVERY JURY THROWS UP its problems, but never – not at the Bar nor on the Bench – have I seen one with as many as in this little case. Still, each problem has been dealt with. The system which puts on the shoulders of ordinary – and extraordinary – people the burden of decision . . . which asks them to care enough to give their time and thought, is working.

So I send juror number one back to the others and call for court to assemble. And now there is the question of Mrs Adams. Will she find the courage to get into the witness-box? And if she does, will she tell the truth? What if the truth is that she let her son store the gun there because she did not feel able to say no to him? What if she wiped the gun clean of his prints because . . . well, after all, she is his mother. If these things are the truth, she is guilty according to the law and I will have to sentence her. This is one of the very few offences in the criminal calendar that carries a minimum as well as a maximum sentence. The least sentence I could give her is one of five years' imprisonment. Unless I can find circumstances which make it unjust to do so. And I know how restricted those circumstances are. And I know they don't apply in her case.

When I walk into court I wonder if Mrs Adams will even find the courage to attend court this morning. Or will I have to send police with a warrant to arrest her. But there she is, in the dock.

'Miss Fontaine, are we ready to sit with the jury?'

'We are, My Lady.' She looks flustered, but so would I in her position.

When the jurors are back in their seats she gets to her feet.

'My Lady, I do not intend to call my client.'

'You don't? But yesterday . . .' No. Be quiet. This is none of your business. Your job is simply to apply the formula that applies in this case. And so I say the words I have said so many times before.

'Have you advised your client that the stage has now been reached at which she may give evidence and, if she chooses not to do so, or having been sworn, without good cause refuses to answer any question, the jury may draw such inferences as appear proper from her failure to do so?'

'I have, My Lady.'

'And being aware of that, is it still her decision not to give evidence?'

'It is, My Lady.'

Well, H was right about one thing – this at least will shorten the trial.

And it does. There is no more evidence. The jury hears counsels' speeches and my summing up, and first thing on Thursday morning I send them out to consider their verdicts. They have two full days to think about things, and more if they need it – because juror eleven has already politely confirmed what I was told about the cancelled holiday. When I thanked her for her public-spiritedness, she said, 'Not at all. This is more important.'

No pressure of time, then. But this jury doesn't need very much time. Neither do they need the rule that allows them to return majority verdicts, rather than a verdict upon which they all agree. Just before lunchtime on Friday they send a note saying they have reached unanimous conclusions in respect of both defendants.

There is no moment in the courtroom like this, when the jury returns with verdicts in a serious case. A silence falls over things. The defendants are asked to stand and so is the foreman of the jury. It is – of course it is – juror number one.

'Madam Foreman,' says my clerk, 'in respect of the first defendant, Michael Adams, on Count One unlawful possession of a sawn-off shotgun, do you find him guilty or not guilty?'

Madam Foreman does not hesitate. 'Guilty,' she says.

'And that is the verdict of you all?'

'It is.'

'In respect of Michael Adams on Count Two, unlawful possession of twenty rounds of ammunition, do you find him guilty or not guilty?'

The answer, of course, is 'guilty'.

I must sentence him, but not today. Instead I say to the dock officer, 'Would you take Mr Adams down to the cells, please?' Normally all defendants remain in the dock until all verdicts are given; and I'm not sure why I have done something different now, except that there is something about the faces of the jurors that ... well, we shall see.

But Michael Adams has other ideas. He has planted his feet in the dock. He stares angrily at the jury, at me, and then at his co-defendant. When he speaks his voice is thick with aggression. 'I want to hear the verdicts on my mother.'

'We'll get a message to you.' I nod to the dock officer who – before Adams knows what is happening – has him through the green baize door.

When he has gone and the sound of his anger has ceased to be audible, my clerk turns back to the jury. 'Madam Foreman, in respect of the second defendant, Michaela Adams, on Count One...'

'Not guilty.'

'And in respect of Count Two...'

'Not guilty.'

The ten jurors turn to the dock and nod or smile, knowing, I suppose, that a little boy learning to face a new and dark world will at least have his grandmother with him. And so a jury fulfils its oath. Who knows the logic they applied. But they believe they have done justice – and we have given them the responsibility to make that decision.

I return to my room. I have developed a habit recently and find myself indulging in it yet again. I go to the Old Bailey archives. Could I possibly find anything there like the case I have just tried? I plump for the mid-eighteenth century and sure enough, here is something. And here. And here. Plenty of them over the following centuries. Not mothers and sons but the same pattern of someone under pressure from a person they love or to whom at least they believe they owe the loyalty of family.

Almost all of these trials involve wives who were relying on a law I had forgotten about – though it wasn't actually finally removed from the statute books until 2014.* Before that there was a presumption that every wife who acted wrongfully was under the coercion of her husband, at least when he was present at the time of her offending. You will recall what Dickens's Mr Bumble said about that,[†] but despite the protests of the beadle, the defence was thought to be a proper one (in all cases but murder and treason), and frequently used over centuries, the principle being extended to the coercive effect by fathers on daughters too.

Why did Parliament ever create such a defence in the beginning? The answer may lie in no more than the historical fact that women were treated as chattels of their husbands. But perhaps Parliament

---

* Section 177 of the Anti-social Behaviour, Crime and Policing Act finally abolished what remained of the defence of marital coercion.
† When told the law supposes his wife acts under his direction, he says, 'If the law supposes that . . . the law is a ass – a idiot. If that's the eye of the law, the law is a bachelor; and the worst I wish the law is, that his eye may be opened by experience.'

had also seen that women who offend alone most often committed low-level, non-violent crime, while those who co-defend with a male family member or partner were likely to be involved in more serious and violent offences. It is so in the archives. It is often so in the courts now.

But if this is right, why then did Parliament legislate to remove the defence? It seems to be out of respect for the autonomy of women in more modern society. Well, none of us would be against that. If the reason for the abolition is that women are rational human beings with as much free choice as anyone, that is certainly true. Still, it is possible for free choice to be eroded by endless daily coercion. Women who commit crimes with their male partner often say they offended out of fear of violence or out of 'love'. Are women persuaded to commit crime by the words 'if you love me, you'll do it', just as they used to be persuaded by those words to have sex? Worse, do particular groups of women whose cultural heritage is that of the patriarchy, find themselves expected to submit to the will of their men?

At present, coercive pressure by a man is no defence except in the rare instances when it goes so far as to amount to duress* – and perhaps that is the right approach. Or perhaps it is only the practical one. After all, each of us must take responsibility for our own behaviour. But we might at least recognize that women in relationships with coercive men can love or believe they love those who abuse them, feel loyalty to them, and often are inextricably tied to them by children. They may fear being without a man as much as they fear being with him. These are deep waters, and we have barely begun to navigate them. At some point we are going to have to take a breath and do just that.

---

* See Appendix P.

CONCLUSIONS

IN THIS BOOK, I have sat on the Bench with you, looking at the lives of people as they unfold before us. This includes the lives of barristers and juries, even of judges. But the heart of each story belongs to those who have been torn apart by the events that brought them to this courtroom. It is the thing that makes the criminal court different from any other.

Civil courts concern themselves with broken contracts or broken collarbones, with patents and probate and any sort of situation where two (or more) parties have got themselves into some sort of relationship and wish they hadn't. One side is complaining about the conduct of the other and wants the judge to put things right. It's not like that in a Crown Court. And the differences are vital. Here are two of them. Firstly, in a criminal court, almost always, one of the parties – the prosecutor – has nothing to do with either complainant or defendant. Rather, the prosecution is most often brought in the name of the Crown – in the name of our society, representing all of us. Secondly, whereas in a civil court the decision about who wins or loses is made by the judge, in a Crown Court it is made by you – or at least by people like you, your family, your friends and neighbours – by anyone who has cared enough about our society to have put their name on the electoral register, and so has become a juror.

So how have we, as a society, decided what behaviour should amount to a crime? I suppose at bottom it is behaviour that we have resolved to stop, or at least signal our collective disapproval of. After all, the whole purpose of the criminal law is to keep us safe, to allow us all to live peacefully and without fear.

And if the criminal law is about 'us all', surely that law should treat 'us all' the same. Don't we believe we all have an equal right to be heard and judged, whether we are male, female or anything else – whatever our colour, whatever our creed; whatever? It's what we would expect of any decent system of justice. But do we get it? If you've stuck with me this far, you may now be seriously wondering whether we do all have equal access to the law and the courts. And whether when we get there, we are all treated equally.

There is a lot to be written about how different groups fare in the criminal justice system, but you can't cover everything in one small book, and in this one I have chosen to focus on women and girls. I haven't ventured into the prison system, about which many people know more than me. I have concentrated on females in the trial process, on the Susans and Lesleys, the Mercys and Michaelas, the women at the Bar and in the jury-box – on all those in the courtroom and the corridors that lead there.

They are all caught up in a 'system', and women often suffer under systems. Just look at the Bar. The women barristers we need to succeed and to become the next generation of judges must come to court every morning as pristine and well prepared as the men, even if they have been up all night with a sick child or a distraught teenager. They have to be as sharp at 2 p.m. as anyone else, even if they have spent their lunch hour on the phone to childcarers, schools or doctors' surgeries. Of course, these days many men play their part in family responsibilities, but every year able women leave the Bar to have children, and find it very difficult to return. I see many jurors, women and men too, who struggle to balance their commitment to a trial with the commitments they have in their personal lives.

What about the women defendants? A comparison of statistics between cases in the archives and those in today's courts makes fascinating reading. I recognize that misinterpretation of statistics is all too easy, but some general points leap out. Between 1674 and 1913 the Old Bailey archives record 43,235 female defendants compared to 161,475 males. The men have roughly 79 per cent of the dock space. The Ministry of Justice's published figures for the year 2020–21 show that 79 per cent of those prosecuted for criminal offences were male. No doubt there have been, at various times, profound population changes, but the percentage suggests that it isn't now and never has been women who committed the most crime. Moreover, statistics issued by the Ministry of Justice show that the crimes for which women are prosecuted are overall less serious, less violent.

The fact that women comprise more than 50 per cent of the overall population but only 4 per cent of the prison population makes the point. But it risks missing another point. Just because women as a whole cause less of a problem than men, does not mean that any individual female defendant is less important. Each must be our concern, just as any defendant must be. The story of each is as important as any other. It can be particularly revealing to examine the background of female defendants, and the pressures that led them to offend (if they have). In 'No Evil Angel' I have looked at how women can be coerced into crime by men. In 'The Way to Dusty Death', at how feelings of family responsibility can draw girls into the most serious of wrongdoing. How many other stories are there of women who offend because they are struggling to support children, to care for parents, to make ends meet when there just isn't enough in a threadbare purse to do it? How often are those women trying to deal at the same time with their own health problems – physical and mental? And when will we recognize that the line between those two can be wafer-thin? Of course, none of that is a defence to committing crime. It isn't for me to say it should be, and I don't. But I do say what a pity it is that we concern ourselves with punishing and reforming and rehabilitating women offenders when, if the same thought and care had been given to their problems beforehand, they might never have offended at all. What Mercy Marsh endured cannot justify her killing her husband, but at least we can question how society tolerated one of its number living through twenty years of daily abuse before things came to a head.

And finally, what about the women and girls who are victims of crime? True it is they are fewer in recorded number than men, but they tend to be victims of dreadful offences, including sexual and domestic violence and murder at the hands of a partner or ex-partner. And we can be sure that the available figures fall far short of the real numbers, because so many female victims never speak of what has happened to them. With our new understanding of the problems they face, we recognize that many need encouragement and support to make their complaint and then to stick with a system which can be heart-wrenchingly slow. We need to find a better way to balance the rights of the victim with those of the defendant. As I have described in 'The Evil That Men Do', there are many ways in which we can help a witness get through the ordeal of giving evidence, but the key is to get it done speedily without sacrificing fairness. We are constantly trying to adapt our courtrooms to this end – with curtains and cameras and pre-recorded evidence. And we are getting better at it. But the improvement is creeping. We need to be able to measure our progress in results. Perhaps money spent on purpose-built courts with purpose-trained judges would amply repay the investment.

And here is the old drum that I keep beating. Rather than prosecute and punish men who offend against women, shouldn't our first aim be to stop them offending? Of course, and mercifully, most men abhor violence as much as women do. Most are right-thinking and responsible. But most is a long way from all. How are we to reduce the number of women victims of physical, sexual and emotional violence? As with any other problem, we need to understand it before we can solve it. There are many causes of nature and of nurture and of lifestyle that lead to violence.

There is, of course, no easy solution. If there were, we wouldn't be still seeking it. But one place to start – as ever – is with our children. We want girls to grow up knowing that they have rights, including those over their own bodies. We want them to understand that if those rights are interfered with, they can safely complain, can expect to be heard, should never be so dismayed by the system that they drop out of it. But don't we equally want our boys to grow up knowing these things? Isn't it as important – perhaps more important – that they should all understand this than that they should understand quadratic equations and the parts of French speech? And for those who are at risk of being violent, or those teenagers and adults who already find themselves along this path, is it really beyond us to help them identify themselves and to find ways to control themselves? And if this is right, doesn't it need to be done long before they put a woman in the witness-box or in the dock or in a coffin?

So what is the answer to the question I asked at the very beginning of this book? Are we achieving justice for all? Clearly not. Are we even coming closer to it than we were in the past? The most one can say is, perhaps. But here is the good news. I wouldn't be writing and no one would be reading a book like this unless we had got to the point where we recognized the faults and cared about making them better. And caring is the first step to doing just that. Now we have the problems firmly in our sights, can't we work together to sort them out? It needs funding at a time when funds are short, but still . . . whatever the financial cost, it can't compare with the human cost of leaving things as they are.

Appendices

APPENDIX A

History of Newgate Prison

If, around 1184, you had stood at the northern end of the little road we call Old Bailey, you would have found yourself near the latest-built of the city gates, New Gate. Behind you was a city struggling to come to terms with an influx of people including soldiers returning from wars abroad. They brought with them a flood of crime, and Henry II was having none of it. He hoped to deter bad behaviour by creating a whole lot of new crimes but the result was only to create a whole lot of new criminals. Soon he had filled up the cell-space in the Tower of London and other gaols. His eye fell on New Gate, with its huge flanking towers, each with a guard room and guards who could usefully watch his prisoners. It worked so well that soon a few more cells were built adjacent to the gate, and then more and more. Within a hundred and fifty years, the footprint of what was to become Newgate Prison had been laid out. It was to last for seven hundred years, and those who suffered and died within its walls are beyond count. It was technically a gaol rather than a prison, holding first those awaiting trial, and later many debtors too. It wasn't designed to hold convicted prisoners because by and large they were either acquitted or punished in other ways . . . pilloried or put in stocks, branded or fined or (later) transported or hanged (disembowelling, quartering, their heads boiled and displayed around the city being optional extras).

The gaol was the responsibility of the Sheriffs of London, who contracted out its running to a Keeper, who in turn employed Turnkeys. It was a private enterprise and the Keeper aimed to make a profit. Everything was charged for. So a prisoner with means could buy a better cell, bedding, alcohol, food, light, water. Gentleman prisoners and debtors could make themselves pretty comfortable. On the Master's Side you might enjoy evening concerts or discussions about literature or philosophy. Sir Thomas Malory completed *Le Morte d'Arthur* there. Christopher

Marlowe, Ben Jonson and Daniel Defoe all made stays there. But the place marked even these men – Malory wrote of death, Marlowe of Hell, Jonson of men and women burned to death. It was Defoe who wrote of the real place – of Moll Flanders and life barely lived on the Common's Side. Unless you could pay for more, your daily lot was half a loaf of bread and a cup of water, and what the charities might give of anything else.

There was gaming and whoring. There were mock trials and organized punishments and unorganized violence. There was rape and murder.

Women occupied large communal cells, sleeping on boards that folded back during the day. Their children came in with them. Their babies were born there. Among the things a male prisoner could purchase was access to the female cells and gin to secure compliance in the night. Among the things a woman might want was the chance to become pregnant, because she could then plead her belly and gain herself another year of life.

People died there in their thousands – from starvation, from gaol fever, from being pressed to death when they refused to enter a plea at trial, from murder – and of course many were sentenced to hanging. Innumerable dead were buried there under passages or behind walls. Over the centuries shocked citizens, from Dick Whittington to Elizabeth Fry, tried to improve the lot of its inmates, but it wasn't really until Charles Dickens brought its shame to public attention that the matter was taken seriously. And it wasn't until 1902 that the building, which had recovered after the Great Fire and been rebuilt before and after the Gordon Riots, was finally razed to the ground. Out of its ashes rose the Central Criminal Court, moving from its historical site further down Old Bailey. Its doors opened in 1907. In the judges' dining room, in the part of the building added between 1968 and 1972, is one of the door knockers from the nineteenth-century prison, and one of its historical key cupboards. Lest we forget.

APPENDIX B

1. Generally the jury is asked to return a verdict of either 'guilty' or 'not guilty'. In most cases it is for the prosecution to make the jury sure that the defendant did the wrongful act (or omission) *and* at that time had any required wrongful state of mind. If the prosecution can make the jury sure of this, the defendant is guilty. If the jurors are not sure, their verdict is not guilty. However, there are situations where juries are asked to return other sorts of verdicts.

2. Where the defence is 'not guilty by reason of insanity', the issue for the jury is whether:
   (a) at the time he/she did the wrongful act, the defendant was suffering from a disease of the mind which gave rise to a defect of reason such that
   (b) he/she either did not know the nature and quality of his/her act, or
   (c) did not know that it was wrong legally or by the standards of ordinary, reasonable people.

   If so, he/she is entitled to be found 'not guilty by reason of insanity'. However, everyone is presumed to be sane and to possess a sufficient degree of reason to be responsible for his/her crimes unless the contrary is proved. It is for the defence to prove his/her assertion on the balance of probabilities (i.e. that it is more likely than not).

3. Another issue that can arise is whether a defendant is fit to enter a plea or to stand trial.
   (a) The judge alone decides this, considering the defendant's ability to understand the charges and the plea, to challenge jurors, to instruct legal representatives, to understand the course of the trial and to give evidence if he/she chooses.

(b) If he/she is found fit, the trial proceeds in the usual way. If he/she is found unfit, a different procedure follows.
   (i) The court must ensure the defendant is appropriately represented.
   (ii) Jurors are empanelled. They do not have to make any finding about the defendant's state of mind, but must decide if they are satisfied the defendant did the act/made the omission charged. If they are not sure, he/she is not guilty. If they are sure, they make a finding that he/she did the act/made the omission.

For more detail, see the Criminal Procedure (Insanity) Act 1964 and Domestic Violence, Crime and Victims Act 2004.

APPENDIX C

Generally it is for the prosecution to prove a defendant is guilty, not for the defendant to prove his innocence. To succeed, the prosecution must make the jury sure of guilt. Nothing less will do. Juries are told that if, after considering all of the evidence, they are sure the defendant is guilty, their verdict must be 'guilty'. If they are not sure the defendant is guilty, their verdict must be 'not guilty'.

Occasionally the burden of proving an issue in the case falls on the defendant. He/she succeeds if they satisfy the jury their case is more likely than not.

In our jurisdiction in England and Wales, we have no equivalent of the Scottish 'not proven'. It is likely though not certain that this verdict will be removed as an option for Scottish juries (see The Victims, Witnesses and Justice Reform [Scotland] Bill).

APPENDIX D

The Youth Justice and Criminal Evidence Act (YJCEA) 1999 identifies eligible vulnerable witnesses:

- (section 16) those under eighteen, those suffering from mental disorder, having a significant impairment of intelligence and social functioning, or a physical disability or disorder, and whose quality of evidence is thereby likely to be diminished
- (section 17) victims in allegations of sexual offences or offences under sections 1 or 2 of the Modern Slavery Act 2015, or domestic abuse, or concerned in a violent offence, or any other witness where the court is satisfied that the quality of their evidence is likely to be diminished by reason of fear or distress in connection with testifying

Special measures available may include screens (section 23), live link (section 24), giving evidence in private (section 25), removal of wigs and gowns by judges and barristers (section 26), pre-recorded video interview (section 27), pre-trial recorded cross-examination (section 28), intermediaries (section 29) and aids to communication (section 30).

In addition, an unrepresented defendant is prohibited from personally cross-examining:

- the victim in a sexual offence (section 34)
- certain 'protected witnesses', child victims and other child witnesses (section 35)

The court may prohibit:

- an unrepresented defendant from personally cross-examining others, e.g. intimidated witnesses in domestic abuse cases (section 36)
- publication of any matter during the witness's lifetime if it is likely to lead members of the public to identify the individual as a witness in criminal proceedings (section 46)

For fuller detail see the Act itself. By using the www.legislation.gov.uk website you can see any amendments to Acts that have taken place since their original iteration.

APPENDIX E

Youth Justice and Criminal Evidence Act 1999 section 27: Video recorded evidence in chief

1. A special measures direction may provide for a video recording of an interview of the witness to be admitted as evidence-in-chief of the witness.

2. [Unless] ... the court is of the opinion, having regard to all the circumstances of the case, that in the interests of justice the recording, or that part of it, should not be so admitted.

3. In considering ... subsection (2) ... the court must consider whether any prejudice to the accused which might result from that part being so admitted is outweighed by the desirability of showing the whole, or substantially the whole, of the recorded interview.

4. *For fuller detail see the Act itself. By using the www.legislation.gov.uk website you can see any amendments to Acts that have taken place since their original iteration.*

APPENDIX F

Youth Justice and Criminal Evidence Act 1999 section 34: Complainants in proceedings for sexual offences

1. No person charged with a sexual offence may in any criminal proceedings cross-examine in person a witness who is the complainant, either –
   (a) in connection with that offence, or
   (b) in connection with any other offence (of whatever nature) with which that person is charged in the proceedings.

Youth Justice and Criminal Evidence Act 1999 section 35: Child complainants and other child witnesses

1. No person charged with an offence to which this section applies may in any criminal proceedings cross-examine in person a protected witness, either –
   (a) in connection with that offence, or
   (b) in connection with any other offence (of whatever nature) with which that person is charged in the proceedings.

For fuller detail see the Act itself.

APPENDIX G

Ground Rules Hearings (see Criminal Procedure Rules 2020 and Criminal Practice Directions 2023) take place before the trial itself, and allow the judge to make directions to ensure that both vulnerable witnesses and defendants are treated fairly and can participate effectively, giving of their best.

At the hearing the judge considers with the advocates and any intermediary or other professionals what special measures and other reasonable adjustments are needed. These may include adjustment of language and complexity of sentence structure, the number and length of breaks, where defendants sit, whether judge and Bar should remove robes, etc.

Intermediaries are self-employed communication specialists with experience in, e.g. speech and language therapy, social work or teaching. They should be appropriately trained, then registered with the National Crime Agency and approved by the Ministry of Justice. They help witnesses and defendants who need help communicating with police and the court because of their age, or a disability or disorder, mental or physical.

For detail about how this system works see The Advocate's Gateway: Ground Rules Hearings and fair treatment of vulnerable people in court.

APPENDIX H

Youth Justice and Criminal Evidence Act 1999 section 28: Video recorded cross-examination or re-examination

1. Where a special measures direction provides for a video recording to be admitted under section 27* as evidence-in-chief of the witness, the direction may also provide –
   (a) for any cross-examination of the witness, and any re-examination, to be recorded by means of a video recording; and
   (b) for such a recording to be admitted ... as evidence of the witness's ... cross-examination or ... re-examination ...

2. Such a recording must be made in the presence of ...
   (a) the judge ... and legal representatives acting in the proceedings [must be] able to see and hear the examination of the witness and to communicate with the persons in whose presence the recording is being made, and
   (b) the accused [must be] able to see and hear any such examination and to communicate with any legal representative acting for him.

For fuller detail see the Act itself.

---

* See Appendix E.

APPENDIX I

Anonymity

The fundamental principle in our system of criminal justice is that the defendant must receive a fair trial. The importance of open justice and a defendant's entitlement to be confronted by and cross-examine their accuser in court is also well established.

If potential witnesses fear to give evidence or fear that revelation of their identity to the defendant or their associates, or to the wider public, will put them or their family or friends at risk of serious harm, various options are available.

Set out below are some relevant measures that can be taken to help.

1. Special measures under YJCEA 1999 (see appendices D, E, F, H above).

2. Reporting restrictions for those under eighteen include the following:
   - Section 49 of the Children and Young Persons Act 1933 provides for automatic reporting restrictions for those under eighteen who are defendants or witnesses in criminal proceedings in or on appeal from lower courts. Such restrictions lapse once the person in question reaches the age of eighteen. The provisions are complex. For more detail, including the rare occasions when the prohibition can be dispensed with, see the Act itself.
   - Section 44 of YJCEA 1999 sets out the circumstances where an investigation has begun in respect of an alleged offence. No matter relating to any person involved in the offence shall, while he is under the age of eighteen, be included in any publication if it is likely to lead members of the public to identify him as a person involved in the offence. This includes a person by whom the offence is alleged to have been committed, or a person against or in respect of whom the offence is alleged to have been committed, or a person

who is alleged to have been a witness to the commission of the offence. The prohibited information includes name, address, identity of educational establishment or place of work attended, and any still or moving picture of him. The court may dispense with the restrictions if satisfied that it is necessary in the interests of justice to do so after having regard to the welfare of that person. Once a defendant reaches the age of eighteen the restriction ceases.

- Section 45 YJCEA 1999 provides for discretionary reporting restrictions for those under eighteen who are defendants or witnesses in other criminal proceedings. Again, such restrictions lapse once the person in question reaches the age of eighteen. The provisions are complex. For more detail, including the rare occasions when the prohibition can be dispensed with, see the Act itself.
- Section 45A YJCEA 1999 provides for discretionary lifelong reporting restrictions for victims and witnesses who are under eighteen when the proceedings commence. The court must be satisfied that,
  (a) the quality of any evidence given by the person, or
  (b) the level of cooperation given by the person to any party to the proceedings in connection with that party's preparation of its case is likely to be diminished by reason of fear or distress on the part of the person in connection with being identified by members of the public as a person concerned in the proceedings.
- Section 46 YJCEA 1999 provides a similar (discretionary, lifelong) power to section 45A in respect of adult victims and witnesses.
- The Sexual Offences (Amendment) Act 1992 creates an automatic prohibition on the publication of details that identify a victim of rape or other serious sexual offences, and there is a similar provision in respect of victims of female genital mutilation under schedule 1 to the Female Genital Mutilation Act 2003.
- There are also automatic reporting restrictions on certain pre-trial hearings (see the Contempt of Court, Reporting Restrictions and

Restriction on Public Access to Hearings legal guidance). However, such restrictions generally only last until the conclusion of the trial(s).

3. Restricting public access: some relevant aspects are set out here –
   - There is statutory restriction on who may be present in a Youth Court (section 47(2) CYPA 1933).
   - Section 37(1) CYPA 1933 gives a power to exclude the public (not bona fide representatives of the media) when a child or young person gives evidence in certain proceedings.
   - There is common law power to restrict public access to any courtroom and to hear part or all of a trial in private if it is necessary to avoid the administration of justice being frustrated or rendered impractical.
   - Section 25 YJCEA 1999 provides a special measure for exclusion from the court during the giving of a witness's evidence of specific persons though not the accused, legal representatives acting in the case, or any interpreter or other person appointed to assist the witness. One named person may represent the media. This provision is used where it appears to the court there are reasonable grounds for believing that any person other than the accused has sought, or will seek, to intimidate the witness in connection with testifying in the proceedings.

4. Withholding the name and address of a witness from the public: courts have a common law power to withhold the name of a witness or other information about them, such as an address, from the public.

5. Other forms of witness protection: in rare and serious cases the risk of serious personal harm to a witness as a result of their involvement in giving evidence, etc., may be such that they need to relocate to another part of the country or even change their identity. Serious Organised Crime and Police Act 2005 Chapter 4 of Part 2.

6. Witness Anonymity Order (Coroners and Justice Act 2009 section 86).

The order involves appropriate measures to ensure that the identity of a witness is not disclosed in, or in connection with, the proceedings. It may include withholding the witness's name and the use of a pseudonym, screening or voice modification, or that they may not be asked questions which might identify them.

Section 88 of the 2009 Act sets out Conditions A to C, all of which must be met before the court may make a Witness Anonymity Order:

- Condition A: the proposed order is necessary –
  (a) having regard to any reasonable fear of the witness, to protect the safety of the witness or another person or to prevent any serious damage to property, or
  (b) in order to prevent real harm to the public interest (whether affecting the carrying on of any activities in the public interest or the safety of a person involved in carrying on such activities, or otherwise).
- Condition B: having regard to all the circumstances, the effect of the proposed order would be consistent with the defendant receiving a fair trial.
- Condition C: the importance of the witness's testimony is such that in the interests of justice the witness ought to testify and –
  (a) the witness would not testify if the proposed order were not made, or
  (b) there would be real harm to the public interest if the witness were to testify without the proposed order being made.

A witness anonymity order is a measure of last resort and there are many complicated hoops to be jumped through before one can be granted. There are strict conditions and procedures designed to protect the witness and to ensure the defendant is not prejudiced. If you are interested in this detail, there is a useful article issued online by the CPS.*

---

* At: www.cps.gov.uk/legal-guidance/witness-protection-and-anonymity

APPENDICES

It is worth noting the ever-increasing movement towards greater transparency most notably in the Family Courts (see changes in the The Family Procedures Rules in effect from 27th January 2025). It remains to be seen what, if any, effect this will have on Criminal Courts.

APPENDIX J

Restriction on evidence or questions about a complainant's sexual history, YJCEA 1999 section 41. Part of it is set out below:

(1) If at a trial a person is charged with a sexual offence, then, except with the leave of the court –
   (a) no evidence may be adduced, and
   (b) no question may be asked in cross-examination by or on behalf of any accused at the trial, about any sexual behaviour of the complainant.

(2) The court may give leave ... only on an application made by or on behalf of an accused, and may not give such leave unless it is satisfied –
   (a) that subsection (3) or (5) applies, and
   (b) that a refusal of leave might have the result of rendering unsafe a conclusion of the jury or ... the court on any relevant issue in the case.

(3) This subsection applies if the evidence or question relates to a relevant issue in the case and either –
   (a) that issue is not an issue of consent, or
   (b) it is an issue of consent and the sexual behaviour of the complainant to which the evidence or question relates is alleged to have taken place at or about the same time as the event which is the subject matter of the charge against the accused, or
   (c) it is an issue of consent and the sexual behaviour of the complainant to which the evidence or question relates is alleged to have been, in any respect, so similar –
      (i) to any sexual behaviour of the complainant which (according to evidence adduced or to be adduced by or on behalf

>   of the accused) took place as part of the event which is the
>   subject matter of the charge against the accused, or
> (ii) to any other sexual behaviour of the complainant which
>   (according to such evidence) took place at or about the same
>   time as that event, that the similarity cannot reasonably be
>   explained as a coincidence.

(4) For the purposes of subsection (3) no evidence or question shall be regarded as relating to a relevant issue in the case if it appears to the court to be reasonable to assume that the purpose (or main purpose) for which it would be adduced or asked is to establish or elicit material for impugning the credibility of the complainant as a witness.

APPENDIX K

Judges sitting on cases of sexual offences are likely, these days, to warn the jury against making assumptions about these and other things. The warning against these assumptions applies to all complainants, but can be particularly acute where the complainant is a woman or girl. What follows is the kind of thing I might say to a jury (For more detail see the Crown Court Bench Book.)

- Late complaint: there is no typical rape, typical rapist or typical person that is raped. Rape can take place in almost any circumstance, between all different kinds of people. There is no typical response to rape. People can react in many different ways. These reactions may not be what you would expect. You must make sure you do not let any false assumptions or stereotypes about rape affect your verdict but make your decision in this case based only on the evidence you hear from the witnesses and the law as I explain that to you.
- Delay in complaining: you must not assume that because there was a delay in making a complaint, it is untrue. Any more than an immediate complaint must be true. Different people react in different ways. Some may tell someone about it straight away. Others may not feel able to do so out of shame, shock, confusion, fear of getting into trouble or of not being believed, or of causing problems for other people.
- If a witness makes a complaint for the first time when giving evidence, or gives an account inconsistent with an earlier one, this doesn't necessarily mean she is inventing her evidence. Sometimes a memory can be triggered as the witness answers detailed questions. A shocking or upsetting experience can affect the memory and the ability to take things in and recall them later. Sometimes going over an event many times afterwards can make a memory

clearer. But sometimes people try to avoid thinking about an event, and have difficulty recalling it at all.
- Displays of emotion/distress or lack of them at the time of first complaint: bear in mind there is no 'normal' reaction to sexual assault. Some people show emotion, others don't. It is possible for someone to put on an act if they choose. You should avoid making an assessment based on any preconceived idea you may have about how you think someone should behave in this situation.
- Display of emotion/distress or lack of it in any interview with police played to the jury and/or when giving evidence: you should not assume that the way a witness gave evidence indicates if the allegation is true. Witnesses react to giving evidence about such allegations in different ways. The presence or absence of emotion or distress when giving evidence is not a good indication of whether the person is telling the truth or not.
- Wearing revealing clothes: do not assume that the way the complainant was dressed means she was looking to have sex or willing to have sex if the opportunity came up. Just because someone wears revealing clothing does not mean that. Nor does it mean someone seeing and interacting with the complainant could reasonably believe she would consent to sex simply because of the way she was dressed.
- Intoxication (drink and/or drugs): do not assume that because a complainant was very drunk it means he/she was looking for, or willing to have, sex. Just because someone is drunk does not mean that. Nor does it mean someone seeing and interacting with that person could reasonably believe that person would consent to sex.
- Previous sexual activity between the complainant and the defendant: just because they had consensual sex previously, does not mean the complainant must have consented on this occasion. Nor does it necessarily mean the defendant had grounds for reasonably believing there was consent on this occasion. A person may want to have sex with someone on one occasion, but not on another. You must decide this issue by looking at all of the evidence.

- Consenting to some sexual contact short of intercourse: just because a complainant consented to some sexual contact, e.g. kissing, does not mean that she must have wanted and consented to intercourse. A person is entitled to choose how far sexual activity goes, and entitled to say 'no' if the other person tries to go further. And you must not assume that because she kissed the defendant willingly, this gave the defendant reasonable grounds for believing she consented to having sexual intercourse.
- Fear: the fact that the defendant did not use or threaten force, and that the complainant did not put up a struggle, does not mean she must have been consenting. It is possible for someone to be 'frozen with fear'. People respond differently. Some may resist, others may find themselves unable to resist. In law there is a difference between consent and submission. A person consents if they agree to something when they are capable of making a choice about it and are free to do so. Consent can be given enthusiastically or reluctantly, but it is still consent. But when a person gives in to something against his/her free will, out of fear or hopelessness or after persistent psychological coercion, that is not consent but submission.
- If the defendant is in an established sexual relationship with another person, it is not disputed that the complainant was raped. What is disputed is whether it was the defendant who committed the rape. The evidence that identifies the defendant as the person responsible for the rape is challenged. You may hear from the defendant and also from their partner that they have a mutually fulfilling sex life, so the defendant claims he/she had no need to have sexual intercourse with a stranger and had much to lose by doing so. You will consider this evidence when you decide whether it was the defendant who raped the complainant. But
- You must not assume that a person who is in a relationship, and/or has a fulfilling sex life, will not want to engage in sexual activity with someone else.
- Background of domestic abuse: experience shows that people in an abusive relationship may struggle to extricate themselves from

it through fear, lack of resources, family responsibilities, cultural or societal concerns and/or their own conflicting emotions towards their abuser. Further, their capacity to react to events may be compromised or blunted by their lived experience. Where the abuse is not physical but psychological, emotional and/or financial, those subject to it may not even recognize themselves as victims of abuse, particularly where the behaviours develop over time. Do not assess someone's behaviour by reference to how you think you may have acted in their position. Put aside any assumptions you may have had and make your judgements in this case based only on the evidence which you have heard, and assess the evidence within the context of their wider relationship.

When giving these and other warnings, judges make clear they are not expressing an opinion but explaining these points so the jurors can think about them in their deliberations.

APPENDIX L

Some important aspects of the job of the prosecutor:

1. Preparation

The CPS will deliver to the advocate, in good time, instructions which address the issues in the case and its history, etc. The advocate must on receipt consider the papers and advise on such issues as the acceptability of plea, amendment of indictment, the need for additional evidence, or if there is no longer a realistic prospect of conviction; or if the advocate believes it is not in the public interest to continue the prosecution, etc. If deciding whether or not to continue a prosecution, the CPS will always consider the consequences for the victim and take into account views expressed by the victim or the victim's family. The prosecution advocate will follow agreed procedures and guidance on the care and treatment of victims and witnesses, particularly those who may be vulnerable or have special needs. The advocate will also advise on admissions, disclosure and presentation. The advocate will prepare if required a case summary and schedules. The CPS will prepare a Case Management Plan which will be maintained and regularly reviewed to reflect the progress of the case. Until the conclusion of the trial the prosecution advocate and CPS have a continuing duty to keep under review decisions regarding disclosure of material. Disclosure must always follow the established law and procedure.

2. Policy matters

Sometimes at trial 'policy' decisions need to be made, e.g. non-evidential decisions on such things as accepting pleas of guilty to lesser counts or available alternatives; offering no evidence on particular counts; whether to have a retrial; whether to lodge an appeal; certification of a point of law; of withdrawing the prosecution. Wherever possible, such matters

APPENDICES

should always be discussed between CPS and advocate. If there is an unresolved matter between them it may be referred to the Chief Crown Prosecutor, the Director of Casework or in the last resort to the Director of Public Prosecutions, who may refer the matter to the Attorney-General.

3. Accepting pleas of guilty

The prosecution advocate may ask the defence advocate whether a plea will be forthcoming, but should not suggest a plea that might be considered acceptable to the prosecution before one is offered. Once it is offered, the prosecution advocate may discuss the matter with the defence to find a plea that reflects the defendant's criminality and provides the court with sufficient sentencing powers. If an acceptable plea is forthcoming, if practicable it should be explained to the victim or victim's family so that their views can be taken into account and they can be kept informed of decisions. A discussion with the judge about the acceptability of a plea or conduct of the case should be held in the presence of the defendant unless exceptional circumstances apply.

4. Sentencing

The prosecution advocate should be in a position to help the court with statutory provisions, sentencing guidelines, aggravating or mitigating features, areas of difficulty, and anything else that might affect the sentence.

For full detail see the Farquharson Guidelines, helpfully set out in the CPS website.

APPENDIX M

Diminished responsibility

A verdict of murder can be reduced to manslaughter if the defendant proves on a balance of probabilities that:

1. they were suffering from an abnormality of mental functioning

2. which arose from a recognized medical condition and

3. there was a substantial impairment of their ability to do one or more of these things:
   (a) understand the nature of his/her conduct;
   (b) form a rational judgement;
   (c) exercise self-control.
   Note: (i) these last need a psychiatric expert's opinion; (ii) there is no legal definition of 'substantial', it is an ordinary English word for the jury to interpret.

4. the abnormality of mental functioning from a recognized medical condition must have been a cause or contributory cause of (or possibly merely an explanation of) the defendant's conduct in killing.

There is currently much public discussion and some disquiet about such verdicts of manslaughter. This is understandable because manslaughter seems to be a lesser offence than murder, whereas 'manslaughter by reason of diminished responsibility' requires proof of murder, followed by proof of an additional element relating to the defendant's state of mind. It may be that a different term to 'manslaughter' is needed to explain the 'diminished responsibility' defence. See Appendix N.

APPENDIX N

Simple manslaughter is a lesser offence than murder because it does not require the element of 'intention to kill or cause really serious harm'. However there are two ways in which full murder can be proved then reduced to other forms of manslaughter. These are a) where the defendant's responsibility for their actions is diminished by reason of their mental state (see Appendix M) and b) where a defendant has lost their self-control by reason of the deceased's conduct. In the not-so-recent past, neither applied to battered women. Now both defences are available to them.

Diminished responsibility requires the defendant to prove on a balance of probabilities that she was suffering from an abnormality of mental functioning which arose from a recognized medical condition. Recent cases have accepted that either battered woman syndrome (BWS) is a recognized medical condition or it is a form of post-traumatic stress disorder (PTSD), which is a recognized medical condition. So there is no bar to a woman advancing this defence, and submitting to the jury that her ability to understand the nature of her conduct, or to form a rational judgement, or to exercise self-control was substantially impaired.

The defence of 'loss of self-control' created by section 54 of the Coroner and Justice Act 2009 replaces the previous defence of provocation. As long ago as 1949 (R v. Duffy [1949] 1 All ER 932) the courts defined provocation as 'some act, or series of acts done (or words spoken) ... which would cause in any reasonable person and actually causes in the accused, a sudden and temporary loss of self-control, rendering the accused so subject to passion as to make him or her for the moment not master of his or her mind'. And noted, 'a long course of conduct causing suffering and anxiety are not by themselves sufficient to constitute provocation ... circumstances such as a history of abuse which induce a desire for revenge are inconsistent with provocation.'

For many years thereafter the slow burn of endless domestic violence against a woman was thought not to give rise to this defence, and as late as 1992 in R v. Thornton ([1992] 1 All ER 306 CA) the counter-argument was still failing. The first crack in the brick wall came later that year, in R v. Ahluwalia (Kiranjit) ([1992] 4 All ER 889), when the Court of Appeal said, 'We accept that the subjective element in the defence of provocation would not as a matter of law be negatived simply because of the delayed reaction in such cases, provided that there was at the time of killing a sudden and temporary loss of self-control caused by the alleged provocation. However, the longer the delay and the stronger the evidence of deliberation on the part of the defendant, the more likely it will be that the prosecution will negative provocation.'

Following this, Emma Humphreys took her own case back to the Court of Appeal. In 1985, at the age of seventeen, she had been convicted of the murder of her thirty-three-year-old abusive boyfriend and pimp. She had already spent a decade behind bars but in 1995 her conviction for murder was quashed and replaced with one of manslaughter, and she was freed.

Sara Thornton too had been convicted of the murder of her drunken and abusive husband in 1989. She and her young daughter had been the victims of his violence for years. She had sought help from her doctor, her church, social services, Alcoholics Anonymous and the Marriage Guidance Council before she stabbed him to death. After a number of failed appeals, in 1995 she succeeded in having her conviction quashed but the Court of Appeal ordered a retrial. The new jury acquitted her of murder and convicted her of manslaughter. It is not clear whether the jury found for diminished responsibility, loss of self-control, or if different jurors took different views. Either way, she had already served the sentence and she too was freed.

A final case worth looking at is that of Sally Challen. She had met her husband when she was only sixteen. He was a charmer, but over time grew to be abusive and highly controlling. She was belittled and bullied. She was not allowed to handle her own money, nor to choose her own friends. She tried to leave but was too emotionally dependent on him. In the end she returned and signed a post-nuptial agreement forbidding her from interrupting him or speaking to strangers. After years of his coercive and controlling behaviour, in 2010 she killed him. Coercive control only became a crime in 2015.* Although Mrs Challen raised the defence of diminished responsibility, the issues discussed in this book were not canvassed before the jury and she was convicted of murder. It wasn't until 2019 that the Court of Appeal heard fresh evidence, overturned her conviction and ordered a retrial. The Crown accepted her plea to manslaughter. She was sentenced to fourteen years, which she had already served, and she walked free.

* See Appendix O.

APPENDIX O

Serious Crime Act 2015 section 76: Controlling or coercive behaviour in an intimate or family relationship*

1. A person (A) commits an offence if
   (a) A repeatedly or continuously engages in behaviour towards another person (B) that is controlling or coercive
   (b) at the time of the behaviour, A and B are personally connected
   (c) the behaviour has a serious effect on B, and
   (d) A knows or ought to know that the behaviour will have a serious effect on B.

2. A and B are 'personally connected' if any of the following applies—
   (a) they are, or have been, married to each other;
   (b) they are, or have been, civil partners of each other;
   (c) they have agreed to marry one another (whether or not the agreement has been terminated);
   (d) they have entered into a civil partnership agreement (whether or not the agreement has been terminated);
   (e) they are, or have been, in an intimate personal relationship with each other;
   (f) they each have, or there has been a time when they each have had, a parental relationship in relation to the same child (see subsection (6A));
   (g) they are relatives.

Note: For the purposes of this section, a person has a parental relationship in relation to a child if—

---

* You can find the full details at legislation.gov.uk.

(a) the person is a parent of the child, or
(b) the person has parental responsibility for the child.

[...]

4. A's behaviour has a 'serious effect' on B if
   (a) it causes B to fear, on at least two occasions, that violence will be used against B, or
   (b) it causes B serious alarm or distress which has a substantial adverse effect on B's usual day-to-day activities.

5. For the purposes of subsection 1(d) A 'ought to know' that which a reasonable person in possession of the same information would know.

[...]

8. In proceedings for an offence under this section it is a defence for A to show that
   (a) in engaging in the behaviour in question, A believed that he/she was acting in B's best interests, and
   (b) the behaviour was in all the circumstances reasonable.

9. A is to be taken to have shown the facts mentioned in subsection 8 if –
   (a) sufficient evidence of the facts is adduced to raise an issue with respect to them, and
   (b) the contrary is not proved beyond reasonable doubt.

10. The defence in subsection 8 is not available to A in relation to behaviour that causes B to fear that violence will be used against B.

11. A person guilty of an offence under this section is liable –
    (a) on conviction on indictment,* to imprisonment for a term not exceeding five years, or a fine, or both
    (b) on summary conviction,† to imprisonment for a term not exceeding twelve months, or a fine, or both.

And here's something new to interest those who are concerned about controlling and coercive behaviour:

In force 29 February 2024, an amendment to the Sentencing Act 2020 (Amendment of schedule 21) Regulations 2024 means that in determining the minimum term to be served by a murderer, the judge must now treat as an aggravating feature (i) repeated or continuous behaviour by the offender towards the victim that was controlling or coercive (as defined in the 2015 Act) and (ii) where the offender used sustained and excessive violence towards the victim. In addition it will be a feature of mitigation if the victim had repeatedly or continuously engaged in behaviour towards the offender that was controlling or coercive when they were personally connected within the meaning of the 2015 Act. Although these new features will only apply to offences committed on or after 24 February 2024, they will provide additional punishment for the abusive partner, and additional mitigation for the victim of that abuse if she ends up killing her abuser.

---

* In the Crown Court.
† In the Magistrates' Court.

APPENDIX P

The defence of duress

This defence is not available in allegations of murder, attempted murder and a few other very serious offences. There is a separate defence for someone who commits a crime as a result of being trafficked (Modern Slavery Act 2015 section 45 and Schedule 4 of the Act).

In a case where, for example, a young man submits he was under duress, the judge might direct the jury as follows:

> The defendant has raised the defence of duress. He says that he was driven to do what he did by threats. It is for the prosecution to prove the defendant's guilt, so it is for the prosecution to prove that the defence of duress does not apply in this case. Follow the steps set out below:
>
> 1. Decide if the threats described by the defendant were made. If you are sure they were not, he is guilty. If you think they were or may have been made, go to step 2.
> 2. Decide if the defendant acted as he did because he genuinely and reasonably believed that if he did not do so, he or a member of his immediate family would be killed or seriously injured either immediately or almost immediately. If you are sure that this was not the case, he is guilty. If you think this was or may have been his belief, go to step 3.
> 3. Before acting as he did, did he have an opportunity to escape from/ avoid the threats without death or serious injury, which a reasonable person in his situation would have taken but he did not? If you are sure there was a course of action he could have taken to avoid the threat without having to commit the crime, he is guilty.

If you think there was or may have been no opportunity to escape or avoid the threatened action, go to step 4.

4. Ask yourselves if a reasonable person, in his situation and believing what he did, would have done what he did. A reasonable person is a sober person of reasonable strength of character of the defendant's age and sex (and with any other relevant characteristics). If you are sure that a reasonable person would not have done what he did, he is guilty. If you think a reasonable person would or may have done what the defendant did, go to step 5.*

5. Finally, ask yourselves if he had voluntarily put himself in a position in which he knew or ought reasonably to have known that he might be compelled to commit crime by threats of violence from other people. If you are sure that he did voluntarily put himself in such a position, he is guilty. If you think he did not do so or may not have done so, the defence of duress does apply and your verdict will be 'not guilty'.

---

* The reasonable person will not share the defendant's vulnerability to pressure, timidity or emotional instability. However, battered woman syndrome may be a factor to be taken into account when considering whether or not an individual is acting under duress.

ACKNOWLEDGEMENTS

The more I write, the more I know what I owe to those who help me do it. As always, my love and gratitude to Alice Lutyens at Curtis Brown, indefatigable agent and friend. Susanna Wadeson my editor at Transworld, I can't say how important you have been to me and I can't thank you enough. To Larry Finlay, wisest and kindest of men, many and most sincere thanks. And to Patsy Irwin who organizes me most wonderfully – I don't know how you put up with me, but I'm so grateful that you do.

To Liv Bignold and Anna Weguelin at Curtis Brown, and the whole wonderful team at Transworld – Katherine Cowdrey, Hannah Winter, Richard Ogle, Dan Prescott, Catriona Hillerton, Viv Thompson, Barbara Thompson, Helen Bleck, Rebecca Wright and Hugh Davis – you have seen me through every step of the way, and I couldn't have done it without you.

As ever, my thanks to Anna Davis whose CB creative writing course kicked it all off . . . never were twelve evenings better spent; and to my good friends from that course (thank you, Aliyah, Ernest, Geoff, Louise, Ziella) whom I still meet regularly and whose good advice never fails.

It goes without saying – though it still needs to be said – how grateful I am to my family who have seen me through so much. And especially to you, Liz, who are always there when I need you.

I have been privileged to work in the Criminal Justice System. I have been privileged to work with wonderful people – fellow judges and clerks and ushers, barristers and solicitors, dock officers and

ACKNOWLEDGEMENTS

security staff and administrative staff, witness and victim support services, probation officers . . . the list is very long, but every one of you plays a part in the running of the Old Bailey, which has been such an important part of my life. My deep thanks to you all.

ABOUT THE AUTHOR

Until March 2022 Her Honour Wendy Joseph KC was a judge at the Old Bailey, sitting on criminal cases, trying mainly allegations of murder and other homicide. She read English and Law at Cambridge, was called to the Bar by Gray's Inn in 1975, became a QC in 1998 and sat as a full-time judge from 2007 to 2022. When she moved to the Old Bailey in 2012 she was the only woman amongst sixteen judges, and only the third woman ever to hold a permanent position there. She was also a Diversity and Community Relations Judge, working to promote understanding between the judiciary and many different sectors of our community, particularly those from less privileged and minority groups. She mentors young people from a variety of backgrounds who hope for a career in law, and has a special interest in helping women. Her first book, *Unlawful Killings*, won the Crime Writers' Association 'Gold Dagger' for Non-Fiction and was a *Sunday Times* bestseller.

**THE INSTANT *SUNDAY TIMES* BESTSELLER
WINNER OF THE CRIME WRITERS' ASSOCIATION
'GOLD DAGGER' FOR NON-FICTION**

With breath-taking skill and deep compassion, Wendy Joseph KC peels apart six jaw-dropping cases in which a life has been snatched away, lifting the lid on what it's like to be a murder trial judge, how our justice system plays out, and what it means to bear witness to human evil.

'Wendy Joseph's gripping account of the law at work reads like a cliffhanger.' *Sunday Times*

'Will make you question all you've come to take for granted about offenders, the crimes that they commit and the punishment they deserve. A page turner.' David Wilson

'A gripping insight . . . beautifully crafted . . . grim tales lifted by humour and honesty.' *The Times*

'Absolutely superb. 5 stars for sheer readability alone. Her Honour entertains as she educates us about murder, about the law and about how we human beings are shaped as we create the culture we live with.' Philippa Perry

'The most exceptional book I have read in a long time.'
Clare Mackintosh

Also by Her Honour Wendy Joseph KC

Unlawful Killings

Praise for *Rough Justice*

'A vivid picture of the thoughts, feelings and actions of a woman judge as she tries cases involving women as victims/perpetrators and asks herself whether we do them justice. A compelling read.' Lady Hale

'*Rough Justice* raises profound questions about what the words guilty and innocent actually mean . . . I would give this to anyone interested in the law, indeed anyone interested in their fellow humans. The criminal law has found its voice: quiet, determined, steely, and yet always humane.' Justin Webb, *Today* Programme presenter and author of *The Gift of a Radio*

'You'll hear a lot of wonderful things being said about Wendy Joseph's *Rough Justice* and I have to tell you that they're all justified . . . This is a book that will make you question what justice is and whether or not it actually gets dispensed by our courts.' Emeritus Professor David Wilson, author of *My Life with Murderers*

'A riveting front-line account of our beleaguered courts . . . Told with clarity and eloquence, it distils an arcane subject with the vigor and pace of a legal thriller. I found it sobering but also deeply moving and resolutely hopeful.' Kia Abdullah, author of *Those People Next Door*

'A fascinating and entertaining view of our criminal justice system from the perspective of the Bench . . . All the characters of the crown court come alive.' Harriet Wistrich, author of *Sister in Law*

'Beautifully written, immensely engaging, powerful and disturbing insight into a judge's work and the choices faced.' Peter James, author of the Detective Superintendent Roy Grace series

www.penguin.co.uk